If The Reds Should Play...In Rome Or Mandalay
Edited by Barney Chilton, Martin Day, Phil Holt & Phil Williams

First published in 1997 by
Juma
Trafalgar Works
44 Wellington Street
Sheffield S1 4HD
Tel. 0114 272 0915
Fax. 0114 278 6550

© 1997

ISBN 1 872204 45 7

The views expressed in each chapter of IF THE REDS SHOULD PLAY are those of the individual contributors, and don't necessarily represent the views of either the Editors or any of the other contributors. All writers submitted their work independently of each other, and each chapter should be considered as a separate piece of work.

You can contact any of the authors within this book at :
If The Reds Should Play, c/o. P.O.Box 384, London, WC1 N 3RJ.

Cover photograph: Rob Ferrari sampling bliss in Rotterdam, 1991

Other photographs by
Teresa McDonald, Carl Hayes, Phil Williams, Steve Wilson and Diane Comyns .

INTRODUCTION

"If the Reds should play...in Rome or Mandalay,
We'll be there, we'll be there,
If The Reds should play...in Rome or Mandalay,
we'll be there, oh we'll be there...
But we'll be drunk, drunk, drunk as fucking skunks,
but we'll be there, oh we'll be there"
Manchester United fans song

Barney Chilton & Phil Holt

Football fans are a diverse bunch, even more so when they travel to see their team play. All types turn out, which is why when we planned this book we wanted to produce something that represented all the different sorts of people who follow United, from the fanzine editor statto type, to the pisshead, the hooligan and many more.

This book contains stories of their travels by United fans from various walks of life, all sharing one passion. You may not agree or associate with some of the chapters, but by the end of the book you will agree that the contributors represent the wide spectrum of supporter who go to matches. This isn't a moral tome, assessing whether some behaviour is wrong or right, certainly not a sociological insight into why we all do what we do, but a truthful account of what actually goes on when following our football team abroad. No exaggerated media clap-trap, all these stories are based on pure facts, which makes them even more remarkable.

We chose the last twenty odd years as the time frame for the book so as to specifically cover the period when we finally qualified for Europe (1976) again after an absence after the success of the 1960s and to give a picture of how things have changed - on and off the pitch - on our travels over the past two decades.

Not only have we started winning games in Europe again (and now looking to emulate that great triumph in 1968), but after a lengthy ban that prevented us from obtaining tickets officially from the club, and following the ridiculous situation of thousands being unable to obtain tickets for Barcelona, we can now, deservedly, buy tickets officially and freely choose how to travel.

As word has spread about the joys of European aways, with an increase in leisure time, more and more people have began travelling abroad resulting in newer generations following in the footsteps of some of the people who have written about those very early games in the 70s and 80s. The violence that led the then Sports Minister, Denis Howell, to tag United fans behaviour as: "quite incomprehensible" has diminished and with cheaper flights to many destinations, each new competitive tie usually results in thousands of United fans packing their assorted bags and beginning new treks with an excitement about what lays ahead.

You'll have the term 'Euro away' engrained in your memory by the end of this book, it's perhaps the expression that many Reds most relate to in their supporting lives, representing the crack that is almost certainly had in every country travelled to and the buzz you receive from each trip. You get to experience countries, cities and towns you most probably would never have seen otherwise, go to extraordinary lengths to get there and do it with a group of like-minded people in the process.

When you go on your first European away trip it is either usually the first of many, or the last , such are the experiences, stories and bizarre sights from it. Quite simply there is nothing in life like it - as you'll appreciate as you read the stories contained within.

This is our culture, not one that Nick Hornby and his ilk would appreciate or relate to, yet one that allows you to spend quality time abroad (sampling other cultures and interesting cities), with your mates (having a chance to spend days with them instead of a few hours on a usual matchday), getting to know new faces, usually getting drunk and making the most of the surroundings, watching Manchester United play. Could you ask for anything more?

Alcohol plays a large part in many of these stories, but then we are on holiday (although it doesn't feel like that on our return). Some people obviously don't imbibe when travelling, but you only have to look at the vast hordes of fans congregating outside the various bars wherever we're playing to realise that it is an important factor of the trip. It's bloody fun at the time as well.

As Porto proved with a travelling Red Army in excess of 10,000, the gospel of European aways is spreading. A chance to see so much, experience the friendliness of the locals (well, usually), where anything can happen, anything at all.

We'd like to thank everyone who made IF THE REDS SHOULD PLAY possible, from all the contributors, Martin Lacey the publisher, and especially the many loyal subscribers.

All these articles certainly disprove the theory that normal football fans are stupid. Each chapter - however different - is intelligently written and not a made-up account of the events like we now see in so many 'new' football books being published. We hope that the book entertains you as much as it has us and please feel free to blame Barney for any mistakes !

You can use a variety of routes to go on a Euro away, spend just a day, a week, travel officially or unofficially, get plastered or stay sober, but if, after reading this book, you're that much more inclined to plan your first European trip then we've succeeded in our aim. Trust us, you'll have the time of your life.

Martin Day

It seems like an age since we looked into this book idea. The four of us have been friends for a number of years, all brought together through the love of the world's greatest football club.

The three other Editors have all been writing in the fanzines for quite a while, but for me it is virtually a new venture. I must remember to send a copy to my old English teacher who, shall we say, was less than hopeful of my success in the outside world. Well, Mrs Edwards, balls to you. Glad I got that off my large chest.

United in Europe. 33 of us have a chapter each, reflecting on 33 competitive away matches in various European competition since 1976. A number of our visits have been well documented by the media, Porto and Galatasaray obviously, but this is the definitive version of events.

I'm sure that all football fans can enjoy this book, even with those with a dislike of our club. The travel, the drinking, some trouble and a bit of football mixed in with more drinking make for a very enjoyable ride throughout Europe, from Wrexham to Warsaw and Dundee to Dortmund. We've even won a trophy on our Roller Coaster ride.

We have tried to get a cross section of people to write in IF THE REDS, which includes an ex-player, professional people, lay-abouts, students (twats), skilled people and even a bleedin' bus driver. Our international writers come from Greece, South Africa, the United States, and, of course, Manchester.

People have used different means of travel, including hitchhiking, flying, train, coach and camper van, staying in brothels, cesspits, that camper van, 5 star hotels and a Turkish prison cell, having to cash in savings, beg, steal or borrow to pay for each trip.

Following your team in Europe is an education and what's more, is like a drug - you just want more and more, visiting countries where licensing laws mean you can only drink for 24 hours in a day.

Finally, I hope that you, the reader, enjoy the book. If you do, please tell all your friends. Don't lend it to them, let the tight bastards buy their own copy. Cheers.

Phil Williams

United (who I've been watching for over 20 years) is not just a hobby, but a religion, a way of life. I have always taken great enjoyment from following the Reds everywhere they play, whether they play in this country or abroad. There are a lot of people who feel the same way about our beloved Reds and I hope that they and everybody else who reads the book will enjoy the various accounts of what watching United is all about to the different writers.

Anybody who has ever watched the Reds abroad - and that runs into many thousands - will tell you that it is an experience never to be forgotten and always one of the highlights of any season.

Over the years I have been fortunate enough to watch United in nearly 20 countries and each trip has had many stories to tell, some more than others! I have taken great pleasure in recording on paper stories that have emanated from watching United abroad.

There is no doubt that European competition is close to the heart of the club and its fans, particularly after the Munich Air Crash in 1958 and then the European Cup triumph 10 years later. I am too young to remember those two events, but hopefully not too old to enjoy many more triumphs at home and abroad in the future.

Enjoy the book.

CONTENTS

It's always a quiet time in Amsterdam!

Ajax 1 - Manchester United 0 (aggregate 1-2)
UEFA Cup, Round One, 1st Leg
September 15th 1976, Olympic Stadium.
Stepney, Nicholl, Houston, Daly, Greenhoff (B), Buchan, Coppell,
McIlroy, Pearson, Macari, Hill. Sub used: McCreery
Attendance: 30,000

Tony Hughes
Tony, 35, is a company director, a collector of movie memorabilia - and United, of course!

It was December 1961 as a baby of six weeks old that my family first introduced me to Italy at a small place just outside San Remo where we continued to holiday for the next 13 years of my life. We were treated as part of the family of the bar/restaurant called "Luigi's". Luigi, you see, was a P.O.W. in England in 1941 and he told us of his time in the Northwest. As a prisoner being invited on Sundays by families of the area to "Sondee lonch" and down "pob". This hospitality lead to his liking of the English.

His son Renato was the ice cream king of the Italian Riviera and he always greeted me in true Italian style by pinching both sides of my facial cheeks and a cry of "Bobbee Charlton" which seemed to signify to Renato - England, but also, as I learned much later - respect. As I mentioned earlier, we were treated as part of the family and shared many explosive moments watching football and road racing; probably Italy's favourite sport. The odd bottle or two thrown in the direction of the TV set was not uncommon. The Italians loved their sport. In May 1968 I watched United play Benfica and win the European Cup - Guess Where? On holiday - In Luigi's! The TV Bar was full of excited Italians cheering on Bobbee, Georgee and Nobbee Stee. . lez!

I really felt I was at home. I guess my love for United started way back to those Bobbee Charlton days when I was 6 years old. I remember my mother allowing me to stay up late at night as a reward to watch a United game in Europe - true excitement at the prospect of actually seeing them play.

It was at this point Manchester United became my team, and how I cried my eyes out in 1969 when United played in Milan to see bottles and stones thrown at my idol John Fitzpatrick as he left the field covered in blood from cuts to his head. How confused I was and very upset because of my love of Italy and its people and of United. The event was hard to understand as a small boy. During 1969 and 1972 when Manchester United visited London I was taken to matches by either my grandfather or older brother. How wonderful this was!

But even those moments were surpassed when I first visited Manchester in 1972. Old Trafford was my mecca! and here I was on the train from Euston to Manchester with my mother. On the train was a group of lads who all seemed much older than me calling themselves the "Cockney Reds". At the time this meant nothing to me as my mother would take me to the restaurant car for breakfast and we therefore had no contact with them as the Reds were mainly in reserved seating.

Reaching Old Trafford, I'd finally arrived. Covered in goosebumps, I climbed up the steps of the main stand eagerly awaiting my first sight of mecca. WOW!! It was all I had dreamed of and more. It must also have been for the new boy's "record signing" £200,000. Little Lou as our song went "Who put the ball in the West Ham net, skip to my Lou Macari" - great player!

On the return journey back to London we went to the restaurant car where we had booked seats for dinner and to my surprise the West Ham team were there. I could not believe I was sitting opposite the now late, great Bobby Moore. When they had eaten I allowed them to deface my program with their signatures. To an eleven year old, this had to be the greatest day of my life and a dream come true. Also one I did not want to come to an end. I wanted more!! How do I get more? By getting 'round mother!

Needless to say, we went to the following game and met Eddie and Shirley on the train. They were the organizers of the London fan club. Sorry Mr.Dobbin (a London branch secretary), I went for the Eurovision Song Contest option. "How much is the fare to Manchester?" was my question. "£1.70" was Shirley's reply. To this I said to my mum, with a smile, "We'll go every week", and we did!! I missed only a handful of games over the next three years. I met many club managers, footballers and show-biz celebrities. Match tickets were always made available to us and I was starry-eyed. However, the people who have had the greater effect are the friends I've made on the train way back in '72-'73 who are still my friends and travelling companions today.

The 1976/77 season, the season was only four weeks old, and United's average attendance was 58,821, 14,000 more than our nearest challengers, Liverpool. Newcastle were ninth in the division with 31,660. Sorry Geordies, not much changes. We had just made the long, dangerous journey to Newcastle the Saturday before.

Forget your trains, planes and automobiles, I travelled trains, boats, buses and cars, progressing to planes for matches in Europe and far off lands. The first European trip with United was to Amsterdam. We met at King's Cross Station and the newspapers reported that the Red Army totalling around 5,000 travelled in a convoy of coaches to Dover for the ferry to Zeebrugge, Belgium and onward to Amsterdam by coach.

David Dryer Travel Company organised our trip at the outrageous price, plus match ticket, of £21.00 per person for a three day excursion. The journey seemed endless, coach and ferry, with the coach driver losing his direction close to the Belgium/Dutch border!

A sixteen hour trip without the luxury of a WC on the coach; imagine the state of some upon arrival having been drinking best part of the 16 hours!! Then where do you think we were dropped? At Cafe Dick's!! of course. Bang on the canal of Amsterdam and there's me at the ripe old age of 14 years, 1 month off 15 - a mere cherub. With friends of 20 years or more let loose in the red light district of Amsterdam, windmills, clogs and tulips were not all I saw on that trip. Thanks Noel & Tim!! A story I can print was when Tim visited an establishment of the night, the young lady offered her services with extras and Tim's reply was "I'd like a nice cup of tea".

Can you remember the fashion of the 1970's? The platform shoes, those Lionel's (flares) and the psychedelic colours of shirts and tank tops - well, in my opinion, if that was not bad enough, football fashion was even more hilarious and far fetched- butcher's coats for jackets covered with United's sew on patches, scarves on the wrist, (incidentally Dortmund fans still carry on this tradition), and the era of the Bay City Rollers. Look, come on, admit, you too had your share of tartan neatly sewn down the side of trousers or on denim jackets, etc. The fashion has returned as the cycle often does. If you can't remember this era, take a look at the invading United fans on the pitch when we were relegated, surrounding Denis Law in trousers we see today ready to blow away in the wind.

Back to Cafe Dick's . . a wilder pub you will not see! My memory is of inebriated Reds sitting at stools around the bar and as one dropped to the floor another one was catapulted from the above chandelier straight on to the vacant stool. This was greeted by the landlord with the ringing of a bell. The alcohol consisted of Dutch lager mainly froth spread by the landlord's spatula, sweet sherry and anything else you could get your hands on. The rest is a bit of a blur!

The riot police came in with their Alsatians, but frivolities just continued. On leaving the pub we discovered a bed left outside. This was used as a springboard to elevate drunken Reds down the street. After such misuse one genius on bouncing fell straight through cutting all his legs on the bedsprings.

The stadium was a fifteen minute walk away. September 15, 1976 UEFA CUP 1st round, 1st leg 8:15 PM kickoff. The ground was the Olympic stadium. Ajax's own stadium was inadequate for the mighty United. The Olympic stadium was barely covered with a roof and in those privileged areas, the best seats were priced at £10.00 compared to O.T.'s best seat for the second leg at £2.00.

The chants I remember were clever links to the Dutch, such as "Violence in Amsterdam" to the tune of 'Tulips from Amsterdam' and "I saw a Red, where?, There on the stair, Where on the stair?, Right there, A little red with clogs on, Well I declare, Going boot, boot, boot, boot on the stair" to the tune of 'I saw a mouse'.

The Austrian referee Paul Schillers started the game and the first half was fairly uneventful, but after 42 minutes Rudi Krol scored off the post from a move starting from midfield. The second half was a different story altogether, with United doing all the pressing. After 47 minutes, Stewart Houston crossed the ball, the goalie fumbled and the ball approached the goalline.

The referee disallowed the goal with Stuart Pearson running in, adamant that we had scored. The newspapers clearly showed we had. We were robbed! The second half flew by with Macari hitting the post from Gordon Hill's corner. Pearson, having a shot cleared off the line, and Ajax keeper Schrivers making a series of super saves, we were still down 1-0 and that's how the game finished. After the match our mass of fans who were congregated behind the goal had coaches waiting outside the ground for the return home and those travelling by other means left the stadium amongst chaotic scenes outside.

On arrival at Dover the customs' officers boarded our coaches. I seemed to remember a lot of tobacco and spirits placed under my seat. Thanks lads!!

The home tie saw us through to the next round, winning 2-0, with goals from McIlroy and Macari as I stood on the Stretford End.

Nowadays I live in Georgia USA and help the New York Supporter's Club promote United. I distribute United Monthly among all the ex-patriots living in the States. I am fortunate to have business interests in England enabling me to see United every two weeks and I'm proud to say that last season I saw all home and away games in Europe leading up to the Champions' Cup semi-final. I suppose the magic of Europe never goes away!

Men against boys

Juventus 3 - Manchester United 0
UEFA Cup Round Two, 2nd Leg
(aggregate: 3-1)
November 3rd 1976, Stadio Comunale.
Stepney, Nicholl, Albiston, Daly, Greenhoff (B), Houston, Coppell,
McIlroy, Pearson, Macari, Hill. Subs used: McCreery, Paterson
Attendance: 66,632

Manchester Mark

Mark, 46, saw his first United game away to West Ham in 1958, his first Old Trafford game came against Spurs in 1963 and his first European adventure was against Racing Strasbourg in 1965. He has visited 23 European countries with the Reds and his best moment in Europe was coming home on the players plane from Vienna in 1969. His influences and underachievements include getting his sportsmaster to reschedule school football matches from 10am to 9.30am so he could catch the 12pm Manchester train from Euston. He once spent an entire English literature 'O' level exam writing a ten page letter to Denis Law (his favourite-ever player) begging him to stay at Old Trafford after he had requested a transfer, and was told by his headmaster that United winning the league was not more important than his 'O' levels. Mark told his it was. He was told by his first boss to choose between United and his job. He chose United, after which he drifted into a lifetime in tickets which at least satisfied at least two of his greatest cravings; music and United.

From glory to elation to ennui and sobriety to stupor. From confectionary cards to an air disaster so horrifying I remember time standing still. From the only Red in the school playground to the only Red on some Northern bound trains. From two Reds in Europe to tens of thousands in Barcelona and Oporto. Times change, teams change, shirts change but one passion remains constant; the love of a football team. An institution named Manchester United which by 1997 had become so easy to admire it had become even more fashionable to hate.

Through over 30 years of European campaign we have experienced a cacophony of highs and lows. The pain and pleasure of defeat or triumph; the goodwill or hostility of opposition support. On occasions the sheer bewilderment of the natives towards the United culture has been the most prized aspect of European travel. From the cordial hospitality of the people of Sarajevo (1967) and Waterford (1968) to the discomfort of prison cells in Vienna and Anderlecht (both 1968) and the seething hostility of Milan (1969) and Valencia (1982). From the mass invasions of Madrid (1968) and Waterford to the splendid isolation in Gornik (Poland, 1969) and Vienna (1968). From the illustrious, irresistible football against Strasbourg (1965) to the chronic disaster of Porto which brings me to why I'm here. My recollections of United's trip to Juve on 3rd November 1976.

United went to Turin on the back of a 1-0 victory at Old Trafford. Common opinion was that the solitary Gordon Hill goal would not be enough to abate the seasoned Italians in their own backyard. We went to Juve courtesy of a David Dryer one day special.

The early morning congregation was full of red eyes and tired faces, a testimony to the previous nights rehearsals. If my memory serves me correctly the flight was at 7.30am, so after a few introductory beers we went in search of our plane. I got a rude awakening when I was refused entry through passport control and instead taken to an interrogation room courtesy of two plain clothes policemen. Apparently internal affairs, then the A10 squad, wanted to interview me regarding a scam at Wimbledon, i.e.; the Lawn Tennis Championships. They said I would be taken to New Scotland Yard as soon as a car was available. At this stage Juve looked a long way away but after swift negotiations they agreed to 'meet' me off the return flight.

Breathing a sigh of relief I took my seat at the back of the plane. Once airborne a frenzied cake flight broke out with assorted varieties flying in every direction much to the chagrin of the organisers. The beer was drunk in next to no time and so it was on to red wine and spirits. The arrival and transfer to the main square seemed interminable. However, just after midday we were nicely settled by a kerbside bar with a table full of Italian food and numerous bottles of wine.

As the wine flowed through our veins so the archives were unlocked and the famous United anthems filled the Turin air. Scallywags returned from their shoplifting sprees, drunks drank with ease and singers sang with pride. Gradually pessimism turned to optimism and even the most sceptical of us could picture the famous Red jerseys cavorting towards us in jubilation. On the coach ride to the stadium the air was indeed filled with expectation.

Many times before, and since, when one is encamped amongst United fans, the outside world can appear not to exist. Yet as we sat down on these cold, concrete steps and viewed the stadia the old misgivings came flooding back. The pitch looked so vast and uninviting and as the players appeared I swear the Italians looked like Gladiators ready to crush the United infidels. Never has the cliché men against boys, been so brutally personified.

Sammy McIlroy and Steve Coppell have since publicly contested to the ruthless game plan of the Italians. Juve spent the first twenty minutes softening United's resistance with a series of very calculated and cynical challenges. Once they had taught United the basics of this primal game they asserted on the football front and cantered to a three goal victory without the Reds once threatening the Juve goal.

All that was left was to drown our sorrows. Out of the ground we filed, in a sorry looking blanket of despondency. Well and truly put in our place by the superior tactics and ability of the opposition. The atmosphere on the coach was quiet and desolate. There was also no drink!

Hords of celebrating Italians passed by the coach in the old age postures of triumph. Sometimes you just have to wipe your mouth. Then, as the coaches are preparing to merge into the night the sinister side of Italian support appear brandishing weapons and hurling missiles at our windows.

After an important defeat one may have thought enough was enough. It always struck me as strange in this ultra curious culture of hooliganism that the victors should provoke the fight. Surely the bitter pill of defeat gave the beaten fans an edge - rather like waving a red flag at a bull. Passions became roused, emotions became reignited and in seconds coaches were empty and the Italians were on the largest scale retreat since the days of Mussolini.

However that didn't get United through to the next round. The morning papers were scathing in their confirmation of United's undistinguished exit. We besieged the airport bar and drank that dry. A large beer fight ensued which was certainly the result of raised spirits following the post match brawl. On the plane home those who could sleep, slept. Those who could drink, drank and most of those sang as well.

The next time I would see these people was at Villa Park on the following Saturday where United were to be defeated by an Andy Gray inspired Villa 3-2, in the midstream of an eight match run of no victories.

At the airport we said our goodbyes and most made their way home or work. I made my way to Scotland Yard.

"Allez Les Rouges"

St Etienne 1 - Manchester United 1
(aggregate 1-3)
European Cup Winners Cup, Round One, 1st Leg
September 14th 1977, Geoffrey Guichard Stadium.
Stepney, Nicholl, Albiston, McIlroy, Greenhoff (B), Buchan,
McGrath, McCreery, Pearson, Coppell, Hill .
Subs used: Grimes, Houston
Scorer: Hill
Attendance: 33,678

Nigel Appleton

Nigel, 39, works as a financial advisor for a major high street bank and was first taken to Old Trafford, in time-honoured fashion, by his Father, who himself is still a season ticket holder. Nigel was hooked immediately, and has since followed United to most points of the globe for both competitive and non-competitive games. He is fortunate enough to have a very understanding employer, which has helped him to build and maintain a more than impressive "games seen" record, which he doesn't broadcast lightly, but those who know him well can testify. In the best tradition of football ancestry, Nigel is now passing his love for United down to his own son, Andrew, who made his first visit to Old Trafford at the age of 6 in 1993. He has become a frequent visitor since that time and would appear to have found the same love and affection for United that his father still enjoys.

I saw my first United game in February 1967 when a Denis Law header at the Scoreboard End secured a 1-0 victory over Nottingham Forest, who were that season to finish runners up to us, in the Championship season preceding the glorious run to the European Cup victory in 1968.

I was 8 at the time and this was to be the only game I was to see that season. For me to be then approaching my 35th birthday by the time we were to next be crowned Champions meant many years of false dawns and heartache - the "newer" United fans of the past decade don't know how fortunate they are with trophy following trophy with almost predictable regularity!

Throughout these mostly barren years and since, I have many varied, unusual, and indeed bizarre memories, many of which have encompassed European nights, both at Old Trafford and abroad. All away trips with United are an experience (and not always good), but nothing generates more anticipation and then leaves die-hard Reds with more unforgettable memories than a "Euro-away". I have been fortunate enough in this respect to have witnessed all but a handful of those played since our return to European competition in 1976.

The match at the Geoffrey Guichard stadium in St Etienne was my second trip to the Continent to watch the Reds and my report also contains one or two anecdotes from mates who were also present on that balmy September evening in 1977.

The English newspaper headlines on the Thursday after the game had an, at the time, familiar ring to them, with headlines such as: *"Red Army Run Amok"* and *"English Fans Riot in France"*, whilst the game itself warranted very little mention. Crowd trouble was, and still is, a better story for the press than a decent football match. It must be remembered that this was 1977 and football hooliganism was at its peak, with neither the police or authorities in general having a clue as how to deal with what became commonly known as 'The English disease'.

In this context the Red Army was in full cry, with violent incidents being experienced at away games as a matter of course and Old Trafford being a no-go area for most visiting fans.

Having said that, on this particular occasion the United fans were, generally speaking, the victims of an inadequate stadium with no segregation and pretty damn awful organisation. How many times have I heard that following an English clubs' visit to Europe? Heysel and Porto immediately spring to mind - for how long must these situations keep on happening?

Not all United fans were angels by any stretch of the imagination, but on this occasion we were definitely more sinned against than sinning.

I had arranged to travel to France overland on a coach trip organised by my Supporters' Club Branch and we departed from a local hostelry, where pre-trip drinks had set the group on the right course for the remainder of the trip, at around closing time on the Monday evening. The departure time was purely coincidental, having been set by the coach firm...honestly!

By the time Southampton was reached, at around breakfast time, there were a few tired souls about, as sleep on a full coach is almost impossible for some, myself included. However the tiredness was soon dispelled as the ferry to Le Havre had a well-stocked bar and enormous quantities of beer were duly consumed.

As it was a lengthy six hour crossing there were some pretty sad cases disembarking in France but most had had the foresight to utilise their Duty Free allowances. After all, it's a long way to St Etienne, and the coach journey would be all the quicker with some alcohol for company.

We were due to stay in Lyon on the Tuesday night but due to massive hold ups and regular stops we didn't check into our hotels until around 11pm, and sad to say only a token drinking effort was made before the bleary eyed travellers retired. I think this must rank as my earliest ever visit to bed on a Euro away...how times change as you become older and wiser!

However the advantage of an early night is that you wake up that much more refreshed, and thirsty! Lyon is an attractive town with many accommodating hostelries and the local beers and wines were being consumed in unheard of quantities for a Wednesday morning, which soon became afternoon, and souvenir hunting came onto the agenda. By the time the coach was due to leave at around 4-ish many St Etienne shirts had been acquired and not all had been accompanied by till receipts!

The 50 or so mile journey to St Etienne was accompanied by enough alcohol to have filled your average off-licence, and one of the party was unable to even move never mind get off the coach on arrival. As kick off was only a couple of hours away sight-seeing was restricted to the nearest bar and wine seemed for some strange reason a lot easier to buy than beer - anyway it was alcoholic and that was all that mattered!

Due to the vast number of drinkers and the smallness of the bar, many spent their time on the roof taking in the sun until, without warning, the ceiling collapsed leaving bodies everywhere! As I recall though, nobody was particularly injured, but it was an excuse for the French riot Police to make our acquaintance for the first time that evening, and one of our party was promptly hauled off and locked up, though he'd been inside the bar at the time with plaster falling around his ears! In fairness he never was the most agile on his feet and was unable to depart in as smart a fashion as some of his more athletic drinking companions!

The poor lad ended up in a French nick for the night and had to catch a taxi back to Lyon, at great personal expense, the following morning.

By this time kick off was almost upon us, and we made our way to the ground. Entry was by a gate in the centre of the main stand with absolutely no segregation, and once inside the choice was yours as to whether you went to the left or right hand terrace.

My personal choice was to turn left, which as it turned out was the best move, though that was more by good luck than judgement. We situated ourselves to the left of the goal amongst a great throng of green shirted Frenchmen all singing: "Allez Les Verts". Was this the only song they sang? Or is my memory doing them a disservice?

It was obvious from where we stood that the majority of United fans (about 4,000 if memory serves me correctly had travelled to France) had gone to the other end of the ground and the group of Reds there was growing, at the same time moving towards the centre of the terrace which was packed with more green shirted Frenchmen. In typical continental fashion they'd been in the ground for hours whilst the Reds had been drinking their bars dry!

Anyway, the sight of all these English fans on their terrace sent the French hordes into a real frenzy. We learnt later that invading that end was the equivalent in England of United fans attempting to take the Kop or the Shed! No wonder they went ballistic!

In what seemed a strange pre-meditated action the French then threw bread of all things at the United fans, whether this had something to do with the bread strike back home is anybody's guess, nonetheless all hell broke loose.

The English, as only the English do, responded with violent attacks on the French and would not retreat, which was again the signal for the riot police to make another attempt at restoring Anglo-French relations by wading in indiscriminately with batons and accosting as many Reds as possible.

After maybe five or so minutes peace was restored, albeit with the majority of the United fans having been pushed out of the stadium. Only the shrewder, wiser Reds managed to mingle in with the French thus avoiding the Draconian expulsion.

The game itself passed by with a very creditable performance from United earning us a 1-1 draw against a team, remember, that had only 16 months earlier been unluckily defeated by the all conquering Bayern Munich in the European Cup Final at Hampden Park.

The majority of the French fans I came across at the opposite end of the ground to where the trouble occurred were, fortunately, not as aggressive, as there were considerably fewer Reds on that terrace and we would have been easy targets if the fancy had taken them.

As previously mentioned, the British press made a great song and dance about the trouble, which I don't think helped United's official stance that they had pleaded with St Etienne to arrange proper segregation within the stadium. UEFA were not impressed either and expelled United from the competition, before retracting on appeal, with the proviso that the 2nd leg be played more than 200 kilometres from Old Trafford - but that's another story.

Anyway, after the game we returned to Lyon, after calling at the local hospital to collect one of our party who'd had the misfortune to put his head in the way of a police baton.

Lyon was returned to at God knows what hour, but a late drink was found, the full details of which escape me - probably due to too much local hospitality!

The journey home on Thursday, as is always the case with coach travel, took about three times as long as going, with the only event worthy of mention being an impromptu International match of World Cup Final proportions, on the car pack of a service station, between the occupants of our coach and a group of French lorry drivers! Don't ask me the score, but suffice to say that they were in a far healthier physical state than us after three days of heavy drinking.

The ferry home was made via the far shorter Calais to Dover crossing, and it was on board that the English papers were purchased. This was when I first became aware of the reaction at home to events in St Etienne, when perhaps not unpredictably, we had been portrayed as rampaging hooligans with no regard for anyone or their property.

Those that were there knew different...

Lucky To Get Nil

FC Porto 4 - Manchester United 0
(aggregate 6-5)
European Cup Winners Cup, Round Two, 1st Leg
October 19th 1977, Estadio Das Antas.
Stepney, Nicholl, Albiston, McIlroy, Houston, Buchan, McGrath,
McCreery, Coppell, Macari, Hill.
Subs used: Grimes, Forsyth
Attendance: 70,000

Mike Dobbin

Mike was born in 1947 in Prestwich, Manchester, and saw his first United game on 9th September 1961, when a goal from Albert Quixall was enough to beat double-holders Spurs. He moved to University in London, and has lived there since, now working as a partner in a firm of chartered accountants. He has been travel secretary of the Manchester United London Fan Club for 26 years, and has not missed a United first team match (competitive or friendly) anywhere in the world since 1991. His other interests are watching cricket, playing squash, and listening to classical music and opera.

United faced a second round European Cup-winners' Cup tie against Portuguese club Porto, after having previously been thrown out of the competition as a result of crowd trouble at the first round match against St Etienne in France. This drastic step had been taken by UEFA, but then rescinded in the light of further evidence submitted by United, who were however forced to play the second leg at Home Park Plymouth, instead of at Old Trafford.

As a result of this much publicised situation, availability of tickets for the away leg in the following round was severely restricted, with United receiving a very limited number. Together with a number of other London-based supporters I had booked a flight from Heathrow to Portugal, and we therefore found ourselves struggling to obtain match tickets. However, we were eventually assured by the travel agents with whom we had booked our flights and hotel, that match tickets for the Estadio das Antas had been obtained for us, and would be waiting at our hotel in Oporto.

So on Wednesday 19th October we boarded the 2.25 TAP flight from London Heathrow to Oporto, in the hope of seeing another United triumph in Portugal to rank alongside their previous game in that country, the famous 5-1 win away to Benfica in 1966.

Following an uneventful flight, we arrived at Oporto, and boarded taxis to take us to our hotel in the city centre, the Dom Henrique. The arrangement made by the travel agents was that the match tickets would be waiting for us at the hotel reception. Once we had confirmed that we were at the right hotel and that our rooms were booked, we asked about the match tickets, only to be confronted with blank incomprehension as to what we were talking about.

Worry began to turn into panic when several other members of the hotel staff were consulted and proved equally unable to find the precious tickets, but eventually the conclusion was reached that they might be in the hotel safe; unfortunately no-one seemed to be able to locate the keys. To our great relief these were eventually found, and the safe did indeed contain an envelope with our tickets. These appeared to be quite good ones, priced at 500 escudos, and for Camarote Maratona No 13, the number however giving some cause for concern to those of a superstitious nature.

Having located our rooms and unpacked, we proceeded to explore the immediate neighbourhood of the hotel. However, the late hour of our arrival in Portugal did not leave a great deal of time for sight-seeing, and it was not long before we decided that there were other more important priorities, and that it was time for a pre-match drink in one of the local bars.

This was followed by more of the same in the hotel bar, where prior to our departure for the ground we decided that it would be a sensible precaution to enquire from one of the waiters as to the availability of food and (more importantly) drink on our return after the match. In view of the of the late kick-off (9.45) we did not expect to be back at the hotel until the early hours of the morning. We were assured that there was no danger of the bar being closed at that time, and the waiter even promised faithfully that he would ensure that we had something to eat.

A couple of hours before the kick-off we left the hotel bar and hailed a taxi to the ground. The ride very quickly sobered us up as we discovered that we had the taxi-driver from hell, and we were extremely relieved when we arrived unscathed at our destination following a nightmare journey at break neck speeds through the streets of Oporto.

The organisation at the ground proved to be chaotic, with no proper indication either on the tickets or around the stadium to give any clue as to where we were supposed to enter (a situation which proved not to have noticeably changed nearly 20 years later, with much more serious consequences). Some time after arriving at the ground, after consulting probably 5 or 6 separate officials, and seemingly circling the ground at least twice outside and inside, we eventually found our way to the Camerotes, which proved to be private boxes, but waited in vain for the rest of our party to emulate our success; we discovered later that they had given up the attempt to find their correct places and deposited themselves in the nearest available seats.

Having established where our seats were, we set off on the search for match programmes, only to eventually come to the conclusion that nothing was available apart from that day's issue of the club's newspaper. This was a 12 page publication costing 5 escudos, giving some coverage to the match, but largely devoted to the various other sports run by the club, and not even including the evening's team line-ups.

We took up our seats and it soon transpired that it was not just the supporters who were having difficulty finding their way round the stadium, as we were joined in our box by Mr David Meek, who had abandoned his search for the press box. As the teams ran out onto the pitch he sought our assistance in identifying the United line-up, which we eventually established as Stepney, Nicholl, Albiston, McIlroy, Houston, Buchan, McGrath, McCreery, Coppell, Macari, Hill. United were below full strength, lacking Stuart Pearson and the Greenhoff brothers because of illness and injury, and Stewart Houston appeared as a makeshift central defender. Oporto lined up in their normal shirts of blue and white stripes with Fonseca, Gabriel, Simoes, Freitas, Murca, Teixeira, Rodolfo, Octavio, Duda, Oliveira, and Seninho. The attendance was variously reported in different publications as 40,000 (Rothmans), 60,000 (Red Devils in Europe) and 70,000 (Daily Mail).

The match was a virtually unmitigated disaster. The first goal was scored by the Brazilian Duda after only eight minutes, when he received a pass near the left hand touchline a considerable distance from the penalty area; he advanced only a couple of paces before unleashing from fully 30 yards a right-footed shot which dipped over Stepney's head into the net before the goalkeeper had even reacted. A bombardment of the United goal, which saw several shots cleared off the line and a fine save from Stepney, was relieved when United managed a rare attack, but they were soon 2-0 down. After 26 minutes a Portuguese corner on the left was nodded on by an Oporto player at the near post, and fell invitingly for the unmarked Duda to volley it left-footed past the bewildered Stepney and a United defender on the line.

Before half-time United were in further disarray when the defence had to be re-organised as Houston left the field injured to be substituted by Alex Forsyth. The story was little different in the second half, and Duda completed his hat-trick after 54 minutes, when a clever dummy from a team-mate allowed him to collect the ball unchallenged on the edge of the area, and shoot right footed past Stepney's despairing dive, just inside the keeper's left-hand post. Worse was to follow six minutes later when Oliveira (who would be somewhat less successful as manager against United twenty years later) scored the fourth goal when his left-footed shot through a crowd of players went in off the post. Late in the game Ashley Grimes came on for Chris McGrath.

Although they could claim that they were below strength United were comprehensively outclassed and fortunate to get away with only a 4-0 defeat. The Reds' diminutive attack got little change from the tall Portuguese defenders, and the home team's speed and skill in attack overwhelmed the bewildered defence.

It was a somewhat crestfallen group which trudged its way back to the hotel, having experienced, rather than a repeat of United's historic win away to Benfica, a defeat by almost as big a margin as their previous European Cup-winners' Cup match in Portugal, the 5-0 humiliation against Sporting Lisbon in 1964.

However, on arrival back at the hotel, we quickly decided that the only cure for our despondency was alcoholic refreshment, and we made our way to the hotel bar which by now had become a disco and was bursting at the seams. Amazingly the waiter had remembered our request for food, and a large plate of sandwiches appeared through the crowded bar. Having consumed a quantity of the local beer we decided that it would be quite inappropriate to leave the city without sampling its speciality, so ordered a few ports before finally staggering up to our rooms in the early hours of the morning.

Our flight from Oporto on the morning after the match was at the unearthly hour of 7.40. I will not dwell on the sorry state of most of the party which assembled in the hotel reception shortly after 6 am, but suffice it to say that several members had to be almost physically dragged out of their bedrooms and into to the waiting taxis.

Having arrived unscathed at Oporto airport we duly checked in at the TAP desk, feeling only marginally better, but in the knowledge that having reached the airport on time nothing could now go wrong. Or could it? Our journey back to London involved an internal flight to Lisbon, which would connect with the TAP flight to Heathrow. The domestic flight duly took off and headed south, but as we approached arrival time we were given the worrying news that there was thick fog at Lisbon airport and that consequently no flights were landing. After circling for a short time we were diverted further south to Faro, where we landed. For what seemed like an interminable wait we sat on the runway at Faro, waiting for any news of our onward journey, and our already fragile state not being helped by the atmosphere in the grounded plane becoming increasingly stuffy and airless.

Eventually the plane took off again, and after the short flight back to Lisbon we were able to complete our collection of all three major airports in Portugal in one day, by landing at a now fog-free airport. Needless to say we arrived at the terminal only to find that our connecting flight had already departed for Heathrow. Various TAP officials proved somewhat less than helpful, and it was only after considerable discussions and various options being tried that we eventually managed to get seats on a British Caledonian flight en route from Rio to London; given the distress that we had suffered the previous night as a result of a Brazilian, it was a pleasant change to find something coming from Brazil which was to our benefit!

Arrival in London then posed another problem for those of us who had taken our cars to Heathrow the previous day, since unfortunately the British Caledonian flight landed at Gatwick! Our somewhat less than perfect trip was therefore completed by a long bus trip from Gatwick to Heathrow, arriving many hours later than we had originally expected.

What had hardly been a very auspicious week for United was rounded off the following Saturday, when they contrived to lose again by 4-0, this time against West Bromwich Albion at The Hawthorns.

The second leg against Oporto at Old Trafford two weeks later did restore some of United's pride, and they in fact managed to score the 5 goals which would have taken them through to the quarter finals, had it not been for Oporto unfortunately getting two. Still - at least we got our revenge 20 years later!

Widzew Lodz 0 - Manchester United 0
UEFA Cup Round One, 2nd Leg
(aggregate: 1-1, lost on away goals)
October 1st 1980, LKS Lodz Stadium.
Bailey, Nicholl, Albiston, McIlroy, Jovanovic, Buchan, Grimes,
Coppell, Jordan, Duxbury, Thomas. Sub used: Moran
Attendance: 40,000

Howard Coomber

Howard was born in Manchester in 1955 and his first United match attended was the 1964 European Cup Winners Cup Quarter Final against Sporting Lisbon. He has not missed a European home tie since then, nor an away one (Wrexham excepted) since 1976. He was a touch miffed at having been "allocated" the Widzew Lodz trip as his part of this compilation. Of all the ludicrous behaviour and hilarious incidents he has witnessed from United followers on European trips, none of them took place on this Polish outing. However, he hopes the reader will find it had some unusual points of interest.

Part One:
Warsaw: Spin Dryers in Poland

"Widzew Lodz on the First of October,
Loads of us there but not many sober,
Stretford Enders taking over,
We're invading Poland"

As soon as the draw for the First Round of the 1980-81 UEFA Cup paired us with the Poles of Widzew Lodz, my mate Paul Gov from Barnsley, always one to come up with a ditty on the spur of the moment, was on the phone yelling this one at me to the tune of "Bobby Shafto went to sea".

Having barely heard of Widzew Lodz, and with his well-oiled Yorkshire accent at the other end of the line, I didn't know what he was on about at first but the penny soon dropped. Another European trip in the offing and this one was to be my first to what was then presented to us via the British media as the mysterious, dangerous and uncharted void beyond the Iron Curtain, the Soviet or Eastern bloc.

At this distance in time - it was 17 years ago - I do not recall how we decided our modus operandi but we booked with the travel agent, David Dryer, who has, over the years, specialised in travel to international sporting events.

Before I go further, may I emphasize I am, in no way, advertising Dryer's company. It is just part of this story that we travelled with him on this occasion and, as he personally took charge of the party, he is an important character in the events which took place.

I do not recall having the hassle of obtaining visas as we were to have for trips to Hungary, Czechoslovakia, Bulgaria and Poland in later years so I guess Dryer organised the visas for us. In the light of those later experiences, that probably saved me a couple of days off work queuing at an Embassy.

Those travelling in our party were to meet at Heathrow at 8.30am on Tuesday 30th September. The flight was, I think at 10.30. The recommendation to arrive two hours early to clear security checks, as required nowadays at airports, did not exist in those days. I was booked to share with my pal Norman from Chessington, who will be remembered by Reds of the 1960's-80s for his portly appearance (lost in one summer of abstinence), his wild untended beard and matted hair, his ability to immediately ingratiate himself with every barman he ever met and his other great quality, which was to drink interminable amounts of bacardi and vodka.

Everyone down to travel duly arrived, except Norman. I tried to explain to Dryer that, when the specified time was 8.30am, that was about 9.45am in Norman time and he would turn up, no problem. As time passed, Dryer became increasingly agitated by Norman's tardiness until he could wait no longer. Just as he was handing over Norman's tickets to an information desk, the man himself turned up.

The conversation went:

Dryer: What time do you call this? You're late.

Norman: Bollocks. I'm 45 minutes early. The flight's not 'til half ten.

Dryer: Where's your luggage?

Norman: (pulling items from his jacket pockets) I've a toothbrush here and a change of shirt in case I throw up over the one I'm wearing.

Dryer: Good God, man. We're going away for three days.

Norman: Not much time, then. Where's the bar?

Dryer: Everything you want is this way. Passport control, shops, departure gate.

Norman: You stupid twat. I'm off to the bar.

So, after a couple of quick ones, to the airport bus, which Norman and I literally fell on to at the last second. Said Dryer: "I can tell I'm going to have trouble with you two". Says I: "Don't worry, Spin. It'll all come out in the wash". It took Spin Dryer a moment or two to realise what I had called him before he replied: "That's good, I've never been called that before". It reminded me of Monty Python when Mr. Smoketoomuch commented that no-one had before told him to "cut down a little, then".

For the anoraks who may be reading, our airline was Lot (the Polish state airline), the plane on loan from Aeroflot. Having flown on Aeroflot planes a few times now, I have found (apart from one surreal internal Russian flight, mentioned elsewhere in this compilation) that they do not deserve their reputation, all airlines being much the same so long as they get you there. Don't ask me the type of aircraft we were on. I know more about the thought processes of Lichen.

The flight was not memorable, no doubt passing by in the usual steward/esses rush to feed and water us as quickly and as plastically as possible before hitting the duty-free sales pitch in an effort to up their bonus pay. Two hours after leaving Heathrow, we landed at Warsaw.

Those who have travelled with United to Moscow in recent years, for Torpedo in 1992 and en route to Volgograd in 1995, will know what I mean when I say that the queue to get through passport and other controls at the airport took longer than the flight itself. Every person's documents were minutely inspected. In my case, my passport had been purchased nine years before and was coming up for renewal so the photo of a spotty 17 year old bore little resemblance to the suave 26 year old the official saw before him. To ensure it was me (what other reason could there have been?) he took the photo clean off the page before trying to replace it with one bash of his fist. It never stuck down again, which caused me slight hassles when leaving Poland later in the week and on re-entering Britain.

After passport demolition came our first (and only legal) bout of money-changing. We all had to change £7 sterling into Polish Zlotys for each day our visa covered us. So, having completed a form about what we were taking into the country (Norman correctly ticked the toothbrush box), we handed over £21 in return for a pile of strange notes. In effect, this was a Polish government rip-off. The Eastern bloc economies were desperate for Western currency and this was a foolproof way of getting it from every Western visitor. Also the exchange rate was the official government rate not the black (or free) market rate openly (though supposedly illegally) available just about everywhere.

We were met by a local tour guide, whose name I forget and who was, on the whole, as forgettable an individual as you can forget. He gave some amusement to the party as we drove from airport to hotel by his unusual turns of English phrases and his patter which was clearly aimed at the parties of pensioners who must have been his usual British tourist groups. He spoke a little of Warsaw's old town, history and architecture and a great deal of the war, which presumably interested the pensioners as they had been through it. Some of our group took an interest in his mincing walk and those inclined to speculate on such matters decided he must be homosexual, although I was too polite to ask what their interest in his sexuality might have been. A show of hands was taken to see how many of our group may be interested in a guided tour of the city. As there was an overwhelming majority who showed interest in such a tour and as this was not a democracy, no mention of the tour was made again.

We checked into our hotel, which was of the type often encountered in Eastern Europe in that it existed solely for Western visitors and its prices were accordingly high. In the lift to our room, the attendant uttered the words which were to follow us everywhere in the next couple of days. You may think they were the jovial "We will beat you three-nil" or some such as usually encountered when following a football team abroad. Not here. Here, and as we discovered in the next few years in other Eastern bloc countries, the immortal phrase on all lips was: "Change money, change money".

The man was offering about three times the rate to the pound as we had been given by the government officials at the airport. A short negotiation secured a rate of about three-and-a-half times the official rate and we did a deal with him.

After a quick swill, Norman and I decided to go for a stroll as we had a couple of hours to kill before our hotel evening meal. As we passed through the hotel foyer we stopped to look at the Bureau de Change desk offering the official exchange rates and were joined in our bemusement by old Spin Dryer, who had just had a pleasant experience similar to ours with the lift attendant. He agreed an exploratory walk was a good idea and so joined us.

As we left the hotel we ran a gauntlet of dodgy characters hanging around waiting to solicit any Westerner coming or going with a view to a "Change Money" deal. And as we walked away from the area, we were followed by a couple of taxis whose drivers, whilst they would have provided a taxi service had one been required, clearly had day jobs in the more lucrative business of changing money.

The three of us took a walk around the streets for no real reason except, perhaps, to get a feel of the place. I was interested to try to get an insight into what it was really like as I didn't trust the British media presentation of Soviet bloc states as lands of shortages and queues.

You must bear in mind that, at the time of this visit, the Solidarnosc demonstrations in the Northern Polish port of Gdansk were at their height. There, in defiance of the government, the dock workers had formed an illegal trade union, independent of the government-run unions and had held strikes, demonstrations and a campaign of disruption in defiance of the (Soviet controlled) Polish government. This had encouraged others, first around Gdansk and then elsewhere in Poland to hold illegal protests. Comparisons were being made with similar attempts to defy Soviet authority in Hungary in 1956 and Czechoslovakia in 1968, where in both cases, the Soviet Army had violently suppressed the protesters slaughtering thousands of ordinary citizens in the streets. Lech Walesa, the Gdansk dockers leader, was being presented by the Western media as a great hero of democracy and potential saviour of Poland, by which was meant deliver of Poland from the hands of the Soviet Union into the hands of the United States.

Always one to take with a pinch of salt that which I perceive as propaganda rather than objective media reporting, my suspicions about how much was truth and how much was mind-manipulation had been enhanced when Margaret Thatcher had lauded Lech Walesa and Solidarnosc and had spoken out in support of free and independent trade unions. As far as the free and independents trade unions in Britain were concerned, Mrs Thatcher was of the view that they had too much power and should be crushed.

Not that the answer to these complex problems was to be found in a half-hour stroll around Warsaw, of course. All I managed to glean was that it seemed the same atmosphere as any inner-city area around dusk and that the butcher's shop we passed, where the door was wide open and staff were busy cutting up carcasses, seemed as well-stocked as any back home.

Our walk came to an end when I spotted Paul from New Malden on the other side of the road. Paul, known as Acid because someone once reckoned he always looked as though he was out of his head on the stuff, had travelled by train and we had arranged beforehand that he was to find us at our hotel. He had just arrived and was on his way there.

When I pointed Acid out to Norman, old Spin laughed: "Don't be ridiculous, you can't know anyone. This is Poland". This man had previously run trips taking the likes of West Ham and Spurs supporters abroad, where it seems the only visiting fans there were on his trip. Over the course of the next couple of days, he was to realise United fans are a different breed and he was to express his amazement at the numbers who had found their way to Poland without his help - or even without a compass.

*<Advocates of the findings of the Taylor Report that, to assist supporters to find their place in a football stadium, areas of stadia should be named after points of the compass, please pay careful attention here: Football fans **never** carry compasses.>*

With Acid on board, we returned to our hotel. Acid booked in - £25 a night, ouch! A ludicrous sum in those days, especially for a cheap place like Poland. Our hotel price had been hidden in the package so we had not noticed it. No wonder that after we flew home, Acid, staying on for a few days, found a local girlfriend to stay with whom he continued to visit from time to time in the next few years.

Having found his room he joined us in the bar for a pre-dinner drink. It was here that I met, for the first time, Noah from Pontefract who was to become a great friend. A fine United regular both domestically and on European trips, he and his mate, whom I found playing chess together on the bar, had been in Warsaw since the weekend, having booked a package for a week.

The bar quickly filled up with the rest of our party. The talk was almost exclusively of changing money and what rate people had been able to negotiate. The extremes seemed to be two-and-a-half and five times the official rate with most having obtained three to four times that rate.

None of us had ever come across the black market in currency before and it was vague to us as to what it all meant. In the bar, however, were a handful of Britons who were on business and, as regular visitors, they were able to explain it to us thus:

Certain 'luxury' items, such as televisions, fridges, washing machines, spin dryers and the like were in short supply. There were two ways the locals could buy them. One was by getting on a waiting list, which took so long it was pointless to try. The other was by buying them from 'Dollar Shops', which were run by the government but took only 'hard' or Western, currency. So for the average Mr or Mrs Pole to get, for example, a spin dryer, they had to accumulate enough cash in Dollars, Francs, Deutsch marks, Pounds or whatever and make their purchase at a Dollar Shop. They could not legally change their Zlotys into foreign currency without a foreign passport so had to do so illegally.

Hence, the lift attendant or taxi driver would buy currency from me at three-and-a-half times the official exchange rate and use it to buy a spin dryer. Or, more likely, he sold the currency on at, say, five times the official rate to someone saving up to buy a spin dryer, and pocketed the profit.

This changing money racket was technically illegal and people were sometimes arrested for it but it was clearly so widespread that a blind eye was usually turned. The police were probably at it as well and, in any case, all of this illegally changed Western currency would end up in government coffers in the end as the government owned the Dollar Shops.

This was all good training for us as, in coming years, we were to 'change money' in Czechoslovakia and Bulgaria although, for some reason, the practise barely existed in Hungary and, when it did, the exchange rates on offer were not worthwhile bothering with.

All this talk of money and economics led to politics and the businessmen, Tories to a man, soon left the bar after receiving a torrent of abuse from a group which included several Yorkshire miners. Only one brave Thatcherite remained to continue arguing their case.

Had it not been time for our evening meal, or if the meal had not been paid for as part of our package already, we may never have moved from the bar. As it was a group of us had already decided to speedily devour the repast as a pre-requisite to a night out in the bars of Warsaw.

The food itself was adequate without being sensational but, whether by design or incompetence, the service was slower than the airport passport queue had been. At the time I was paranoid enough to decide it was plot to keep us out of the bars so we could not mix with the locals. Or at best, it kept us spending our drinking money in the hotel rather than elsewhere.

After the borscht soup, came (eventually) the veal. After this main course, our dissatisfaction at the snailpace service became more vociferous. In our party was a red-haired, middle-aged woman, named Eileen. I knew her slightly, as, at that time, she was involved in running transport for one of the supporters' branches. Being used to running branch trips and with some of her regulars on this trip, she had latched herself on to the tour-guide and appeared to believe she had assumed control of the party. She was indignant at our pleas for the waiters to get a move on and expressed amazement that we wanted to leave the hotel for an evening out as everything we could want was there.

<I think Eileen liked hotels because the following year, she travelled to Valencia but refused to leave the hotel to attend the match as she had heard vague rumours the local fans might be violent. Nasty places, these foreign parts!>

Our view was that we may never come to Warsaw again and our philosophy was always that one of the points of travelling was to see something of the place and get on the piss with the locals. After putting this unequivocally to Eileen, a handful of us decided we had wasted enough time, left the lobotomees for Judgement Day or their chocolate pudding, whichever was to arrive first, and we set off into the Polish night.

The first place we came to was a self-service cafe-bar type of place. We joined the queue but, again, the service was slow. That, and the sight of the greenish soupy dish the locals were tucking into, put us off and we moved on without making a purchase.

Round a couple of corners, we found a gem of a place, just what we were looking for. We entered through a double door. Between the two doors was a cloakroom desk manned by the archetypal Eastern-bloc female athlete type. Built like a brick outhouse, hair tied back in a bun and a world-championship scowl, it was she who attracted us to the establishment in the first place.

We might have walked past had we not seen her open the outer door, push out a somewhat imbibed customer and, before he hit the deck, boot him up the backside so he flew about five feet forward before collapsing on the pavement. Seemed like our sort of place so in we went.

As we entered, Norman turned to me and said: "Have a look, every drunk in Poland is in here". The place was clearly where the local working men went to relax after the days toil. Basic, though not unclean, an uncovered floor but with a few tables and chairs dotted along the walls of the L-shaped room. In one corner, a group of drunks were singing. In the middle of the bar area, two men were shouting at each other, whilst their pals tried to join in but were not quite up to the decibellic capabilities of the main duo. A couple of others were standing on tables and the whole atmosphere was one of unstoppable, alcohol-induced chaos.

We approached the bar and, being in Poland, ordered vodkas all round. This turned out to be the equivalent of going to a well-stocked pub bar and requesting "a drink". With a gesture at the optics and a shrug which meant "Which one?", the barmaid gave us a look which said, in any language, "You're obviously imbeciles". The bar, which was about ten yards in length, had behind it two rows of vodka bottle optics, each one a different kind made with, for example, lemon, lime, herbs, etc, ad infinitum.

We settled for the plain vodka which looked familiar and each received a brim full glass equivalent to about eight measures at home. We asked for orange with it and were each given a tall, half-litre or so, bottle of orange.

Taking a seat, I sipped the top from the vodka to make room to add orange to it. As I and others continued to do this, adding orange little by little, we attracted the bemused attention of some of the locals, one of whom asked what we were doing with our drinks. "Adding orange to it, you know, vodka and orange" came our reply. The astounded Polish response was "But you don't dilute our vodka!". In the one phrase, not only was the ice broken between us and the locals, but we were put firmly in our place as far as the drinking stakes were concerned.

We asked why the bar sold no beer, only vodka. The reply was, again, one of state economics. It was illegal to sell beer in Poland after 7pm because that's when most drinking took place and it aided the economy to sell Polish vodka rather than beer, which was imported. I was inclined to say that another reason was that the state ensured the workers only drank vodka because it got them too pissed to be capable of contemplating joining Mr. Walesa's agitations but I didn't dare mention this because, whilst in this bar, we had become aware of a young couple so totally out of place that it was most suspicious they were there at all.

This was a very basic, cheap Warsaw working men's bar, yet these two were dressed for the London Hilton. The locals paid no heed to them one way or another but, after a while, they spoke to us very nicely in impeccable English. We spoke a little of football and they asked if we had heard of the recent troubles in Poland, to which we were wary enough only to say it was big news in Britain.

Either it was a remarkable coincidence that they should be in such a bar when we were - it was remarkable that they were there at all - or they were police, dressed for the hotel, who had followed us. These days, football fans get used to being shadowed by supposedly undercover police, especially on overseas trips. At that time, it was not so common and, with the image we had been fed of sinister Eastern bloc dictatorships, it worried us a little so we moved on to a couple of other, unfortunately quieter and more characterless, bars.

The bars were supposed to close at 11pm but, by that time, we were installed and, of course, spending money in one which was selling us beer so we ended up with illegal 'lates' as well as illegal beer. By this time we had worked out the going price of drinks and calculated that, with the cash we had obtained via the money-changing merchants, it would be hard-going to spend it all before we left the country on Thursday. Zlotys could not be changed outside Poland, nor even spent at the airport.

On the stroll back to the hotel, we had to step over the man who had been kicked out of the working men's bar as he still lay where the cloakroom lady had booted him to and we could not help noticing a few other prostrate vodka enthusiasts on the route.

In short, I have never seen so many pissheads in one place at one time as I did that night in Warsaw.

PART TWO:
LODZ: THE MYSTERY OF THE MAN WITH THE BRIEFCASE

So match day dawned. Lodz (pronounced Wodj) is about 80 miles from Warsaw and a coach had been arranged to take us there, First we had the morning to kill. It's always a problem on European trips , is this. The match is in the evening. We are on holiday and want to enjoy ourselves (i.e.; have a drink) but want to be sober enough to appreciate what we are seeing on the football field at the end of a long day. So, after a now legal beer (before 7pm you see), we went to look at the shops.

Although old-fashioned in appearance, like something out of a 1950s or even 1930s film, the shops were apparently well-stocked and assistants helpful. On noticing our interest in the alcohol counter, one assistant was helpful enough to recommend Polish white spirit. It is virtually pure alcohol. I brought a bottle home and soon after, spent an evening indoors with a friend sampling it. On later mentioning this to an acquaintance of Polish extraction, I was told it was not for spending a session drinking. Poles take one slug, and one only, at bedtime to help them get to sleep. Oh well, too late by then.

Whether or not the average Warsovian could afford the prices in the shops is a question I cannot answer but, to us, it was cheap and the shortages and queues, which were portrayed by the Western media, were not in evidence. Postcards were bought and posted, presents and souvenirs purchased and Tim from Farnborough bought some excellent crystal for his mother which was, as shall be seen, to lead into a crystal maze all of his own at the airport on the way out.

Time came to get on the coach to Lodz. There were about 40 of us on board including some staying at the hotel but not in our party. With the First Leg at Old Trafford having ended in a 1-1 draw, we had the away goal against us. The driver's son, who was taking the opportunity to get to the match, was the only passenger confident of a United win. Three-one he predicted. This vote of confidence from a Polish teenager and the lad's enthusiasm to both practice his English and talk football lifted our spirits on the journey.

We got to Lodz about 3pm and so had over four hours before kick-off. The gang who had been out together the previous evening set off to get on the piss with this lot (or Lodz) of locals. Couldn't find a bar open anywhere. Asking locals we encountered, the consensus was that the bars don't open on match days as the local fans get pissed and fight at the football. And they call it the English disease!

We asked a couple of well-dressed, businessmen types, if they knew a bar that was open. Having ascertained that we did not want to change money, one of them opened his briefcase to show its contents - two bottles of lime vodka! As our chances of finding an open bar appeared to be doomed, we bought them from him (in sterling, of course - he didn't want zlotys) and sat down in a convenient park to chat and enjoy them. What was this man in a suit doing wandering around Lodz with two bottles of vodka in his briefcase on the off-chance of meeting someone who was looking for a drink and had Western currency? One for Arthur C.Clarke, I think.

As the evening began to set in, we slowly made our way to the stadium, exchanging friendly greetings with local supporters as we went. A golden rule when following your team abroad: Be sportingly friendly to the locals because, if any of them is inclined to violence, he is less likely to gain assistance from his fellows if you are grinning, shaking hands and exchanging drinks with them. At an away match in England, you can blend in with the locals. In somewhere like Poland, unless you can successfully make out you are deaf and dumb, the language barrier renders this virtually impossible.

On the last stretch down to the stadium, a gang of exuberant United fans came round a corner and we sang our way down through the gates and up on to the terrace beneath the electronic scoreboard, behind a goal. Looking around, we spotted a knot of Reds in the middle of the terrace to our left, just about on the half-way line. That's where we should have been. There was not the police control or segregation in those days to the extent there is today. We had walked straight in to the wrong area - about 50 of us.

However, no problem. The locals were bemused, but not hostile, at our presence as we made our way down the gangway towards the front. Seeing us coming, some police gathered at the bottom to greet us but they did not impede us as we climbed on to the running track and walked round to where the United contingent were sitting. They gave us the customary round of applause as we clambered over the hoardings to join them.

Getting on for 200 United fans had somehow got there and were in good, vodka-propelled voice, despite being up against some 40,000 locals. There was something of an eerie atmosphere amongst the Polish supporters who were surprisingly subdued. After all, this was one of the biggest matches in their history against a club with a prestigious reputation, if not a currently outstanding team, and with a 1-1 away result under their belts.

Soon after kick-off, the reason for the quiet crowd started to become clear. We noticed a disturbance in the crowd on the larger terrace opposite. Missiles were being thrown. They appeared to consist, in the main, of rolls or loaves of bread (so much for bread shortages). The explanation was that the stadium where the match was being played was not Widzew's home ground which did not have sufficient capacity for the expected crowd, but that of their rivals LKS Lodz. LKS were the less successful club in the city but had a bigger stadium.

LKS fans took umbrage at their rivals' supporters in their stadium so the trouble had broken out. The crowd were subdued because half of them did not support Widzew and many who did were wary of showing themselves for fear of being singled out by LKS troublemakers.

Whilst we were watching all this an old drinking pal of ours turned up. Slug, from Manchester, is the brother of Tony who runs the programme and souvenir stall which is well known to Old Trafford regulars. Slug had actually emigrated to Poland some two or three years before, presumably after going there on a work contract and taking up an offer to stay. He had made his way round the crowd to the United section to see if any of his old pals had made the journey. The lime vodka came out to celebrate the re-union. Imagine the shock on the face of a young local lad, who spent the evening pestering us for coppers, when Slug told him where to go in perfect Polish.

At half-time, I would have liked to have joined in the general applause which greeted an impromptu show of international goodwill, when a couple of United supporters paraded the pitch waving a Union Flag and a red-and-white banner and were joined by both Widzew and LKS fans showing their colours, but the vodka had got to my bladder. Spin took me to where he had found a toilet before the game. It was up against a perimeter fence. So much for the straight-laced travel agent.

The game itself was not very memorable and, at this length of time, little detail stands out. Widzew, whom the locals generally expected to lose, packed the midfield and defence to try to hold on to their away goal advantage, as 0-0 would see them through, and hoped to catch United on the break.

United had to go forward but this was not one of the best United teams and their attempts to break through the Widzew wall were broken down time and again. The nearest we got was a, long-range, curling Steve Coppell shot which bashed against a post. With United getting increasingly frustrated and Widzew increasingly confident as they saw United repeatedly falter against their tactics, the game petered out into a goalless draw. We were out of the UEFA Cup.

Straight back to the coach for a return to Warsaw. By now, Spin had realised the extent Reds will go to see their team, even in this kind of obscure place, and the coach, only two-thirds full on the journey to Lodz, was now overfull with standing-room only as numerous Reds, who had planned to stay overnight in Lodz, had taken the opportunity to hitch a lift to Warsaw where they could make a quicker getaway to their plane or train home.

Spin, who had clearly also met a man with a briefcase, had made friends with Big Fred of Stretford, who had apparently been serenading Spin throughout the match. Spin seemed to think Fred was the greatest thing since sliced bread and insisted he use the coach tannoy to go through the full repertoire of United songs, which Fred duly did with Spin hanging on to him round his neck. A comic scene as the difference in height was such that Spin had to stand on a seat to do this.

Some joined in with Fred's concert but others were subdued, the effects of travelling, vodka, a long day and defeat taking their toll. On our return to Warsaw, it was a short stint in the hotel bar, some of those who had hitched a lift on the coach footing the bill both by way of thanks and to get rid of surplus Zlotys. After a night's sleep, it was a last quick look round Warsaw and a coach to the airport.

By the last morning of a European trip, especially when United have lost, everyone is spent and just wants to be home. The last couple of days have been a holiday with a build-up to the crescendo of the reason for the visit. That is the match. After one last blow-out on the night after the match, the reason for being there no longer exists and the effects of a couple of days drinking as well as the thought of an impending return to the realities of work are adding pain to the equation. It's an anti-climax, a downer, and you wish it was over.

The trip home was uneventful, save for Tim's encounter with a female customs official at Warsaw airport, who invented a veritable crystal maze of questions which had to be negotiated before Tim was allowed out of the country. Tim, not being one to tolerate fools easily nor to admit defeat in any argument, nearly didn't make it.

You'll remember he had bought a crystal vase in Warsaw to take home to his mother. At some £15, it was excellent value. At the airport, all our luggage was searched and Tim's vase was discovered.

The stroppy official first accused Tim of trying to conceal it, which was rubbish, not least because he had no idea there may be a difficulty. Then she demanded £40 export duty. First incredulous and then believing this to be a con, Tim refused in most impolite terms. After an altercation a customs supervisor turned up, calmed down his officer while we calmed Tim, and confirmed £40 duty was payable before the vase could be exported from the country. Tim offered the vase to both officials as a gift as, at £15, it was a bargain but not at £55. He was accused of offering a bribe to the officials. A bribe, so he did not have to pay a tariff which, if the gift was accepted, would not be payable. Work that one out.

A policeman came to arrest Tim but he was the most sensible of the lot. Tim did not have £40 but a whip round was organised with the Polish police collecting it and we quickly dragged Tim, cursing and swearing, on to the plane.

And so home to save up for next year's European adventures.

Valencia Vacation

**Valencia 2 - Manchester United 1
UEFA Cup Quarter-Final, 2nd Leg
(aggregate: 2-1)
September 29th 1982, La Mestalla Stadium.
Bailey, Duxbury, Albiston, Wilkins, Moran, Buchan, Robson,
Grimes, Stapleton, Whiteside, Moses. Subs used: Macari, Coppell.
Scorer: Robson.
Attendance: 35,000**

John
John, much older than he looks and a 'wide-boy', has supported United all his life . His writing skills, however, leave much to the imagination.

Some random memory jerkers from one of the most violent episodes in United's past:-

▌ 39 United fans being arrested and jailed for weeks following a bar brawl in Benidorm. The Spanish press then showed another 200 incarcerated Reds looking like animals behind bars.
▌ A naive Cockney Dave taking all the waiter's tip money for the week out of a saucer and then being chased out of the bar because he thought it was his change.
▌ Sitting in a bar at a crossroads the day before the match and being pelted with hard boiled eggs from the top floor of an overlooking high rise block of flats - shit do they hurt when they connect.
▌ Going sunbathing on the beach and seeing several naive young Reds get very burnt as they fail to appreciate the strength of the Mediterranean sun.
▌ Returning to the hotel to find approx. 200 police with guns pointed at the entrance (supposedly for our protection!).
▌ Everyone in the hotel lobby being scared witless and several people making an instantaneous decision not to go to the match because the atmosphere was so intimidating.
▌ The Utd firm considering all this a challenge and treating the hostility as a form of protecting the name of United!
▌ We being so pissed we got our tickets from 'Spin Dryer' and marched through the armed police and baying fans like real heroes when we were in fact just too drunk to realise the seriousness of the situation.
▌ Shortly after, whilst looking through a brothel window we bumped into Mick from Blackpool who was on holiday in Majorca and got himself run over as he ran to greet us - the first United fans (and friendly faces) he had seen all day!
▌ Police sirens sounding so loud it was unbelievable throughout the trip and in the

mistaken belief that they were chasing us we all dived into a silk scarf shop and pretended to buy scarves!

▌ Drinking mega bottles of wine outside the ground and applauding the team as they arrived. The police response being to baton charge us with horses attacking every English person in sight. Fat Ron, Norman and Arthur all go mad on the coach and urge us all to steam in.

▌ Being bombarded in the ground with everything from chairs to bottles.

▌ Several upper tier Reds being forced to move down via a gauntlet of police truncheons.

▌ United fans singing "You'll Never Walk Alone" at half-time - bastards!

▌ Police waving guns in our faces and laughing when Valencia win - see *Daily Star* cover of the following day for the best photo ever.

▌ Me leaving the ground with my massive Union Jack stuck down my shorts.

▌ Our coach going down a dead end, having to reverse and getting every window put through.

▌ Every other coach having their windows put through on the main road anyway, although ours was more scary as we were trapped in!

▌ Most people being so scared that they stayed in all night yet us being so stupid and drunk we stayed out all night right in the middle of town. Which was, er, eventful.

▌ Spending half the night chatting up prostitutes who we found to be transvestites when Howard went for a jump.

▌ Burgo pinching Martin's bed even though he wasn't supposed to be in our town, let alone hotel!

▌ Last drink at about 5am and twenty armed police jogging in, scaring us to death and then simply sitting down to have a coffee.

▌ Getting home unscathed (unlike so many others) to find Dave Smith say United would never take supporters abroad again as someone was going to get killed due to all the problems - what problems!

Czech Mates

Dukla Prague 2 - Manchester United 2
European Cup Winners Cup Round One, 2nd Leg
(aggregate: 3-3, won on away goals)
September 27th 1983, Na Julisce Stadium.
Bailey, Duxbury, Albiston, Wilkins, Moran, McQueen, Robson,
Muhren, Stapleton, Whiteside, Graham.
Scorers: Robson, Stapleton.
Attendance: 28,850

Phil Holt

Phil, 40 (going on 20), has supported United all his life. He has carried a lifetime ambition to see United win the European Cup in person, although with this level of drinking going on doubts whether he will ever be able to see anything ever again without blurred vision.
"He loves the life and lives the life".

In the full knowledge that some 13 years later Fergie would be signing Euro '96 star Karel Poborsky, we thought it only right that we should visit his homeland on an early scouting mission, ensuring that he ate all his greens and most of all, assassinating every known barber in the country so that our future substitute could cultivate that most ridiculous haircut ever in time for his Old Trafford arrival.

So it was that in Autumn 1983 eight of us embarked upon an epic train journey to see Mummy and Daddy Poborsky with the sole intention of taking in the second leg of our Cup Winners Cup away tie to Dukla Prague.

Ever since the late seventies I had dreamed of playing Dukla for the somewhat obscure reasons that my favourite single of the period had been the post punk anthem: "All I want for Christmas is a Dukla Prague Away kit" by those redoubtable Tranmere fans Half Man/Half Biscuit. Prague at the time was still under Communist rule and presented a much more formidable proposition than today's tourist attraction with its trendiest city in Europe tag. Nevertheless our visa applications were all granted (due most definitely to the "reason for visit question" being answered with "In order to purchase several Dukla kits!") and off we went straight after another episode in United's magnificent Scouse conquering escapades of the eighties.

It was therefore in good heart that we boarded the 21.00 hours boat train from Victoria in company with several other waifs and strays from Red Planet - who amongst us can ever forget Norman setting off for another week away with just a toothbrush for company or a young Taylor with his crew of jibbers who spent the entire trip avoiding Herr Ticket Inspector to much amusement from the rest of the train?!

Already well oiled from the pre-match and Manchester to London session we stocked up with duty free on the ferry and fell blissfully asleep until Cologne where we made our first stop for drinkies.

The fact that we hit Cologne at 9am on a Sunday morning did nothing to prevent us embarking upon on our first pub crawl of the trip. Civilised bars serving coffee to families on their way to church were suddenly presented with several English beer monsters quaffing German beers as fast as the harassed bar staff could fill them up. This worked massively to our advantage as we became so popular that, filled with goodwill following their church attendances, one particular set of bar owners took it upon themselves to provide free ale for all their thirsty English guests - I've always liked the Germans!

Giving a cursory glance towards the awe inspiring Cologne cathedral we eventually took our leave in time to catch the 3pm train to Nuremberg and promptly fell asleep until arrival.

The centre of Nuremberg on a Sunday night is a very quiet place with hardly a sole to be seen, but we made sure that the locals were soon out on the streets. We'd visited a few empty bars and had a very welcome steak when one of our party began to chat the barmaid up in a particularly quiet venue.

His chat up line (followed by many in differing forms over the years) referred to him being a United player, Bryan Robson, out for a quiet drink with some of his team-mates, whilst undertaking pre-match training in Nuremberg prior to moving on to Czechoslovakia for the game. The barmaid fell for the story (why do they always do?) hook, line and sinker (Steve did after all slightly resemble Robbo, i.e; head, two arms and legs, etc!) and promptly telephoned her boyfriend who just happened to be the sports reporter from the local paper. She also shouted the landlord down and informed him of his famous visitors. Within minutes the bar was full of Wolfgangs, Fritz, Helmuts, et al and every single one of them believing that we were in fact eight members of the famous Manchester United Football Club.

Now anyone who knows me will realise that myself and my chums are all fat, ugly, drunken bastards, and for so many people to mistake us for professional footballers was beyond belief, however, believe us they did and before long we had a bar full of people wanting to shake hands and hug us. The boyfriend was so impressed with his scoop he got the newspaper photographer out of his bed in order to take our picture and the landlord was so impressed he provided a constant flow of free drinks and threw together a superb feast fit for a King.

This was truly the life - Mick was impressing everyone with his tales of gruesome injuries (as he was supposed to be Kevin Moran!), Martin (Gordon McQueen) promptly declared that he was the gay lover of a United centre-forward Joe Jordan and Steve was still trying to shag the Robbo obsessed barmaid. We departed about four hours later having not paid for a single drink and they must all have been very impressed by the players devotion to the team as we all sang United songs at the top of our voices!

All that is except Carl who was exceptionally pissed from free Schnapps and had gotten into a big argument with an American ex-marine serving all-night hot dogs from a kiosk on the street. The marine was so upset with whatever Carl had said that he produced the biggest knife I've ever seen and chased him into the railway station where we found him hiding behind the lockers.

Time to go and the 4am overnight service to Prague provided our intended beds for the night. It was, however, difficult getting much sleep as we had our first encounter with the Communist red-tape when we were rudely woken up by surly border control guards sending their sniffer dogs into our carriage. Fortunately the dogs were friendlier than their owners and no-one suffered more than a few licks on the face but the guards were intent on searching every bag at least twice and made sure we got no more sleep.

It was actually quite comical watching them search the train so thoroughly both inside and out as if anyone would actually want to sneak into their God forsaken country or attempt to sell anything to the peasants therein.

By the time we reached Prague we were a weary bunch but a £4 hotel room and a 40p bottle of lemon vodka soon cheered us all up. Our first destination was a travel agency where we had arranged to pick up match tickets, imagine how gutted we were when we got there and the assistant informed us that we would have to pay a booking charge of 4p per ticket on top of the ticket price making the total cost all of 24p each!

Would this be alright we were asked! We managed to cope somehow and off we went in search of Prague's famous Pilsner beer. Nowadays Prague may well be construed as both trendy and lively but back then it was as drab as could possibly be imagined. Everyone wore grey, no-one smiled, there were queues everywhere and worse of all the bars were extremely hard to find. The city is undoubtedly beautiful with lots of superb architecture but the only sights we were after were the insides of bars and these were few and far between.

Our first was like a works canteen with bench after bench of thirsty locals downing large glasses of beer. We were escorted to our seats and ordered the same as the locals. The bar was crap but the beer was tremendous and we built up a fair few notches on our tab so it was with some trepidation that we approached the check out desk. We were right to worry because the cost was heart attack inducing - we had drunk 32 large beers and were asked to pay the equivalent of 64p!

This pattern was to be repeated throughout the trip and I have to say that we loved every minute despite our drab surroundings. As night approached we adjourned for something to eat and took our places in the only restaurant we could find. An attempt to sit with the locals soon earned us a rebuke and we were quickly ordered to a place of prominence on a large stage overlooking the rest of the gaff. This was a seriously posh establishment showing signs of faded elegance dating back to pre-Communist times so we decided to give the old place the respect it deserved and went to town on the menu. So little had been spent during the day that we could afford to spend on the food and we ordered accordingly. No-one had any idea of the cost as there were no prices quoted and the following is a fairly accurate summary of what the eight of us ate and drank that night: - soup for eight, caviar for six, salad for six, fillet steak with veg and chips for eight, sorbet for eight, dessert for eight, 45 large beers, 12 bottles of champagne, 2 bottles of Jack Daniels, 2 bottles of vodka, 16 liqueurs' and six coffees.

Bearing in mind that this was probably the best restaurant in Prague we were somewhat apprehensive about the bill. We hadn't understood most of what we were ordering but had simply asked for the best they had so we were more than a little pleased when the total bill for all eight of us came to the princely sum of £22! We tried to round the payment up to £25 but they had never heard of tipping and thought we were trying to pay for sexual favours!

Stubbs was indeed trying to gain favour with our waitress as for some reason he had developed an obsession for the little white socks she was wearing (these could be attractive on the right person but in Prague everyone wore them, from your daughter to your grandma and the rest of us were fairly sick of the sight of them).

She was in fact so grateful for our custom that she posed for several photos on his lap and promised to meet him the following evening - a date he drunkenly arranged to coincide with kick-off and of course she never saw him again - the poor girl having thought she had copped off with some rich foreign type.

The fact that she even spoke to him at all showed remarkably poor taste as he had spent the whole trip looking a proper prat due to anticipating it being so cold that the only footwear he had bought with him was a pair of snow boots.

It was actually very sunny throughout the week and Stubbs never got the opportunity to buy new shoes until we got back into Western Europe and even then he bought a pair of even more stupid looking cowboy boots - and this from the man who classes himself as a style guru and is now the owner of Lytham's most stylish menswear shop!

Back to our wonderful night in downtown Prague and off we went in search of some life - this proved very difficult and the best we came up with was a sort of bastardised night club in the middle of a shopping centre. We paid our entrance fee to the "Western Disco" and were greeted with the sight of hundred of Prague's teenage life dancing away to non-stop Abba. The DJ only had about four singles, the bar only sold neat vodka and the girls all had boyfriends - what a dump!

However, we made the most of the vodka and the boys were so interested in speaking to Western football fans that they offered their girlfriends up in exchange! Not bad all in all but even so, you can only listen to 'Waterloo' so many times before it drives you completely up the wall and we had to take our leave before too long. The night held few further entertainment options and we settled for playing toy roulette with our hotel porter who had a bottle of vodka to share around.

The next day heralded severe hangovers and only a few brave souls managed what has to go down as the worst breakfast ever. We shot off for some entertaining money exchanges with dodgy men in raincoats stood on street corners - you are warned not to do this as every so often they rip you off and it is highly illegal - but several of the money men were policemen anyway, even if you did lose out occasionally you still made tons the other times as we were getting up to ten times the official exchange rate and most of all it was extremely funny.

The only time I saw anyone suffer was when Stubbs purchased a load of old Rumanian currency from a Gypsy type and this even came in useful later when he palmed it off on a grateful taxi driver.

The next step was obviously a game of football in the park to work off our hangovers and we duly purchased the only ball for sale in the whole of the city. Off to the park, where we found the must superb facilities ever, goal nets, a little stand, training bibs, corner flags, the lot. After a few minutes we were surprised to see a small crowd of uniformed army types taking their seats to watch and even applaud us!

The numbers built up gradually until we were not far off a pre-Keegan Newcastle home crowd and at this stage one of the soldiers told us in broken English that we were using the army training facility reserved for Sparta Prague and although they were very pleased to see us enjoying ourselves everyone was waiting to watch an actual Sparta training session and wondered when our game would be over so that the real players could come out!

We spent the afternoon in the players hotel where we had to pay the exorbitant sum of 50p per beer but it was good watching our heroes (or our team-mates if you were in Nuremberg) mixing freely with a few fans who had travelled. Downsey, later to be immortalised in Bill Buford's book, was holding court in the bar and was keeping everyone entertained with outrageous tales about his exploits, helping to make an enjoyable afternoon pass quickly.

It was almost match time and we couldn't find a taxi so we set off by tram only to get hopelessly lost. We eventually found the ground with minutes to spare and took our seats bang in the middle of yet more army guys - this was getting ridiculous. These guys were real nasty jobs and pointed guns in your face for obstructing their view at half-time!

The game itself is one of my greatest ever United experiences - end to end stuff throughout, a thrilling 2-2 draw that takes us through on away goals and a Schmeichel-like last minute save from Gary Bailey which ensures we have more away days to look forward to. The soldiers were none too happy with the result and one went absolutely bananas at me for reaching over a seat on my way out. Downsey was keen to ensure everyone kept together as it appeared there could be trouble ahead but overall it was a happy bunch who marched off together back to the team hotel for an epic night long drinking session about which I can remember little other than a constant stream of dodgy looking prostitutes trying to charge extremely high rates whilst their potential customers were rolling around in clearly drunken stupors and rather worryingly seeing several Reds actually disappearing with them.

The day after was comedown time and rather than spend another day in the cheap but drab home of Mr and Mrs Poborsky we decided that a stop-off in Amsterdam was far more appropriate and it was red light area 'here we come' after another lengthy journey where border guards with their dogs did everything they could to prevent us sleeping.

Amsterdam provided an excellent end to the trip and everybody had a jolly good time as is always guaranteed there. In particular I shall never forget one certain unnamed member of the party (a large fat bastard) who I swear lost his virginity with a lovely young prostitute whilst the rest of us were, rather pathetically I admit, stood outside the window with ears cocked. The cries from within were most impressive and our matey thought he was performing well until the young lady turned out to be screaming in pain because the fat slob was squashing her so much!

Happy days indeed and it is with great pleasure that I can report that the vast majority of our number are still going, still drinking and certain ones are still indulging in some carnal Amsterdam type activity!

A bender in the Balkans

Spartak Varna 1 - Manchester United 2
European Cup Winners Cup Round Two, 1st Leg
(aggregate: 1-4)
October 19th 1983, Yuri Gargarin Stadium.
Bailey, Duxbury, Albiston, Wilkins, Moran, McQueen, Robson,
Muhren, Stapleton, Whiteside, Graham.
Scorers: Robson, Graham
Attendance: 40,000

Carl Hayes
Carl, 33, is a training designer/developer in the Civil Service who has been a member of the Blackpool, Preston & Fylde United Supporters Club for many years. He used to sit on a fence in United Road and in later years has sat in K Stand and now in J Stand. He fortunately missed most of the Ralph Milne years (thank God) due to playing cricket and travelling in Australia. He will only miss United games through cricket - either playing or through watching Lancashire and England (overseas). He has enjoyed the great friendship with other Reds that he has met on European away trips over the years, and feels it is a great honour to write about his favourite one, Spartak Varna in 1983.

The second round of United's European Cup Winners Cup campaign of the 1983/ 84 season saw us being drawn away to Spartak Varna of Bulgaria for the first leg.
We learned of the draw on the Friday afternoon after spending a week travelling to Prague on the train and back. "Spartak who?" and "Where are they from?" were the questions everybody asked. The trip to Norwich on the train the following day was spent looking at maps and train timetables to see if Varna was possible by train. It was to be a small group who did eventually make it by train, albeit five minutes before the kick off, but it wasn't for me and the three others from our group who were making the trip to Bulgaria.
Looking at the miles, border crossings and visas involved, flying was definitely the easier option. Phil Holt, Mick Burgess, Dave Rossiter and myself opted to travel by Ross Travel, a small London travel company headed by proprietor Michael Ross who at that time specialised in football and sports travel. Along with one other unofficial trip and the four on the train we were to be the only travellers.
We opted for Ross Travel as we had spoken to one or two lads who had travelled with them to Prague and had recommended them. Ross used to get a lot of stick from some elements of United's support, and the club, but he was certainly the best option on this occasion. Remember, in 1983 the club had banned fans travelling to European away matches and there was no official travel organised after the events in Valencia the year before.
The cost of our three day return trip, including flight from Luton, a four star hotel,

visa and match ticket was to be £230.

The Thursday before we departed we got a phone call to say that the arrangements for the trip had changed. Our first reaction was: "Shit, it's being cancelled", but it turned out to be tremendous news and very much in our favour. The trip was to commence on the Sunday before, making it a four day excursion and better still we would be flying from Manchester with a £20 refund - bonus!

Phil, Mick, Dave and I were a motley foursome indeed - our love for United wasn't shared on the clothes front. Whatever we wore back then must have looked pretty smart in Communist Bulgaria. In those days I preferred Roberto Carlo and Gabbici Italian knit sweaters, Ben Sherman shirts (nothing changes much does it?), French mac and beret. Phil used to be sponsored by Lacoste as all his t-shirts, polo and round neck contained the fashionable (and still) crocodile of the early 80s, together with an array of brightly coloured Pringle golf sweaters.

Burgo, soon to be known as "Low Profile" by the end of the trip used to wear pink mohair hand-crotchet jumpers (as worn by Rat Scabies of The Damned), dodgy leather jackets and brightly coloured sky blue t-shirts. To finish off Mick would tie his 'Gardeners Arms' Union Jack flag round his neck like a huge napkin. Dave on the other hand preferred the sporty look of Adidas tracksuits and Gazelle trainers along with his Head Bag, Donnay and Tachini jumpers. He took loads of the stuff to try and flog (on the advice of a clothes shop owner!) but the asking price for his trainers was equivalent to a months Bulgarian wage which proved too much for our East European hosts. The only thing we all had in common was a love for Clark Desert Boots.

We eventually set off from Manchester airport at midday on a small Balkan Airways (Bulgarian state owned) aircraft which felt and looked like it had been in operation since the sixties. Little did I know then that my second European away excursion was to be one of the best (if not the best) trips I've ever had. The three and a half hour flight soon passed and allowed enough time for everyone to get in the right spirit (vodka mainly).

After getting through passport and visa control we were met by the local cab drivers. They weren't offering their transport services but were asking in very broken English "Change Money?". Some of us changed the odd tenner (this was to last nearly the whole trip!) for what can only be described as brown coloured monopoly size paper notes, worth four times more than on the official exchange rate. Remembering the size of these notes was to prove useful a little later.

An organised bus was ready to take us from Varna to the beautiful (not) Bulgarian premier holiday resort of Golden Sands, some 10 miles away. Years later this resort became popular for many Westeners seeking a cheap holiday on the Black Sea. Back in 83' it was mainly used by their rich cousins from the Soviet Union.

From the outside, our digs, an eight storey hotel, looked okay, with trees lining the whole building on the esplanade, overlooking the Black Sea. After checking in it came as no surprise that I was to share Room 510 with Burgo. I'd had the pleasure of Mick's incredible snoring in Prague, so this time I came prepared with ear plugs. Besides I was determined to get so inebriated that I couldn't hear Mick's noise. We checked out the facilities and found that the hotel had a bar and a night club, but the club was closed on our first night.

Golden Sands in October was like any U.K. seaside resort in the Autumn (Blackpool being the exception), it was dead and it was dark, with hardly any street lights. We ventured out following a meal of watery soup, cabbage, potatoes and hard bread into the dimly lit streets to find hardly·any bars. We did find some in the other hotels along the front but everywhere was dead. We soon found our way back to our abode where our fellow supporters, 70 in total, had had similar problems. Not to be perturbed we made it a night to remember in the hotel bar. This is where many new acquaintances and long standing friendships began with other fanatical Reds. The hotel was drunk dry of vodka and it wasn't long before I realised that this was the biggest bunch of pissheads I'd ever come across in my life!

The following morning my room mate was flat out cold at the entrance of the lift along with "Nutty" Norman who's hair was matted in spew, still with his belongings intact - a solitary toothbrush in his shirt top pocket! Along with these two was a lad from Manchester, who spent most of his four days out cold - face down! There were people sprawled across the smart sofa chairs and some lads who hadn't made it to bed, still drinking.

We made our way to breakfast for more nourishing hard bread and cheese. We shared a table with tour organiser Ross and his courier Jackie (who was to have a dangerous liaison with Gary the Tax Inspector from Manchester later that evening). Mr Ross had already arranged our entertainment for part of the evening - he had organised a visit to a traditional Bulgarian folk night which was to include a three course meal, free drinks and dancing - all for £8.

As we left the hotel on our first morning we were confronted by a fleet of taxi drivers. Again they weren't haggling for business but were wanting us to change for money on the black market. This time though it was five 'dib-dobs' to the pound. We eventually got to the town of Varna by help of a 2p municipal bus ride to the centre. The bus was full of miserable but rather fat ladies, many of them wearing white socks over their tights in true communist style. Burgo clasped his eyes on the hugest pair of breasts he'd ever seen and was soon next to her (or should that read him?) as he skilfully manoeuvred himself close to the lady as the bus swerved corners and jolted to let off other passengers.

On the way to the town you couldn't help noticing row upon row of urban Stalinist tower blocks. This grey concrete jungle wasn't my kind of socialist utopia. Everyone appeared to be oppressed and depressed. Varna itself wasn't up to much and there certainly wasn't anything to spend all this extra black market money on. Apart from, that is, the 10p beers! It wasn't long before we needed the loo and we were being directed to public toilets in the middle of the square.

These loos were absolutely disgusting. I've had to squat in many far away places but these were the smelliest holes in the ground I've ever come across. We sat relaxing in the sunshine for the rest of the afternoon drinking beer when we spotted Barry Ellison (God rest his soul) and his (ex) wife Jenny and cordially invite them to join us for the afternoon.

They look pretty pleased with themselves and promptly show us a 650 'dib-dob' note which they had exchanged for English notes. Barry informs us that it's worth ten times more than anyone else has got so far. To us this note looks dodgy. When have you ever heard of a 650 dib-dob note before? Besides, the size of the note doesn't match up to the monopoly size ones we'd exchanged earlier with our friendly cab drivers. He'd been had! It turns out that these notes are produced by

Bulgarian gypsies who are notorious for fooling foreign tourists.

The Ellison's had already been to the Spartak stadium that morning and Barry's holding a carrier bag full of match programmes (4p each). He's ordered another box of programmes which he's to pick up on the day of the match. Barry earned his living dealing in football programmes and was the man behind 'Chorley Programmes'. I also shared a passion for collecting programmes so Barry and I spent the afternoon talking rare United Reviews, testimonials and friendlies. Barry, incidentally, met Jenny in the Stretford Paddock in the early 70s and he always thought that United should have issued Season Tickets for the Paddock. See his letter in the United Review No.4 versus Notts Forest, season 1974/75 to prove it!

We eventually board the rush-hour bus back to the hotel. A quick shower and we are soon in the hotel bar ready for the short coach ride to the restaurant for the Bulgarian folk evening.

It was to be a superb night with the best food of the whole trip being had with copious amounts of beer and vodka. The folk dancing in national costumes had just got under way when in walked the United official party of Chairman and Directors, which included Bobby Charlton and Jimmy Murphy. Some of their faces dropped when they saw us, the 'unofficial guests', but they were all warmly clapped in by our party.

Unfortunately for Martin Edwards we had only got through our first course and he was soon to find out what was the main dish! An enormous food fight had erupted between our lot which seemed to stop suddenly with everybody throwing things in the direction of Mr Edwards!

After things had quietened down, one or two of our sensible crowd used a bit of diplomacy with the Chairman, he saw the funny side of it and we left! We head back to the hotel disco, where at first we were all refused entry as it was for high class clientele only. When the doormen saw the colour of our monopoly money, he soon changed his mind.

The club was pretty spacious with a cover band on stage singing Beatles songs in broken English. We went to the upstairs bit which looked down onto the huge dance floor. We're feeling pretty flush and splash out on the best champagne in the house. At 50p a bottle we're drowning in the stuff! Immediately a large group of girls (or is that a large girl - my eyes are failing me now) are round us like flies. These lads must have a bit of dosh they must have thought...and we did. We were loaded compared to other people in the disco. There weren't many locals in the place, this would be too expensive for them. We quickly find out that the people around us are Russian and are part of a TV production team but it is impossible to get a conversation going with them, let alone ourselves.

As the night wears on bottle after bottle of champers is drunk. At some point the police arrive with Alsatian dogs and some people are led away, but everything is a bit hazy now. Two of our group leave with two Russians to discuss Glasnost, Stalin, Trotsky and Lee Harvey Oswald's wife (not). The other two decide to go for a swim in the Black Sea. Whilst they are swimming somebody from our trip who is stood on the balcony notices them in the water. Thinking that they are drowning he calls the police. Spotlights along the coast are now shining even brighter in the direction of the naked swimmers. They are faced with the Bulgarian police force who are all rifled up. These spotlights incidentally are used by the authorities to stop people trying to escape Communism, not for people trying to swim in! After successfully negotiating re-entry to Golden Sands the swimmers head back to the hotel for a shower. Meanwhile the other two are still trying to bring an end to the Cold War. Whilst Burgo is in the shower, our room has been 'done over' with mattresses, bedding, clothes and furniture everywhere and he's locked in without a key. Still pissed, he climbs over the balcony into next door's balcony - five floors up! He bangs on the window and wakes the neighbours. The middle aged couple (who we find out the next day are Swiss and are on honeymoon) absolutely crap themselves when they see this shadow of a mad-man or monster banging on their balcony window.

They let him in (he's naked remember) and he runs out of their room and down to reception claiming he's been robbed. The Swiss couple call reception accusing Mick of breaking into their room. The receptionist acts and calls the police. It's the same police that were on the beach a little under an hour ago. They recognise Mick's manhood and they want to arrest him. By this time Phil intervenes and manages to calm things down. The ranting and raving goes on for another good half-hour and after the police have left we find out that it was actually Phil who has turned over the room!

The next morning a message is pushed through the gap between the floor and the bottom of the door which says: "Hayes and Burgess - Room 510, please tidy your room and come to reception". I go to reception and explain that neither of us had wrecked the room. The receptionist clearly wasn't listening and just says: "Any more and you two are out".

Most of Tuesday is spent at the players hotel. We enjoy the afternoon playing ten pin bowling with Steve Coppell and soon we are on the razzle again (not Coppell though!). The hotel has one or two exclusive lounge bars to which we frequent. We're soon discussing politics with people from all over the globe whilst Mick is chatting to some fat, haggard Communist women. We meet a black guy who claims to be a Prince from some Marxist-backed African nation and who is in Bulgaria on business. He's a top geezer who clearly knows how to mix business with pleasure.

Later on in the day we head to the ground for the customary souvenirs. In all the games I've watched United abroad, those who know me will know that my habits have not changed. This includes obtaining umpteen match programmes at least 24 hours before kick-off. I like to ensure I have a bag of goodies to take back and Spartak Varna was no different. Pin badges, pennants, souvenir match poster and a floppy blue 'n' white bush hat (as worn at Sunderland on the Saturday). But best of all was the Spartak Varna signature tune on 7" vinyl and in a picture sleeve!

Tuesday night is spent mostly in the hotel bar. One of our group successfully negotiates a realistic price for one of the ladies of the night, he then to his horror realises that the woman's parrot on her shoulder has become dislodged but the wooden leg is still intact. The poor peasant is ordered (almost thrown) out!

We leave the hotel bar and head into town. But which town? My memory has faded at this point and all I can remember is being in some really shady downstairs nightclub with Dave. There are some dodgy looking Bulgarian sailors around and what appear to be more prostitutes. The place is full of them. I leave, I've lost Dave and I pass out in the taxi. The next thing I know the taxi driver is waking me up at the hotel entrance chasing me for the fare. I stagger into the hotel bar and the usual faces are there with beers in hand.

The day of the game finally arrives and the morning is spent breakfasting, relaxing and a quick trip to the players hotel for photos and well wishes. We jump on the players coach to take some snaps and have chats with Mike Duxbury, Gordon McQueen, Kevin Moran and Norman Davies who thank us for coming and for our support. This is United's first ever visit to Bulgaria and they have had a warm reception from the locals.

Kick off time is 4.30pm and we arrive at the ground by coach transfer in good time. A standing area has been cordoned off by ticker tape which is reserved for about 500 travelling fans. There's only 150 to 200 Reds that have made the trip! As we came into the ground a huge cheer greeted us from the Spartak crowd. I think the public address must have told them that the United VIPs including Bobby Charlton had arrived. We waved back and thanked them for their reception!

The Yuri Gargarin stadium, the second largest stadium in Bulgaria, was typically communist, oval shaped with a running track separating the pitch and the stands. There is an electronic scoreboard behind each of the goals and the numerous blocks of flats overlooking the ground are clearly visible due to there being no roofs. The concrete steps are used as seats as well as standing and we've got so much space it's ridiculous.

The unorthodox Jewish solicitors and accountants from London park themselves in front of a huge Macclesfield Reds flag. They've been the quiet, sensible types on this trip. The four lads who have come by train have just made it in time with a 300 mile taxi ride from Sofia to round off their four days of non-stop travelling, a taxi which they have to get straight back after the game to get the return train!

We are all standing level with the half way line with the best view in the house. That is, if you were sober. Opposite us there isn't a stand at all. It's open with the United coach parked behind the team benches and advertising boards.

In the match programme Spartak welcome their English guests by saying: "We believe that the football competition between Manchester United and Spartak Varna will arouse enormous satisfaction and pleasure among all football fans in our two countries". "Receive our best wishes for a most pleasant stay in our sunny attractive and beautiful town- Varna".

This is only the second time that Spartak have qualified for Europe, the last time was also in the Cup Winners Cup in the 1961/62 season. They've made it this time through the back door after losing the Bulgarian Cup Final 4-0 to CSKA Sofia, who did the double. In the first round Spartak had beaten Mersin IY of Turkey 1-0 on aggregate.

The game played in front of 40,000 seemed to pass by before our very eyes and the 2-1 win sets us up nicely for the return leg at Old Trafford. The Reds dominated the game and were always in control following an early goal from Robbo. This silences the home crowd who had earlier been jumping up and down and chanting for a good half hour before the match. Arthur Graham had a stormer and he deservedly got the second.

Phil spent much of the game wandering around in his sheepskin coat and centre-parting haircut looking for more beer. The beer I can't remember but the salty pretzels I do.

We head straight to the airport after the game to catch the 9pm flight which is delayed for two hours. This gives us plenty of time to get rid of the monopoly money and plastic coins over the bar before we leave. As I'm queuing up Gary Bailey steams in and says: "You don't mind if I jump in front of you do you?". He proceeds to buy numerous cans of Tuborg for the players. Having been served we stand around chatting to the players. Macari is brilliant, really enthusiastic about the support and the effort the fans had made.

As we're boarding the flight I begin to think about the last few days. Varna itself wasn't up too much, Golden Sands was okay and everything was dead cheap. But what made it such a superb trip was the great people and characters on board.

The group go home two people short as they decided to rob a bank, stealing wads of Bulgarian notes which cannot be used anywhere else in the world! They spend the next few months in a Bulgarian jail.

This wasn't the end though. Our flight delayed already we couldn't believe it when we saw the Balkan aircraft we were about to board. This was the worst aircraft you had ever seen and it was even older than the one we came on. It was propeller controlled and as we got going it was the loudest aircraft I'd ever been on. As we climbed into the air, ice appeared on the doors and windows. If you were sober I swear you would have been worried. The other unofficial trip were also on the same flight coming home.

We were promptly served with drinks and cold dinner. An enormous food fight went off again with the plastic lumps of cheese and hard cobs of bread being thrown everywhere. The hostesses were agitated and got extremely upset as they were hassled and harassed by some now-naughty supporters. In the end they gave up and left everyone to it. If you wanted a drink and duty free good you could ask them nicely at the back of the plane and they would serve you.

Meanwhile the lad from Manchester was face down on the floor in front of the exit door. Did he see the game I wondered? The noise in the aircraft turned to 'Hisses' as yellow life jackets were being inflated. As we left the aircraft at 3am numerous people were wearing them including one of our group (later to be seen wearing it again at Coventry on Boxing Day).

Nearly done we thought but he had to play on the revolving baggage claim conveyor belt acting like Dylan from the Magic Roundabout. When he eventually got home he woke the entire street, singing at the top of his voice and then proceeded to cook a joint of meat in a frying pan and butter the dog!

It took a full day to sober up and recover. A great trip with great memories. One of the best...if not the best.

DISPATCHES FROM
OLD TRAFFORD

Barcelona 2 - Manchester United 0
European Cup Winners Cup Round Three, 1st Leg
(2nd leg that tremendous 3-0!, aggregate: 2-3)
March 7th 1984, Camp Nou, Barcelona.
Bailey, Duxbury, Albiston, Wilkins, Moran, Hogg, Robson, Muhren,
Stapleton, Hughes, Moses. Sub used: A.Graham
Attendance: 70,000

Arthur Albiston

*Arthur Albiston, 40, is a former Manchester United great, who made 482
appearances for the side at left-back in a career at Old Trafford spanning 15
years. Regarded with much affection by the United fans for his powerful surging
runs and masterful defending, Arthur played in twenty-seven competitive
European games (thirteen abroad) , playing in cities as diverse as Prague,
Oporto and Varna in Bulgaria. He is currently helping coach the next batch of
budding United youngsters twice a week at Old Trafford.*

The very name of Barcelona Football Club has a great ring to it. Every player wants
to play in big European matches like this and I was no exception. Earlier in the
competition we had overcome Dukla Prague on "away goals" and Spartak Varna
4-1 on aggregate, hardly household names, but now we were in for a real test. In
the Barcelona side were the great Maradona - who went off injured in the away
leg - and Schuster, the West German amongst a sprinkling of Spanish internationals.

We approached the match in good spirits having just won away at Aston Villa 3-
0, which was no mean feat, and were unbeaten in the league since early
December. However, we'd had a couple of disastrous results in Cup competitions,
losing to Oxford Utd in the Milk Cup and Bournemouth in the Third Round of the FA
Cup. Nevertheless the European Cup Winners Cup gave us all a chance to
redeem ourselves.

Preparations for the match followed a familiar routine. After the Villa game
everyone was given Sunday off, unless you were injured, in which case you'd have
to report to the Cliff for treatment from physio Jim McGregor. The squad players
who didn't play against Villa would also report to train. Monday training would not
be too strenuous as we were approaching the last quarter of the season. Tuesday
would be mostly set-piece routines and a brief rundown on how Barcelona would
play before departing early afternoon for the airport and our charter flight to
Barcelona. As soon as we boarded the plane the card-schools would take shape.
Ours consisted of Lou, Bryan, Kevin and myself. Sometimes invitations would be
sent out to the "junior" school, but usually there were no takers.

As a youngster I had once lost my passport with Scotland U-21's, so I always carried a small holdall, this was convenient for the other card members to lumber me with the cards and also information on who owed money to who. The other players would sort out the card "table". This would involve occupying six seats and folding down the middle two. There's been many an argument over seating arrangements before the plane has taken-off, but normally a glare from Bryan or Kevin did the trick!

We played a game called nomination trumps in which you had to predict how many "hands" you would achieve. If you didn't get exactly what you predicted, you didn't score. I can't remember who came out on top on this particular trip but I seem to recall Lou and his family having the holiday of a lifetime that summer!

The main thing was it took our minds off the job in hand, which was to get a decent result from the first leg. Other players had different ways of relaxing, some would read, some would sleep and others would listen to music on their walkmans. A few would try to chat up the air hostesses, usually to no avail. After landing it would be straight onto a bus to take us to our city centre hotel. The cards would continue at the back of the bus. As Tommy Cavanagh once said, there could be a bomb scare or terrorist alerts but nothing stops the card schools!

On arrival at the hotel it was a quick change into our training gear and off to the stadium. The Camp Nou must be one of the best stadiums in the world and I'm sure most of the lads were looking forward to playing there. The session wouldn't be too long, it was mostly to give everyone a feel for the place and also to see how bright the lights may be. We'd finish with a light-hearted eight-a-side game and play until Ron's team won. Ron wasn't a bad player, not too mobile, but he talked a great game.

Back to the hotel where everyone would eat together. It's funny how things stick in your mind but I recall one of the lads ordering for desert, half a pineapple filled with custard and raspberries with cream on top. So much for weight-watchers! Everyone had a taste and soon most of the lads were on for it, much to the disappointment of the other guests in the restaurant.

Wednesday and the day of the game and the nerves would begin to surface. I always got up for breakfast, Lou was another early riser and we'd usually eat with some of the press or radio lads that were covering the match. Most of the players would have a long lie in bed before everyone would go for a stroll around 10.30. Some players who were doubtful for the game would have treatment and perhaps a fitness test to see how they could cope.

Having two young sons at home, I couldn't go home empty handed so I'd be looking for something suitable for them as we strolled around the city centre. One of the bonuses of playing in Europe, apart from the different football, was some of the places you'd get to visit. Barcelona being a "football" city, we'd get some good natured ribbing from the people who recognised us and also the best wishes off the United fans who'd arrived early for the game. Back to the hotel for more cards before we had lunch together and then off to bed for a sleep or rest and getting your mind focused on the game. We'd have tea and toast around 5pm and I remember the hotel being extremely busy with quite a few familiar faces of lads that we knew from Manchester coming to the hotel to wish us good luck.

My memories from the match are quite vague but I do recall us having a fair amount of possession and felt quite hard done by the 0-2 scoreline.

Unfortunately the first goal took a wicked deflection off a young Graeme Hogg, who was making his European debut. At 0-1 it wasn't so bad but very near the end one of their defenders, Rojo, strode forward and rifled one into the top corner giving Gary no chance in nets. We flew home immediately after the game, everyone a bit subdued, but still hopeful for the return leg.

You don't get too much time to feel sorry for yourself in football as the games come thick and fast in March and April. Two home wins against Leicester City (2-0) and Arsenal (4-0) set us up nicely for the second leg at Old Trafford which was to prove unforgettable.

TURIN TURNOVER

Juventus 2 - Manchester United 1
European Cup Winners Cup Semi-Final, 2nd Leg
(aggregate: 3-2)
April 25th 1984, Stadio Comunale.
Bailey, Duxbury, Albiston, Wilkins, Moran, Hogg, McGrath, Moses,
Stapleton, Hughes, Graham. Sub used: Whiteside
Attendance: 64,655

Steve

Steve, 39, Cockney Red and Manchester United fanatic since the day he can remember, has supported them throughout the glory days when the 'buzz' was something to remember. He believes United are the one and only religion. Known by many, he would class himself amongst the 'hooligan' fraternity and believes what he's done in the past - although he says it sounds hard to believe - was for the benefit of MUFC. He believes Man Utd are - and should be - No.1 in anything and everything they do.
Having met and conversed with an American journalist who has also done a story in a book with regard to these events (and holds him in the utmost respect), Steve has no need to paint a more vivid picture than it really was...

Semi-Final. Cup Winners Cup. Should have been the biggest game I've ever been to. Little did I know what drama was to unfold...

Unusually for me I booked on a two-day trip, travelling the day of the game and not the normal three day, simply because I went on a trip guaranteeing a match ticket as this was when United fans were banned from Europe. Suffice to say the match ticket never materialised at the end of the day.

I booked it with that lovely character Mr.Ross, the latter day version of UF Tours. I'll put it down to Mr.Ross' normal style - he never got in contact about the trip at all, and if it wasn't for the fact that I phoned his office the day before travelling - which was the Tuesday - only to be told that the airport had been changed and we had to be in London, at Marble Arch, at 5am to catch a poxy mini-bus to Manchester to get the plane I would never have got there.

So after all the normal nonsense of getting out of bed nice and early, all that crap, sleepy eyes it was up to London and then to Manchester to get the charter.

There wasn't anything exciting on the way out other than the fact that we were pestered continually by journalists on the plane. There were lots of stupid Daily Star reporters - who we'd also had trouble with on the previous trip to Barcelona - hellbent on talking about trouble and trying to instigate trouble, going on about 'United fans being barred', etc, 'British hooligan at his best'.

We arrived in Turin on the Wednesday lunchtime to be met by the sight of only about - at that time - 100 or 200 United fans scattered about the main square with several Union Jacks dangling from balustrades. The afternoon of the game was spent in that normal English delightful pastime of getting plastered, especially that young slim fellow, Michael from Blackpool.

By mid afternoon the number had swelled to about 300 or 400. But still quite surprising to me because United were in the prime of Red Army on manoeuvres, plus it was the Semi-Final of the Cup and I honestly expected there to be several thousand United fans there, and not maybe 1,500 at the end of the day. I was very disappointed with the turn out.

What also surprised me - in that main square - was that the police let us do whatever we wanted. With United fans drinking everywhere, and cars having difficulty swerving through the Red & White, the police closed the road off, so that no traffic could actually knock any of us over whilst we fell around drunkenly in the street.

The afternoon was beautiful sunshine, a normal, plenty of drinking session, with nobody really venturing from the square, with no trouble, a heavy police presence and us like performing monkeys with a massive Italian audience. Everyone was just - as is the way - standing getting drunk and Mick got nicked for some drunken behaviour, still not sure why, but this becomes a relevant part of my story, the fact that he'd been nicked.

And so towards kick-off. We - i.e. the firm, as such - all caught a bus down to the ground arriving fairly late. Although promised match tickets we never actually had them, and there was obviously not a United section to get into. This didn't seem a problem at the time and everyone was ushered towards one set of turnstiles and was just allowed in to be met when we walked in there by everybody else who was standing on the forecourt.

They were all saying that they couldn't get out on the terracing as every time they stepped on to it they got bombarded by missiles. Being the brave honchos that we were and completely up for it as always, we just walked straight through this tunnel without any hesitation, turned, went up straight over the first crash barriers as you come down the terracing and walked straight on and upwards.

The Italians were just clearing out of our way as we went, completely just opening up, backing off and disappearing. Whilst this was happening everybody else who'd come out on to the terracing before we'd arrived and been bombarded with everything and anything and had to go back under , were following us.

We took up position on the terracing, with very little policing. The police that were there were extremely young, it was if they'd drafted everybody in from school and put them in a uniform. The Italians were allowed to walk round the pitch with these massive flags, which in themselves were a really great sight, on these massive fibre glass poles, which looked the business, but not so much when they were trying to stick them through the fences at you! But they were just allowed to do it. It was a good sight, but typical foreigners just allowed to do what they like against the English because the English are fair game for anything, as Rome '97 proved.

The atmosphere in the ground was brilliant, probably the best abroad apart from Galatasaray that I've ever been in. The stadium was rocking, when the teams came out the whole stadium was just red everywhere, the flares, the smoke was amazing.

The game - shit! Obviously we lost. Gutted. With the last minute goal knocking us out I was destroyed. We were stuck in a poxy little bit but right at the bottom of the terraces. But after we'd first arrived we'd had no more trouble whatsoever.

We were locked in, but certainly not for the time a certain American correspondent put down in his report. We came out to be faced by Italians in a semi-circle, across the road from our gate, around our exit was a baying mob, hurling the odd item, with our coaches that we were supposed to be put on, on the other side of the road, with the police ushering you towards these coaches.

Approximately 60 of us burnt off to the right as we came out and just completely broke away from the police escort. Really we weren't as annoyed as we would have been if we'd been back in England after a defeat, a bit wary of the circumstances, not particularly sure of what we were going to do, but as always bang up for it. It was a good little team. We burnt off in the direction away from our turnstiles, still no police and, basically, caused absolute mayhem as we went down, around the ground.

Then we turned left across that main park dead opposite the old ground. Juventus, at the time although I didn't realise it, are the team, a bit like the Manchester United of Italy, where they have a massive travelling support, and all the way through this park there are just hundreds of coaches from all over Italy. It's got all the Supporters Clubs and everything else, all parked there, one coach after another, and we've turned into the darkness of this park.

We were going to go through the whole park on the rampage. We've started off and passed two or three coaches and got about thirty or forty yards into the park and gone straight into the first coach. We're actually in the coach, with reckless abandonment. We've done one coach, we've come off and then repeated this all the way through. There were hot dog stalls, big stalls with scarves, they've all been tipped over.

Some youngish guy, about 19/20, who I've never seen before and never seen again since this day, and I remember it clearly, he had in his hand this big fork like you hold the roast beef down to do the carving and he's brandished the fork like he's the devil in a sceptre and he's jabbing it going through this park and giggling everytime he's done it.

It's a massive park and we've done the whole thing with no police. By the time we were in the middle of the park we must have been outnumbered by five hundred to one if they'd all turned and we literally took on each coach, one at a time. They never got their act together and joined up, and we just went through the park on a complete collision course with anything and everything that came in our way, taking the odd time out to actually go up the steps of each coach.

Contrary to that American journalists report I never saw any building catch fire, nor any shop windows put in, simply because there weren't any shop windows as we were going through a park! He hasn't even mentioned it's a fucking park.

It was really a case of we were a steam train and nothing was going to stop us, I suppose carried through by adrenalin and possibly a bit of fear that it could have all back-fired at any moment and we would have been trapped in the fucking darkness and absolutely battered to shit.

We got right through the park, thinking we were all superheroes and had done our bit for the cause seeing as the cheeky Italians had knocked us out of the cup, and proceeded to walk another two miles - which certainly took everything out of us and brought us back down to earth - from the park to the town.

On reaching the town 70% of the group that were with us turned right into the station to their midnight train on towards the next destination, leaving a mere handful of us to cross into the square, which was at this time completely filled with a baying mob of Italians, with cars driving round with them hanging out of the roofs.

We crossed into the square towards this hotel where we'd all arranged to go back for a drink and I was walking under a covered walkway, got about twenty yards down towards the hotel when, bumph. Two Italians smack-bang standing right in front of me, nowhere to go.

All of a sudden this police car pulls up to my right hand side, door opens up and Mick falls out of the back-seat, just released from the cop-shop. He walks over, says: "Alright Steve", turns round and knocks out the first Italian standing in front of me. The coppers jump back out of the car, run round, grab him and pull him straight back in the car and drive off! Which is contrary again to reports from my American friend who says that when we got back to the hotel Mick was back in the bar. Mick got arrested as soon as he got released.

This was a great relief to me because these were rather large Italians. He was left sprawled on the floor and I just stepped over and walked into the bar.

We couldn't get out of the hotel for the rest of the night. The Italians were out there all night long, just waiting for the odds and sods to come out in ones and twos. We all stayed there, had a drink, until it was time to go to bed.

I read what Bill Buford wrote and I haven't a clue where he came out with this fucking armoured car nonsense, because I certainly don't remember it. I can also categorically state that unlike his report , twelve year-old boys were not systematically kicked to pieces by six or seven Utd fans and we most certainly didn't go into that park with 200. Basically he went a little bit overboard with his descriptions.

It was in the bar that I first consciously met Buford, even though he was on the trip out with us. We turned round and met this American journalist who said he was working for the Sunday Times at the time. He said he'd been with us on the way back after the game, little known to me, and that it was the "best guerilla warfare" that he'd ever encountered.

The day after - as with all European trips - straight up into the bar, starting as if we'd just begun. Another heavy drinking session and then back to the airport for a sight which I have never seen anything like in my life. The journey back (with Buford) was something to be seen, and no-one believes you when you tell them that how the plane arrived back was.

The plane was completely overcrowded. Untold amount of jibbers on the plane, it could have been up to 20 jibbers. The police have come on saying they're looking for someone who hadn't got a ticket, rushed over the plane for about two minutes, and then walked off without taking anyone with them. There were people under the seats, people squashed up so where there should have been two people there were four. It had to be seen to be believed.

The way back was just some massive session. No-one had seats, and when we came down to descend into Manchester airport, there were people standing up in the aisles still drinking. One of the funniest sights I've ever seen was someone with this big bottle - vodka or beer - and when we hit the Tarmac he shot along the aisle from one end of the plane to the other, and then come back again, without falling over or without the bottle coming away from his mouth.

The jibbers did it without any problems whatsoever. Got through customs at Manchester, and the police did nothing, everyone just walked through. If you tell people that people jib planes they'll never believe you - but this was a mass jibb. Absolutely unbelievable.

Oh Good, we've drawn Raba Vasas ETO Gyor

Raba Vasas ETO Gyor 2 - Manchester United 2
UEFA Cup Round One, 2nd Leg
(aggregate: 2-5)
October 3rd 1984, Raba ETO Stadium.
Bailey, Duxbury, Albiston, Moses, Moran, Hogg, Robson,
Muhren, Hughes, Brazil, Olsen. Sub used: Gidman
Scorers: Brazil, Muhren
Attendance: 26,000
(and just why are nearly all European away attendances exactly spot on the 0,000 mark!)

Stephen Sozzledallthetime
Stephen, 40, is still watching United on a regular basis but as he is such a law abiding citizen he has refused to take a drink since Maggie introduced the ban on drinking before sporting events. As a result he has now become very boring and sits in the library all day reading Dicken's novels about the old times when you were allowed to drink in the street. He is still having regular fantasies about a certain element of the following story.

This one definitely takes the biscuit in a world of 'What?', 'Where?', 'Who?' and 'How to get there?' series of questions following the European draw on that Friday in the middle of the summer that we all look forward to so much each year.

A team that has no European history that anyone has ever heard of, no recognisable location on the map and no entry in Simon Inglis' "Guide to Football Grounds In Europe". It hardly sets the imagination running wild with anticipation and so it came to pass that come the day of reckoning my little crew that had numbered 25 for our last sortie to Juventus was actually reduced to three; two by plane, one by train.

I always reckoned that the difference you saved by going on the train would probably be eaten up by extra spends during a longer time away and so made an instant choice to travel on one of Michael Ross' by now legendary flights direct to Budapest with a two night stopover.

Arrangements for the trip were duly made and it was pleasing to report that Mr.Ross had employed a new secretary to make arrangements/take bookings, etc. Her name was Jackie and accounts from those who had been into the Charing Cross Road shop where Ross was based tended to indicate that she was an absolute stunner and what was more she would be accompanying us on the actual trip.

This was to be a crucial occurrence as every single traveller subsequently fell in love with her and spent the whole trip drooling over her. I have never laughed so much as the number of times that that fat bloke from Blackpool kept asking Jackie: "Please could he check that her tits, sorry tickets, were in order". This was a theme that ran through the three days we were away and I reckon she must have heard the words 'tits' more often in those three pre PC days than in the rest of her life put together.

Mind you, it must be stated that they were in fact an exceptional pair of breasts, which served to fully complement the rest of her luscious figure, and still figures vividly in my fantasies to this day - and those of several others bearing in mind the drunken conversations that still occur with my fellow travellers.

Anyway, on with the trip, and it's to Heathrow airport we go for an early morning meet and first sighting of Jackie's lovely tits (calm down, that's enough now, Ed). We arrive at 6am, for a departure some three hours later and adopt our normal positions at the bar. There is something distinctly lacking in the atmosphere of a trip where we are going somewhere no-one wants to go to, we are winning 3-0 from the first leg and hardly anyone has bothered to make the effort for the trip. Nevertheless a fully stocked bar does throw temptation your way and in time honoured, inimitable fashion, I move from beer onto treble vodkas way too early.

This is a spectacular vodka attack even by previous standards and death cannot be far away. I am going through a Paul Wellor Style Council phase and my Burberry raincoated image is not matched by my outrageous behaviour as we seek to board the plane. This drunken person cannot wait for the drinks trolley and starts drinking neat from a bottle of Blue Label inducing an incredible vomit attack all over my yellow cashmere Lacoste sweater, my co-drinkers and best of all a very concerned stewardess.

I manage to explain that I need some air and try to climb out of the window only to be restrained by our tour guide, the lovely Jackie - oh well, that's one way of making an instant impression even if it's not quite the correct one! My next action is to try to make my way into first class as I spy some empty seats which I have not yet managed to be sick over. This is a lovely area, full of well to do people enjoying some polite conversation until Paul Wellor suddenly decides to collapse into an unconscious heap across the aisle thus stopping any further trolleys entering first class for the rest of the trip!

No-one is able to wake me until, miraculously, two minutes before landing I come to and am back to normal (if there is such a thing in the world of the Martin Edwards lover).

A coach then takes us to our hotel which is the magnificent Astoria Palace overlooking the river with an enormous fountain in the lobby - shortly to be seen as the venue for the world: "Manchester United supporter's water splashing on posh hotel guests Championships".

We make our way into a wet, drab and grey Budapest where we quickly locate a bar that serves up our good old friend Eastern Bloc vodka for approx 20p per glass. Coupled with my earlier intake, this does me no good whatsoever and my health/behaviour deteriorates rapidly. Jackie is coming in for more stick and takes to her bed early, refusing all requests for company for some reason.

The rest of us astound central Budapest with some amazing drinking exploits with some excelling themselves. A good sing-song rounds the night off and we all fall into either bed or the fountain as very happy souls.

The day of the game heralds a Mr.Ross sight-seeing tour by coach on the way to the ground some two hours away. To a man we all decline this thoughtful offer and decide to make our own way by train to this cesspit of a town that awaits us. The train takes less than an hour and we get 10p taxis to the ground where a good splattering of Reds have already arrived.

We congregate around a social club and sit in the sunshine drinking beer with the locals at approx. 15p per pint. This is very pleasant and gets even better as the lemon vodka appears. There is to be no alcohol in the ground yet out hosts are so genial and the police so lenient that we march in for the game with a bottle of vodka apiece and no-one asking any questions - why can't we do this nowadays?

In the ground we meet up with several friends who have come by train and van and listen eagerly to their travelling tales. Breakdowns, muggings and late trains all play their part in convincing us that flying was the best way - and Jackie's tits of course!

The game passes quickly and a 2-2 draw even provides some entertainment despite the first leg lead. There are lots of humorous songs (celebrating an Alan Brazil goal) and good banter with the opposition fans and again it is a happy bunch who depart for the coaches and the journey back to Budapest. On the way Mr.Ross has booked us into a Miner's Welfare Club for some much needed food but comes into a torrent of abuse when we realise that there is no alcohol but just coke to be had (and not the nasal type!). Noah, however, sneaks back to the bus and returns triumphant with several bottles of lemon vodka still remaining from the game which are much appreciated by all the locals as well.

We return to the hotel for a last tour of Budapest's bars and a last dance in the hotel fountain - naked this time! The only thing remaining is for me to clear my room bill only to find that I have fallen asleep the night before whilst ringing home and not replaced the receiver which has rang up a massive phone bill of £82 - not bad for 1984!

The trip ends very happily for Low Profile when Jackie accepts his offer of a night out in London and even invites him to stay at her place. This is later ruined however when she walks into her bedroom during his stopover and catches him sniffing her underwear!

End of another great romance!!

The Naked Truth

PSV Eindhoven 0 - Manchester United 0
UEFA Cup Round Two, 1st Leg
(aggregate: 0-1)
October 24th 1984, Philips Stadium.
Bailey, Gidman, Albiston, Moses, Moran, Hogg, Robson,
Strachan, Hughes, Brazil, Olsen.
Attendance: 27,500

Mick
Mick, aged 34, is married, a purveyor of fine wines, beers, spirits, liqueurs, pies,
burgers, Kentucky, curry and Blackpool rock.

Whenever your team qualifies for Europe, one of the most eagerly awaited moments is on the day of the draw itself. Home or away first? Who've we drawn? Where's that? Are you going? These questions will all have been asked and answered by the many thousands of Man Utd fans who have followed their team overseas over the years.

And so it came to pass that Manchester United would play PSV Eindhoven on 24th October 1984. Not bad, people thought, at least it might still be warm in cloggy land in October and not too far to go. As per usual (and quite comical in the early days) the modes of transport to these games were feverishly discussed dependant on money, time off work, if you were a wanker and couldn't fly, etc. One of the funnies that received quite a bit of attention was the ferry that would leave Sam Platts (as it is now) and sail down the Manchester ship canal to the Irish sea, circumnavigating Britain, turning left or right at Liverpool depending on whether the weather was good or bad and head for Holland - and all for £39 return.

The best trip that we could come up with was the boat-train to Harwich, then ferry to the Hook of Holland and usually a 100 mile route march by the local constabulary to knock all that fighting spirit, ale, and enthusiasm out of you. Tickets for this journey cost about £50, but don't forget that this was the era of Persil tickets, where upon begging mothers, girlfriends, wives, aunties and anybody else who used Persil washing powder, travel tickets could be purchased on a 2-for-1 basis.

The Veevers Arms next to the bus station on Talbot Road was the meeting point for the Blackpool Reds before an away game and so the motley crew assembled there on Tuesday dinner time for a quick session before going to Piccadilly for the tea-time boat-train to Harwich. There were eight of us (including one female, Suzanne), who left Blackpool North for the hours ride to Piccadilly, and although I was only 22 at the time I was a veteran of about a dozen trips abroad watching footy. I had mainly travelled by air with Ross Travel in the early eighties and so did not know many of the 'faces' that went on the train.

We left Piccadilly about 5pm and settled down for the four hour journey. Although this was supposed to be a dry train the Old Bill did not have much luck in enforcing it. There were almost as many Hectors as Old Bill on the train as the jib was a cheap, if not troublesome, way of seeing the Reds. A few people got lobbed off the train before Harwich but some of the die-hard experienced jibbers "pissed it". Much ale and singing were the order of the day on trains in the Eighties and nobody let the side down, much to the annoyance of the Old Bill.

When we got to Harwich we waited for what seemed like an eternity in a large booking area of the station. During this wait I was asked by the police to accompany them to one of their interview rooms. Everything seemed civilised until I entered one of the rooms. This was locked behind me and then I noticed one of the Old Bill who was dressed in plain clothes as one of the "passengers" on the train. The mood of the place was quite hostile and aggressive with the plain clothes policeman wanting to know who I was, where I lived, where I'd come from, etc? Pretty thick bastard I thought, seeing as I had just come from exactly the same place as him!

When I enquired what the problem was I was met with a chorus of: "You're the fucking problem". Why was I the problem I replied rather drunken and sheepishly? Was I the only person singing and drinking on that train? No, I don't think so! This reply did not please our friend from the constabulary and bearing in mind that I was still on our side of the North Sea, I decided to do nothing to provoke them. This did not satisfy the police so they picked up my Head Bag and emptied the contents onto the table in front of me, rummaging and searching for anything that might incriminate me and satisfy their pathetic macho egos. When no illicit substances or incriminating materials were found they came up with something that defied belief to further have a dig at me.

"Take all your clothes off", said the British Transport Policeman. "Why" said I. "Just take them off, this is not a fucking quiz" replied the copper. Sobering up by the minute I did what the police had said and was soon bollock naked in the interview room. As soon as the last bit of clothing came off, the copper said: "Right, put your clothes back on". This episode had merely been an exercise to show they had control over me whether I had done anything wrong or not. Packing my gear back into my bag I Thought: 'what an absolute bunch of wankers'.

When fully clothed and my bag repacked the plain clothed copper sneered: "Now fuck off, we don't want to see you again. Just wait till the Dutch police get hold of you. They won't be as fucking kind as we were". As I left the interview room and saw Suzanne and Gaz, another of my co-travellers I couldn't help but think 'what the fuck was all that about!'.

Gaz and Ian were not happy chappies when I told them what had gone on but I told them if we gave them any grief none of us would see cloggy land for the match. Over at the top of the booking hall the crowd of people had now formed something of a queue with British Rail and port staff checking tickets and bags. Within an hour everybody was on the ferry and people without cabins (99%) were staking their particular patch to doss down for the night when the nightclub and casino had shut.

Not giving a toss where I was going to sleep I headed for the bar with our lot only to find it absolutely mobbed. Olly shouted 'Duty Free anyone" and produced a bottle of Vodka which served as a nice aperitif for what was to come later.

Not being a great ferry traveller I headed for the outside fearing I was going to chuck up. This is quite a regular occurrence for me and in no way does it impede my drinking capabilities although it doesn't do much for my facial features.

Chris and Wiz went for a jolly round the ship whilst the rest found a spot for our gear. When I came in from the deck the nightclub had just opened and we all piled in for a bevy. Now nightclub discos on ferries are normally crap, and this was no exception. But looking forward to the game (which would kick off in 20 hours), everybody was hyped up, pissed up, some drugged up and the night went pretty well though losing £30 at Blackjack put a dampener on things.

Suzanne kicked me at 6am. "We're here" she said as I tried to get up. When on deck you could see the lights of the Hook of Holland and as we docked you could also see quite a lot of Dutch policemen, some with shields and riot gear, some with Alsatians and doberman dogs and some with just the basics. Disembarking went pretty smoothly except for two lads who were picked up by ferry staff, presumably because they had interpreted the sign 'Duty Free' in the shop a little too literally.

With customs cleared the police herded us onto waiting buses and took us to a bus depot in Eindhoven. Anybody who had a match ticket was then allowed to go their own way but those without tickets were made to walk 3 miles (with bags) to the ground.

We were the lucky ones, many other Reds using various (coaches, etc) forms of travel and collecting tickets at the ground were stopped by border police and refused entry into the country - facing an unhappy journey back home.

PSV's ground is a neat compact one with a running track and fences around the pitch perimeter. I had wondered if they took the fences down for athletic meetings because you would be a bit pissed off watching the long jump through a grille!

After buying tickets for the United end, it was back into the centre for a drink, something to eat and to get cleaned up, though not in any particular order.

The weather was warm and sunny and many Reds were sat outside on the pavements of cafe's and bars. "Don't have any proper pubs" moaned Ian but he soon picked up when it was pointed out that you still got pissed up in them whatever they're called and whatever they looked like.

Big Belly, Suzanne and Marshy decided on something to eat and with Big Belly's legendary dislike of foreign grub they went to the Holiday Inn. Sirloin Steak and chips is about the limit for Big Belly and no salads, sauces or vegetables whatsoever. The other two had something more adventurous containing garlic which proved to be their undoing as they missed the last half of the match with suspected food poisoning.

The rest of us found a bar which was packed with Reds and decided that this would do us for the day. No point in traipsing about different bars if they all look the same!

With about three hours to go now until kick off people started to wander to the bars nearer to the ground and the city centre bars became frequented by more and more cheeseheads as they finished work.

We didn't see any problems or grief between any of the supporters, just plenty of drinking and the usual piss-taking.

With about an hour to go, we made our way towards the ground. If you didn't know before who sponsored PSV Eindhoven, then you certainly did by the time you got to the ground. Almost every corner or road was illuminated by a giant flashing neon sign proclaiming 'Philips' or 'Philips Electronics' or 'Philips this, that and the bloody other'.

When we got to the ground there was a very large police presence. Although there had been no trouble in town, Anglo-Dutch games always have that little needle in them that could swing either way.

Anyhow, once inside it was down to business. This is what we were here for and a good result in the first leg was vitally important. Yet the match didn't get going and there wasn't much to ignite the Reds in the ground. The defence coped quite adequately with anything the Dutch outfit had to offer. Predictably the match ended goalless which the United players regarded as a great result judging by the way they saluted the 4,000 or so United fans who had made the journey to Holland.

After the match the police kept the United fans back for about an hour until all the cheeseheads had left the ground and surrounding streets. Those people going back to the Hook of Holland to catch the Beatrix Kronigen were herded onto buses, which to some people was regarded as a right result seeing as they had been drinking all day and didn't fancy the long walk back to the bus terminal.

This though was not a good result for our mob who had left all our bags in the bar where we had been drinking all day. Walking back there we saw a few skirmishes between Reds and the locals, but nothing to write home about. We got back to the bar at around midnight and began to have a couple of beers, until Suzanne (who was well pissed off with us by now), pointed out that the ferry left in an hour. Taxis ordered, drinks drunk, bags reclaimed and we headed for the Hook of Holland by taxis, slagging off women in general who do not know how to enjoy themselves at football.

We made it onto the ferry with about 10 minutes to spare and crashed out on the first available piece of floor space.

Arriving back at Harwich was pretty sobering, freezing cold and pissing down. Welcome back to Blighty. I wondered if I would bump into the plain clothed wanker I had met at the ferry terminal on the way down, but surprisingly didn't...

Travelling home after a game is usually one of the big downsides to Euro away games. All the buzz has gone, and usually the money but none the less we still had our Duty Free's. "Aperitif" I shouted and produced a bottle of vodka, similar to the scene on the way out. There is nothing like the transparent gold of the Russians for turning a train journey resembling a funeral to that of a boisterous away match service-crew. Our party inspired a few others, but judging by some people's reaction they just wanted us to shut up and die.

Arriving back at Piccadilly shortly after lunch-time we said our farewells to some of the people we had become mates with on the trip and arranged to meet them again at the Trafford or Dog & Partridge before the next game.

We had another hour to kill before the train back home so, surprise, surprise, we decided to go for a drink. Suzanne started whining again and said she was staying where she was which was a result for us as she looked after the bags.

In the pub we gave marks out of ten for the trip. Drinking 10. Football 7. Travel and accommodation 0. Shagging 0 (although Olly tried with guess who). For my part if we qualified for the next round (which we did in extra time of the 2nd leg thanks to a Strachan goal) it would be back to the paraffin budgie.

Now looking back thirteen years later, our trips have become a lot more organised and comfortable but the big buzz is still there the day before, and on the day of the match.

Long may it continue.

Bloody freezing - but at least the bars stay open all day...

Dundee United 2 - Manchester United 3
UEFA Cup Round Two, 1st Leg
(aggregate: 4-5)
December 12th 1984, Tannadice Stadium.
Bailey, Gidman, Albiston, Moses, McQueen, Duxbury, Robson,
Strachan, Hughes, Stapleton, Muhren.
Scorers: Hughes, Muhren, Own Goal.
Attendance: 21,821

Martinez Daze
Please allow me to introduce myself to you. My name is Martinez Daze. I am of large standing with a somewhat less than athletic bronze frame, some may in fact say I'm a fat bastard. Anyway I'm a Red - I don't suppose I would have been invited to take pen in hand in this publication if I had blue tendencies. My first recollection of United wasn't watching a game but having my first kit stolen, at my school, Limeside Infants, Oldham. I loved that white away shirt, this in the late sixties. Well, that's enough of me...enjoy the article.

This was a low time in my life, being on the Nat King Cole and Christmas just round the corner. It was a fairly disappointing European draw - the lure of a crack in some remote corner of Europe being replaced by a game at Dundee - well, in itself remote I suppose.

I didn't order a match ticket and didn't have any intention of going. But as the day before the match arrived, I just couldn't miss a European away, a game being played just four hours or so away and in a land where you could (then) legitimately drink all day.

Therefore I gave Chris Marsh, a mate in the same dire straits as myself a call and we decided to meet up at the bus station in an hour, after Chris had signed on. After meeting it was the first bus down to the motorway, where we showed our thumbs and a bit of leg, or as some might add, quite a large bit of leg. Our first lift picked us up after about 15 minutes and dropped us - approximately twenty miles from home. Each services we passed were awash with Celtic fans travelling down to Old Trafford for their hastily replayed game against Vienna.

By now it was getting dark and sleeting, and as I wore my new heavy sheepskin coat thought I looked like the dogs bollocks. Just as we were beginning to get very wet, cold and disheartened and thinking about going to Manchester with the promise of a good piss up thanks to a coach load of Celtic fans from Dundee, we got a lift in a wagon up to Hamilton services for about 8pm. Desperate for a few beers (and warmth - it was snowing now), we discovered the nearest bar was two miles away and someone at the garage suggested the golf club just over a field. Can you imagine Royal Lytham or St Andrews letting two freezing scruffy vagabonds in their club? Well Hamilton Golf Club - or whatever it was called - welcomed us in with open arms. After a quick chat with the Club Secretary we were fed with soup, pie and chips and a wee dram thrown in (or down).

We must have been the most exciting event of the year as we were introduced to all the present members, all buying us drink after drink. The club steward gave us a lift back to the services about midnight and wished us luck and to call in on the way home.

We were both raving about the Scottish hospitality when a Transit van pulled up. "Where yer going boys?" the driver asked. On reply we jumped in and were off again, freezing again, not helped by the van lacking anything that resembled a heating system. The roads were terrible with the ice and snow everywhere, this didn't seem to bother our chauffeur though as he overtook any vehicle he passed, with a strange sense of humour as he would go around roundabouts the wrong way, etc, as we both stared in astonishment.

Finally he dropped us off at Perth train station. It was now about 2.30am and the first train out to Dundee was 6.30am. We got our heads down in the very cosy waiting room and were awoken by a hive of activity outside as the train was about to depart. Thankfully the train was one of those free ones and 20 minutes later we embarked, at long last after such a short - in reality - journey, at Destination Dundee.

A city at 7am in a blanket of snow with nothing open isn't one of the most welcoming of places and as we couldn't stay at the station with a very desperate Hector (train inspector) chasing after us, we set off for a couple of hours luxurious sleep at the bus station. Of all the plans of mice and Reds. Two fellow United fans, Rob and Bob from Keighley were having a party. Their crate of beer borrowed from a Yorkshire wine merchant was offered to us and we obliged. United matches in Scotland always seem to be more drunken than most and this was no different. So a drinking session started that lasted between the four of us until 7.30pm.

"We four Kings of United are, came to Dundee from afar"

This little ditty we sang in many drinking establishments that day. Other verses were added but, alas, the wee brain cannae remember. By Noon we had met up with many a Red, some with tickets, the majority without. Talk was of a night club opening its doors with a bit of female entertainment. Of course, the thought of naked ladies attracts some people, so we decided to take advantage and just nip in for a drink. Now regular visitors to the Fantasy Bar in Manchester will be wetting their lips in the knowledge of what was to come. Well, as we entered the venue we were met by the sight of a large screen showing porno films.

This looked promising. We grabbed a beer and sat around the stage with about a hundred other perverted Reds. Everything seemed great until the barman said 'sorry, I havnae got any more films'. "That's alright mate, just get the Jack The Rippers *(strippers)* on". 'What strippers?' said the barman. You guessed it, the female entertainment promised was a bleedin' blue friggin' movie! The barman could not understand why we didn't want to stay, so one or two told him in no uncertain terms. On leaving we bought the local evening paper due to it having a photo of us all in merry mood earlier in the day. Above the photo was the headline: **"The**

friendly Red Army".

As is usual again with Scottish games, every bar we went in was packed with friendly Jocko's joining us in different songs. Just before kick-off I met up with fellow Reds from home, two of whom were AWOL after being falsely arrested. Seizing the chance of a lift home for free we thankfully avoided our very own nightmare return leg. Then on to the ground, crossing the bizarre road that separates the two football clubs of the town. What must Derby Day be like there!

The match - to many exciting and fluctuating all the time (like the first leg) - was a blur, but we won, seeing the Reds in the official Utd tier (nearing 1,000) to one side celebrating wildly and Reds in the home end also, er, celebrating wildly. And we'd now get another chance to get somewhere really foreign in the next round.

After such an exciting two legged affair there was still no real animosity, a lot of mutual congratulations and scarf swapping whilst we were kept in. So, for yours truly, began silly game time.

If you have a video tape of the game you can hear me singing whilst Gordon Strachan is being interviewed. This was followed by a game of footy on the pitch without a ball and then a jib into the dressing rooms. On seeing John Gidman I said I was sorry he didn't play as I thought he was the best crosser of the ball at the club. He smiled, shook my hand and walked off towards the waiting coach. It was not until I arrived home and watched the game on video that I noticed that Gidman had played the full 90 minutes. He was later to take the piss out of me at an away game later that season.

Anyway, for such a short destination it proved - again - to be a most illuminating trip. Both me and Chris made many new friends, both North and South of the border.

Oh, and we got into the game with forged tickets. A right result all round.

ANYTHING BUT BLOODY PENALTIES

Videoton 1 - Manchester United 0
UEFA Cup Round Four, 2nd Leg
(aggregate: 1-1. After extra time, lost 5-4 on penalties)
March 20th 1985, Sosto Stadium.
Bailey, Gidman, Albiston, Duxbury, McGrath, Hogg, Robson,
Strachan, Hughes, Stapleton, Whiteside. Sub used: Olsen
Attendance: 25,000

Pete

Pete from Ramsgate, 33, is happily married to a Chelsea 'bitch' with a bonny Busby babe called Brittany. He's been making his way from Ramsgate to Old Trafford for the last 18 years, firstly with the Cockney Reds on the special and more recently with the Invicta Reds. He's seen United play all over Europe, had good and bad times at home and away, seeing at least 700+ games (call him a part-time Cockney bastard if you want). He was born and bred a Stockport Red and is proud of it. Here's his adventure of a visit to Hungary.

So, let me set the scene. March 1985, after a 2-2 draw at West Ham it was straight back home to Ramsgate to pack my bag, this being the second visit to Hungary is as many months, boring Commie bastards. Hopefully this trip will be as successful as Raba Gyor.

So off I set for the long, arduous trip to Dover (if anyone has seen the Warriors, it had nothing on this trip), with Bobby Buttons, with his fuck off flares, Shamus from Littlehampton, with his Wacky Backie in hand, Rocky from Altrincham, who went on the rob in our local chippie, hoping for the till but ending up with a rather nice apron; and numerous other Reds who have since gone their separate ways from our beloved club.

With ferry tickets in hand, we all strolled down the jetty singing that old all time John Denver great: "We're leaving on a Jetfoil, don't know if we'll be back again". We arrived in Ostend, to get the train, well over 1000 miles ahead of us with not a single train ticket in sight - the European jibbers team is back on tour.

This trip is so different to the last one to Gyor where I went on the plane for a three day trip and stayed in a classy 4-star hotel. Now it's dodging the hectors, dossing on the trains and drinking shed-loads of beer and abusing the German b*****ds. First stop was Cologne, after an enjoyable cat and mouse running the gauntlet from the Belgium and German hectors (guards).

On arrival in Cologne we walked outside and bumped into the cathedral, which we were told was the best tourist attraction. Surprisingly the bar opposite stood more ground. After a small aperitif we got back on the train for more fun and games, especially taking money off Bob and the others at cards, only problem being by this time we were on our second four pack whilst Bob was tucking into his 3rd bottle of German Ribena.

We bumped into a German soldier who didn't speak a word of English, but we still punished him with a volley of: "We won the War" and "One World Cup", but he kept laughing as we were laughing at him, especially when Shamus borrowed his cap and made a Hitler moustache with a bit of paper and went Goose stepping up the train, although the oldens on the train did not find it so amusing.

Rocky then entertained us with his speciality - gobbing up a mouthful of flem and hanging it as far as he can out of his mouth and zipping it back up again. This little trick kept us amused for at least 5 minutes. All of a sudden, somewhere near Frankfurt, we had a hector alert, four of the seven of us who were jibbing made haste to the toilet, which baffled the German soldier but passed with no problems.

We pulled into Frankfurt, said our goodbyes to our budding 'SS' officer and set off for a top up of beer, as we hadn't had one for a couple of minutes. Had a nice meal, in fact we thought it was that nice we decided not to pay for it when the German waitress left us unattended.

Back on the train and thankfully we were not too far from Munich as tiredness and drink are taking their toll before our first night's stopover. On arrival at Munich we thought we'd stepped into a Christmas picture postcard, with snow at least two feet deep, which we, of course, were all kitted out for!

Due to the arctic conditions we made our way to one of the first hotels we saw, which we later discovered was more like Colditz than a nice guest hotel in Blackpool, but at £4 a night who was grumbling.

We found directions to the Beerkellar, where we came across some more Barmy Reds - and we thought we were worse for wear. Two Deutschmarks for a litre of beer, tremendous value at half the price. After three hours, and bucket loads of beer, we decided to find a late night kebab shop.

After food we trudged through the snow and came across a German nightclub, but were refused entry for being 'drunken English'. So there was no alternative than to start snow ball fighting with the German bouncers and other unsuspecting Krauts in the queue. After five minutes we decided to have it on our toes as the enemy had had enough, as about twenty of them emerged from the club "wanting it". Arrived back at the camp, forcing our way past the dogs and search lights and back to our warm, cosy hut.

After a nights sleep we made our way back to Munich bidding it a fond farewell. Unfortunately we had to buy a ticket to Vienna as the jib was almost impossible, which made us feel like losers, but not that bad considering the distance we'd so far travelled.

The beer from the day before had worn off so when Shamus pulled out some German cans it made good sense to start all over again. Now travelling legally, we decided to abuse the hectors, which was great fun at the time, with Shamus smoking his finest and Rocky showing them his masterpiece with his flem.

Coming into Vienna the temperature was still -5°, but we were all dressed for the Costa Del Sol, rather than Costa Freeze-Your-Bollocks-Off. We bumped into a mass of United fans who had already checked out the local action. They informed us that one of the lads had booked into a hotel across the road, where we could shower as we were still hanging from the night before. With 12 people in a single room showering, there was a knock on the door. We thought we'd been had, but after opening the door it was only Roger from Margate who just happened to be passing, as you do in Vienna.

We hit the town and like a bloodhound Bob found his favourite restaurant - McDonalds, which made good eating, as we'd only eaten beer suppers and dinners for the last two days. Had a look around Vienna before joining the train on the final leg to Budapest.

On arrival in Budapest, we taxied to the hotel, where everyone was staying on the Michael Ross trip. Four Star luxury, even the players were staying there. Here we found out that Videoton's ground was still an hours train journey away which really pissed us off.

Budapest at night was great, full of bars, all welcoming us as if we were locals as we'd been there a few months previous, during the first round victory over Raba. Went to a strip joint, where believe it or not the Hungarian women were very tasteful, even better when only charging £5 for sex.

The day of the match we travelled to the city where Videoton (so named because they are sponsored by the main employer within the city, a video making company!) play, which I promise you only a Hungarian could pronounce, with only 18 letters in its name. The welcome party of Videoton supporters met us at the station, this made us feel slightly uneasy as we walked through a crowd of mad Hungarians - chanting and singing and looking us up and down as if we'd arrived from another planet.

These so called "angry fans" turned out to be souvenir hunters, who wanted to exchange scarves and hats instead of punches. Walking to the nearest bar, I heard a broken English voice of: "Peter, Peter", and when I turned round it was the very same East German Red who I'd met at Raba months earlier, who had cried on my shoulder saying how lucky we were to be English and able to see United, week in, week out, as there was the matter of a huge wall in his way.

In the bar we made friends again, although I'm sure all he wanted was my scarf and badge, so feeling sorry for him I decided to do so. Instead of a football match it turned into Saturday Morning Swap Shop, expecting to see that Scouse twat Keith Chegwin pop up from somewhere. I acquired a Videoton ski hat, which to this day can still be seen on my barnet at Old Trafford in the winter.

After the first leg 1-0 victory, the Semi-Final was beckoning. We in fact went down 1-0 down to the roar of 25,000 barmy Hungarians (about 400 Reds had made the trip). After extra time penalties loomed which were going fine until Frank Stapleton - scorer of the First Leg goal at Old Trafford - squared up to take the penalty. He hit the ball so fucking hard and high it almost knocked Bill Haley off his comet and to this day you can still see it through the sight of a telescope.

Losing 5-4 on penalties, everyone came out of the ground absolutely gutted, but still the locals wanted to have our Wrigleys Gum, and tempers were not as good as two hours earlier.

Travelling back to Budapest, the only consolation to be had was drinking beer to console ourselves after this so close but so far game. With nowhere to stay we had to find a place so we made our way to a hotel which was actually a castle overlooking the River Danube.

A dormitory type room was sorted, costing only £2 a head. The one major problem we envisaged was fucking Count Dracula coming through the door. We headed back into the city where we sniffed out one of the only topless bars in Budapest where the Hungarian talent was better than Stapleton's bloody rocket. It was 4am and we decided to go back to the Count's Palace, where we'd all made wooden stakes and crucifixes. Good job it was only two hours until day light.

The following morning we checked each other's necks and made our way to Budapest station for the long, hard trip home. Had a few beers at the station and got on the 24 hour train to Calais - this being a non-stop Orient Express. Arrived back home with only my ski hat and tail between my legs but the memories of a fantastic trip, and hopes of many more to come with better results in the future.

Pete from Ramsgate - A Red To The End.

<A drunken bus also made the long trip over to Videoton from England, containing some very well known United faces (such as Tommy Gardener and Mallett) and achieving notoriety whilst causing mayhem all over Europe. Stories of legend were born on this trip (including the song: "The drunken bus went over the hill...") and those involved still speak in awe at all that went on during the week away.

Highlights included the group being stopped at one border control and queuing up with 100's of fellow travellers, and the Utd fans deciding to use their travelling guitar for an impromptu concert whilst dancing on tables and chairs. For some reason they were quickly ushered through the large queues in front of them.

One passenger took all his clothes off on a cross-channel ferry and did a streak through the whole boat and the independent coach driver got so drunk that he went down the Autobahn singing the Blaydon Races with no hands on the wheel. That the driver had even been drinking came as a surprise to the other people on the coach!

The trip is also immortalised by virtue of a tattoo on Drunken Dave's right leg recounting the verses of 'The Drunken bus came over the hill' and in tune with the style of the trip several of the words within have been spelt incorrectly on his leg!

Nevertheless it's quite impressive to think that they only received 10 complaints about their behaviour from the coach company...>

Santa
Wonderland

Pecsi Munkas 0 - Manchester United 1
(aggregate 0-3)
European Cup Winners Cup Round One, 2nd Leg
October 3rd 1990, PMSC Stadium.
Sealey, Anderson, Donaghy, Bruce, Phelan, Pallister,
Webb, Blackmore, McClair, Hughes, Martin.
Sub Used: Sharpe
Scorer: McClair
Attendance: 17,000

Tower Power

Tower Power, 35 and a mini coach driver, was born in Meridan Warwickshire, and whose father was a Red having to work away from his Manchester roots. He is married to Elaine and they have a son, Liam. He now drives for a living after a career as a lazy electrician. His first United match was at home to Burnley in 1971, John Aston scoring in a 1-1 draw. He sat with his father (Les), little realising that this was to become an obsession. The last time he missed a game at Old Trafford nobody had heard of Maggie Thatcher. He believes that like most fans away matches is where you get the buzz - and there is nothing better than a Euro away.

First let me introduce myself and my travelling companions for the journey. My name is Martin, and I spent the trip with six drunken friends; Philip, Tony, Ron, Mick B, Mick R and Phil.

This match was the first European away since the lifting of the ban after the Heysel disaster. Remember the days when you would listen to Radio Two for the 3rd Round Draw of the FA Cup on a Monday lunchtime? Everyone at work would be talking about it all morning with the excitement building up. For some bloody reason the draws for the respective European Cups is somewhat more difficult to hear about.

Eventually word got round that it was going to be live on the radio on a warm Friday lunchtime in July. Well I decided to have the day off work (sad bastard), I tuned in my radio in and sat back from about 10.30 in the morning. The phone never stopped ringing with the same question: "Have you heard anything yet?". 'No...no...no...fucking NO!".

At the 12.30 sports desk the reporter said full details of the European draws would be given out at 1pm. That came and went and still no bleeding news, and then, finally, at 1.20pm we were told that we would be playing the Hungarian side, Pecsi Munkas.

When the draw was made it was a case of 'where on earth is Pecsi Munkas?'. After a bit of detective work we found a town called Pecs in the south of Hungary. These were the days before travel companies offered trips, and United's trip was a one day affair via Budapest, which included a four hour coach trip and costing in the region of £250.

Of course this was not for us. For the next couple of weeks we looked into ways of reaching this far flung destination, and eventually we decided on hiring an eight-birth camper van, complete with toilet, shower, cooker and fridge.

The hire company told us we would get about twenty miles to the gallon. This information was to prove complete and utter bollocks, yet the first problem was the only place we could find to hire these campers was over in Bradford, a mere 80 miles away.

So on Saturday morning we got a City friend to run us over to pick the vehicle up. He was not too pleased when we pointed out that this would be the nearest he would get to seeing European football. This would prove to be wrong when Glynn went to watch United in Gothenburg, blue nose bastard.

On collecting the camper we discovered it was a bloody monster, about the size of a coach. It did baffle us that anyone with a normal driving license could hire one of these. On departing the garage we were told to fill up a.s.a.p. The petrol station was two hundred yards down the road. Unfortunately on entering the forecourt we managed to clip a petrol pump. This was a frightening prospect - with a trip over the Iron Curtain in front of us we had crashed 200 yards into the journey.

Reaching home after a boring home match with Nottingham Forest one of our supposed travelling companions - Sprog - had left a message: 'Sorry, can't make it due to not telling the girlfriend until today. She has burnt my passport'. Well it meant we were down to seven, not the magnificent, I hasten to add.

Sunday morning meant local league football. The team we are connected to - The Mortgage Shop - had an away game in St.Anne's, and Phil who was staying with us could not believe we wasted our precious hang over time watching this shit. Tony had played in the game and needed a shower because of all the running he had done. Phil likened Tony to Ralph Milne, only Ralphie could play a bit!

We departed on Sunday afternoon, Mick B the last to pick up from his local hostelry - The Gardeners Arms. To say Mick was merry would be an understatement, he was cabbaged. His baggage for the week away was a crate of Guinness, a toothbrush and a pair of Marks & Spencers finest.

The fridge was full of beer, a wardrobe full of adult literature, the other wardrobe full of our fancy dress outfits - we were under way.

The journey to Dover was a nightmare, taking ten hours, missing the proposed ferry and the one after. We eventually made it and departed the boat with yet more cans. It was decided before we left home that three of us would share the driving. Up until now it had been Philip and myself who'd driven, and it meant it was Mick B's turn. Unfortunately he forgot to stop drinking, therefore I took the wheel with Mick then telling me how to drive on the other side of the road. He was a past master of Continental driving having gone to the World Cup in Italy that summer. On returning home we found out it was only for one hour - again due to drink.

The day ahead was a long hard drive through the tip of France into Belgium and then down through Germany. Everyone apart from Tony was spending the day looking at the stash of porn mags, he was more interested in looking out of the window at his so called Fatherland, due to his German relations. I should point out that these sightseeing moments for him were between long moments of sleep. Fuck me, this guy could sleep for his country (Ireland, Germany, England?).

One of the main rules had to be that the toilet was for pissing purposes only. Unfortunately both Mick's had other ideas as both were having bowel problems - and so it became a competition who would go the most times in the week ahead. This was, of course, to become a problem for the rest of us. The hire company had informed us that the toilet would probably last us all week without needing to be emptied. Well by Dusk on the Monday the full sign meant someone would have to empty it. Fucking me, who else! The job only entailed pulling a lever back under the toilet tank, but the smell was the worst...well you can imagine.

We decided to drive until about 8pm, and at about 7.30 we broke down and were not happy chappies. It was decided that one of us would have to walk and phone the German A.A. A pack of cards was produced, the drivers were exempt which included a by now very drunken gentleman. Phil lost in a not so honest card deal. He wasn't happy, especially due to the torrential downpour that was now occurring.

When he finally got to the phone he seemed to have communication problems due to the fact that his German wasn't too good. The operator couldn't speak English so he came back and told us his parting words were: "Listen you Kraut cow, get the fucking A.A. man here now!". It seemed to do the trick as within an hour Hans the A.A man was with us laughing because we had simply run out of petrol. Of course I got the blame - and would have to buy the first round. Nothing new there then.

We arrived in Regensberg, a quiet town with no bars. Well, that's what the man said where we changed our pounds. We didn't know if he was joking or just wanted us out of his hometown but we managed to find a bar. It has to be said that it was a gay bar, but at this point we were desperate for a drink, still thinking that bars were thin on the ground round here. How wrong we were. The place was alive, we'd had a bad start but it was kicking now. We then tried an Irish bar and from there went on a Schnapps bar crawl, all the locals were very friendly even when we became a little boisterous.

Three of us - Mick R and Tony as well - retired to bed about 3am, not before we woke the town up with our renditions of musical gems such as 'The Hills Are Alive With The Sound Of Music' and 'If I Were A Rich Man'. It must have been the Schnapps.The other four came to bed about 5am, we could hear them leaving their last bar - a mile away. Now one of Philip's faults is to become very mischievous when drunk, many people and hotels can vouch for that.

This night he thought it would be a hoot to have a disco, the cassette was put on full blast (a punk tape) and resulted in pogo dancing in and out of the camper. This went on for half an hour before he finally hit the sack.

Tuesday morning was Philip's turn to drive, but I was awake at 7am due to the incredibly loud snoring of Mick B. Therefore I set off driving, no one woke until 10.30 but at least today we were to reach our destination by early evening. Unfortunately we didn't account for the Yugoslavian borders. This was shortly before war broke out and we faced a long traffic delay leaving Austria. On crossing over the border the unthinkable happened, Mick B took the wheel. Up to this stage the camper had done about 13 miles per gallon, it was now to do about 8 m.p.g. Mick's driving has to be seen to be believed. He still thought he was driving his Escort. No motorway mattered, roads as well come to that. There were no street lights and the cars and trucks on the roads didn't bother with headlights. We - the passengers - have never been so shit scared as we darted about - the local transport seemed to be cow and cart...we must have killed people.

It also soon became clear that Mick was not now enjoying his passengers company. He became very irate at Philip's map reading, and the constant slagging off of his driving (this is in the main due to the fact that we kept ending up on our backsides - no fucking seat belts!) and all was not well.

Eventually we reached the Hungarian border at about 8pm and were stopped. We thought this was due to the authorities wanting to see our Visas, but alas, no, it became obvious that the border police had never seen a camper van before. They wanted to see every inch and delayed us another half an hour.

Phil decided to have a shower, this was to be a major mistake. Mick B was still at the wheel and taking corners at the same speed as straight pieces of road, resulting in Phil shooting out of the cubicle on every corner.

We finally arrived in Pecs close to the University quarter packed with lots of pretty young girls. We gave them all a porno mag as a goodwill gesture and wished them farewell. On entering the main square of this Hungarian secluded town we knew we were back in Europe. A well known pair of United drunks were lying in the gutter slaughtered.

Pecs was a pretty town with a number of bars to spend our recreation time in. After a quick meal we found a bar with a number of football officials - men from the F.A, men from the police back home and United club officials. They were not too happy with our attendance. When approached it was clear that we were the last people they wanted to converse with.

Their only contribution to our debate was when they parted the hostelry with a sullen: "behave yourselves boys, we don't want to get banned again'. Maybe our reply did not fill them with reassurances, as we basically called into question their fathers.

It was the night before the game and we were still without match tickets. I decided on a visit to the players hotel in the hope of a player or two sorting us out. The only person I recognised was a Club Director. I approached him politely and in no uncertain terms was told to 'go away and behave yourself'. I apologised for asking, and pointed out it surely would be better if all United fans were in the same section. "Go away". This was a man I had idolised all my life, I left hurt and disappointed that a hero could be so rude. A few years later we were to speak again on our way to Benfica in the friendly. This time he had the time to spend an hour discussing various things, he said he did not remember our meeting in Pecs but explained why he was so unfriendly. My hero again?

On returning to the rest of the chaps they had come across more unofficially travelling Reds, some had flown to Budapest, some had come by train and a boat down the Danube. 16 lads had flown to Budapest and climbed into four executive-style Lada taxi's. On reaching Pecs it became clear that there were no hotel beds to be had. Thankfully one of the taxi drivers had his Grandparents living in Pecs. He took all the lads round, moved his Grandparents into the garage and charged them the price of a Big Mac to stay for two nights. Unfortunately these lads had a few too many and decided that the house cat could fly. This meant throwing the poor thing down a cliff. Oh, and they forgot to tidy the property up before leaving. The lengths Reds will go to, all to avoid travelling expensively with the club.

Our last port of call for the evening was the local striptease club, the drink was cheap and beginning to take its toll. Unfortunately the club wouldn't let United fans in - the next days we were to hear that this wasn't due to fear of hooligans but that a certain Chairman was being entertained. The end of the night saw us take the camper up right outside the stadium, where after a few silly photo opportunities we retired until the ticket office opened.

We arose on Wednesday - match day - at about 8am and the stadium was bristling with people. We were taken to the main office where we were told tickets were at the high price of £1.50ish. The seven of us bought 25 - strange you may think but they were to make us many friends that morning.

Kick off was at 1pm, only four hours away by now. We travelled into the main square, where we dressed for the day ahead. During our preparations for the trip I suggested wearing fancy dress on the day of the game, seeming like a good idea at the time.

Therefore the seven of us departed our camper into the main square all dressed as Santa Claus.

It was already seventy degrees outside and the outfits were very warm. The locals couldn't believe their eyes and we soon became quite an attraction. We needed something to eat before the liquid refreshment and we chose the local fried chicken shop - a shame they didn't cook it for longer than the thirty seconds it took.

Anyway, on to the first bar, then the second, third, fourth, when we reached the fifth bar the English press had caught up with us.

At first we were interviewed by B.B.C Radio and then by Clive Tyldesley for I.T.V. The only problem was Ron and myself were on the sick from our work so had to keep the disguises well and truly covering ourselves up.

The interview was to be seen on the Saint and Greavsie show the following Saturday. When it was shown it missed out my part of the interview, which was a drunken speech on why we should be back in Europe. Phil and Mick B got their tenpenniesworth in, followed by a rendition of jingle bells.

Thankfully I kept my Santa beard on throughout, or so I thought, but more of that later.

Shortly after this it became clear that a young Hungarian lady called something like Agnes was hanging onto us. She was quite attractive, spoke good English and had an ample chest. She could not believe how rich we were (!) and soon became our guide and interpreter for the day ahead.

Kick off was approaching and we made our way down to the stadium where we gave out our remaining tickets. On entering the ground we were met by hand-shakes and applause by the so called Hungarian hooligans that the British tabloid press had warned us about.

We decided to make our way over to the United section, and were met by United's new security firm. They were as subtle as the Albanian Police. It was basically made clear that we were not welcome - now call me insane but having

United supporters all together makes for better security.

There was never going to be trouble here, what if we had played in a different more hostile atmosphere and there was a major problem. The first game back after Heysel was obviously a high profile game, because of our own security we ended up watching the game with the Hungarian riot police. Our new friend Agnes became our interpreter and they thought we were great.

The game itself was a pretty uneventful winning one. A 1-0 win thanks to a Brian McClair goal laid on by Clayton Blackmore. The game petered on in the second half and it is worth pointing out that at this stage there were two unofficial people on the United bench - two drunken Reds, John and Wayne, had jibbed it, high security my arse.

At the end of the game the official party were escorted to their waiting coaches and we went on to the pitch where Alex Ferguson came out to chat and have his photo taken with us. He even invited us on to the players coach, apparently we were quite a talking point in the changing rooms.

On boarding the coach some of the players applauded us, Les Sealey was pissing himself and Steve Bruce offered us all a can of beer. We waved the players coach off and made to the nearest bar, about twenty feet away. Parked outside it was a Salford Van Hire mini-bus, United flags draped outside and a party in full swing. Agnes was still with us and drinking beer for beer.

Every round we bought she asked us for a packet of fags, she must have got 800 out of us and every Red in the place was trying to get into her knickers (except me). We ended up having a six hour session in here and it was decided that we would get taxis back into town. Well, six got into one Lada and me and Mick B got into another. Unfortunately the first taxi took Agnes to her house with five gentlemen and word has it that she had quite a game both there and in the taxi. Mick and me ended up having a bloody steak and fried egg instead. In fact to this day Mick has still not forgiven me.

We eventually caught up with each other, with comical stories concerning their little venture with Agnes. Unfortunately two Santa's began arguing about the situation, fell out and had what was described to us as a fight (handbags at dawn) on a patch of grass as a bemused taxi driver looked on for his next fare!

After a beer we were all bosom Santa's again and finished the day off with a full blown bar crawl taking in the strip club. Somewhere along the line Mick B ended up selling his Santa outfit to a happy local for 99 pence and on returning home discovered he had to pay £28 for it!

Once again on the Thursday it was me who got the journey under way, although the thought of the long haul back was not appealing. Everyone was somewhat under the weather and you could tell that the day was going to be a very quiet day.

We stopped the night in Passau, Germany, had a meal and a beer or two and within an hour everyone was back in the holiday mood and another drinking session was under way. Except for yours truly, as I was, to coin a phrase, fucked.

The early morning drive on the Friday saw us have a puncture which we discovered at the services. You have never seen seven more useless bastards in your life. It took us an hour to change it, mainly due to us turning the wrong way trying to get the nuts off.

After this I decided to ring home for the first time that week, and when my wife heard my voice she started crying, repeatedly saying 'Thank God'. Early that day a mini-bus returning from the match had crashed and there were fatalities. My family had thought it was us, it turned out to be Reds from the Hollinwood area of Manchester.

The rest of the morning was a very thoughtful one, firstly to the families of the lads in the mini-bus and secondly to my family. They had been ringing the police to try and find out and on ringing United, Barry Moorehouse, the membership secretary, was brilliant to my wife and reassured her it was not us.

Later that same day we found out who our next opponents were to be. Phil and Mick B went to the phone and on returning I could see the glee in their eyes. "Well who have we got you bastards?", 'Sampdoria' came the reply. Well, it could have been worse...

It took the pair of them two hours to tell us the truth, after listening to all of us going on about how we were going to get there. We'd in fact been drawn against the might of Wales - Wrexham. Welsh Phil thought it was his birthday, Wrexham his local club, only eight miles from home.

The ferry home was to say the least a little choppy, an eight force ferkin storm. The chaps thought it would be a laugh wearing the Santa outfit's again, not realising how rough the cruise would be.

The sight of five Santa's all spewing up in the gents was a sight. You may be wondering why only five out of the seven, well I was busy taking photos and Philip was the only passenger on board propping up the bar drinking. Even the barman was a little green under the gills.

We finally reached Bradford just before lunchtime on the Saturday, sorted out the paperwork and returned home, in time for Saint & Greavsie. There was a ten minute report on Manchester United's return to Europe, the highlight seven Santa's being interviewed with Agnes in the background. Greaves said we were the best ambassadors the club could have wished for.

On Monday it was back to work. I thought it was safe to go back as nobody could have identified me off the Saint & Greavsie show. This was to prove true, the only problem being The Daily Mail had a picture of us after the game - minus our beards! The factory walls were plastered with photo copies. Thankfully my Gaffer saw the funny side.

This was the First Round over with, all our dreams were to come true as we reached the Final and beat Barca. I'd like to take this opportunity of thanking all my companions and also my wife, who gave birth to our son, Liam, exactly nine months after our return. He looks like me, honest.

The sheep track to Wrexham

Wrexham 0 - Manchester United 2
(aggregate 0-5)
European Cup Winners Cup Round Two, 2nd Leg
November 7th 1990, Racecourse Ground.
Sealey, Irwin, Blackmore, Bruce, Phelan, Pallister,
Webb, Ince, McClair, Robins, Wallace.
Subs Used: Donaghy, Martin.
Scorers: Robins, Bruce.
Attendance: 13,327

John Sayer
John, 35, is a hard working newsagent who has been a United freak all his life. Currently living in Ramsgate, Kent, he has been watching United live for about 23 years. He started travelling regularly to home and away games with the Old Folkestone, Kent Branch by coach when he was 14. He is currently secretary of the Invicta Reds which he has been doing for 11 years. On match days he will be found in a pub before kick off having one or two quiet drinks with his many friends from around the country.

Wrexham. In November. Well, how do you put into words such an exciting European away trip?

I still don't know how I drew the short straw to write about such an eagerly awaited European away trip...ha!...ha! I must have been extremely pissed at the time to agree - which is rare for me on a European away, contrary to what some people may say.

Four of us travelled up on the morning of the match. Not many people were using this as an opportunity to use up their holiday leave and there were few Reds who opted for a stay in Wales for the game. Certainly unlike any other European away we've experienced in decades. A few drinks, game, and then home. Thank you who ever made the bloody draw!

With me were Roger from Margate, a veteran of many European games who said it made a pleasant change from jibbing his way across Europe, Fatty Pete, a larger than life poser who is rumoured to have once bought the first round of drinks, and Peter Van Something or other, who for a couple of years, like so many others, went non-stop to every game, fell in love, and has since disappeared up his own arsehole, not to be seen at a United game since.

With a Fiat Tippo hired for the journey we set off on our merry way. After a quick service stop tasting one of those delightful special cold fry-ups that cost an arm and a leg we headed for the little village of Buckley (where a fellow Red lives), about eight miles away from Wrexham. Just as we hit the Welsh border with passports ready someone shouted 'stop'.

As I hit the brakes, causing mayhem behind me on the tiny road, we realised that - without any specially adapted Wellington Boots with nails to cope with any sludge - we'd not be allowed anywhere near the village as mud began increasing in volume with each turn of the wheel.

Without the boots, apparently also used for the catching and shagging of sheep, we couldn't enter Buckley, so we took the main road straight to Wrexham. The journey was getting a bit boring (a European game was round the corner!), I decided to liven things up a little. I said to the others: "Let's see if we can get to Wrexham without slowing down or stopping at any roundabouts". This made the rest of the journey much more fun, as I got more and more cocky with each roundabout. As we approached our destination I decided to increase the speed as we approached each roundabout. Somehow we arrived safely and after dumping the car a few minutes walk from the ground, Roger jumped from the car, wanting to kill me and saying - for some strange reason - that he never wanted to see another roundabout in his life. I couldn't see his problem and suggested we find the nearest pub so I could buy him a drink to calm his nerves.

Perhaps it's a coincidence but I've had complaints about my driving on other European away trips, most notably Gothenburg, when I was removed as co-driver half way through the trip. Again I couldn't see what the problem was,

First pub. Pub and beer crap. Move on. As we passed the ground - which looked a right shit hole from the outside and was even worse when we eventually got in - we met a few Reds who pointed us in the direction of a pub called 'The Turf'.

With the help of Roger's persuasive tongue the goon on the door eventually let us in. It was already four hours to go before the game and we got a few much needed beers in. As could be expected, about half the pub was packed full of Reds, and, also as you'd expect, vocal ones. We worked our way to the back of the pub and joined in the very vocal singing.

With about an hour until kick-off, we learnt that upstairs had a balcony which overlooked the pitch and where you could watch the game from. This seemed like the best idea all day and as the pub started to empty we decided to take a look. Unfortunately the reason the pub had emptied was that half the bar had had the same idea and it was impossible to get up the stairs, let alone the balcony.

A few more and it was to the match, where we were standing in the Marstons Paddock, behind the goal. We managed to get in straight away, just making kick off and to confirm that United were wearing that horrible City blue, multi-coloured (and sickening) shirt, you know the one.

It was fairly vocal in the ground, for the size of the Utd following (about 6,000), but, unfortunately, didn't have the same European away 'feeling'. With United leading 3-0 from the first leg, it was always going to be a bit of a stroll, and it was all pretty unforgettable, with Robins and Bruce scoring within five minutes of each other in the first half and that was that.

At the final whistle it was straight back to the pub for a few more before the long trip home. With the roads deserted it was a pretty boring trip home as well, apart from Pete doing a ton past a police car on the M6 and then shitting himself about getting pulled. Early hours arrival, crashed out.

As European trips go, this was the must boring and uneventful ever, and must surely be bottom of the all-time list.

(Welsh) Phil Williams

Phil is obviously perfectly placed to write about a European away fixture which took place just a few miles away from his home - now how many of us could ever say that!

Europe has many exotic destinations, many of which United have played in at one time or another. After our comfortable 3-0 aggregate victory over the Hungarians of Pecsi Munkas in the previous Round, the minds of United supporters were firmly fixed on a possible dream trip!

A group of us were still making our weary way back from Hungary when the draw for the 2nd Round of the Cup Winners Cup was made. We had stopped for a short while at a service station in Germany when one of the lads phoned home to check up on her indoors (to check the draw was the real reason!). He returned to the vehicle with a huge grin on his face - his first words were: "I hope you like pizza lasagne and spaghetti". We all thought Sampdoria, great, what a trip. Little did we know he actually meant we could be eating in the Pizza Hut in Wrexham.

The consolation from this 'local' draw was exactly that - it was local and for me that was just 10 miles away. It would mean a great saving in holiday time and cash. The other bonus was that I knew plenty of local hostelries to enjoy a pre-match session.

The plans for the day were drawn up a week or so before, and it was arranged that the local based Reds would meet up with a motley crew of other drinkers for an 11am start in my home town of Buckley - for anyone without a detailed map of Wales, that's a town about 10 miles away from Wrexham.

The first couple of hours were relatively tame with some food actually being consumed as well as the drink. A large pool competition was played out and then it was onto the serious matter of a pre-match European session.

The rest of the afternoon and early evening was taken up touring my local drinking haunts, annoying most of the locals in the process by singing in every pub. As the afternoon progressed the group got bigger, the drinking heavier and the songs louder.

As usual, departure for the game was left to the last possible minute. Around 25 Reds (now well inebriated) boarded the mini-bus and it was a tight squeeze during the journey, and approximately half way through, the tight fit got too much for two Blackpool Reds who tried to knock hell out of each other, which was no mean feat under the circumstances!

Tempers were cooled and we roared into Wrexham with just ten minutes to kick-off. After parking the van in a convenient spot for an early post-match getaway I eventually found my seat in the Marstons Stand right on the whistle - it would have been a touch embarrassing to miss the start in this most local of fixtures.

As with the vast majority of European aways, the match seems to be there as a drinking interruption, and this was to be no different as the match became a blur with only the two goals and the half-time oxo and pie living in the post match memory bank.

At the end of the game the team were cheered off and we all looked forward to sunnier days in the Spring. With everyone back on the transport we headed at speed back to my local to celebrate our victory and continue the day long bender. The landlady had thought some of the behaviour before the match was out of order, after the match it got worse. Some of the lads seemed to go overboard and some chundered for Britain, in and around the pub. This did the street cred no end of damage on my next visit a couple of days later!

The landlady of the pub was running the pub in her husband's absence due to hospitalisation (apparently he took a turn for the worse on hearing the nights events - especially as he's a staunch Evertonian!). Bed was eventually reached well after midnight and Thursday was taken up nursing a serious hangover whilst trying to work, but still dreaming of a sunny Springtime jaunt. We were to be rewarded in full with a trip in the South of France, I can't wait.

Once again fond memories from a Euro away!

MONTPELLIER AWAY, AWAY, AWAY

Montpellier Herault 0 - Manchester United 2
European Cup Winners Cup Third Round, 2nd Leg
(aggregate: a superb 1-3)
March 19th 1991, La Mosson Stadium.
Sealey, Irwin, Blackmore, Bruce, Phelan, Pallister,
Robson, Ince, McClair, Hughes, Sharpe.
Sub Used: Martin Scorers: Blackmore, Bruce
Attendance: 18,000

Chally

Chally is 33, married and has two daughters aged 7 and 3. He has followed United, home and away, for 22 years, beginning in the Stretford End as a junior, the memories of queuing for half an hour to pay thirty pence are still vivid. These were the days of the butchers coat and scarves tied to every part of the body. From the Stretford End he went to the Scoreboard Paddock, at the same time he was introduced to Yates Wine Lodge - this became his downfall for two years as he doesn't remember much about many of the home games of that period.

Football became just another form of socialising with friends, the friendships were developed through United and the North Wales branch of the supporters' club.

The eighties were not a great time for football, epitomised by the three disasters. During this time Chally obtained a season ticket in G Stand. Tickets for the away matches were very easy to get hold of and some good times were had. Paying at the turnstile to get into both of the Cup Finals in 1983 and then the 1985 Cup Final against Everton summed up the era.

Then came 1990, the year that changed Chally's life. His first daughter was born and England got into the Semi-Final of the World Cup. Up until that year he had never seen a football match off the British mainland and he was now in Italy watching a World Cup Semi-final. From that experience he wanted to watch United in Europe, so when the ban was lifted he attended every game in the Cup Winners Cup that following season.

Once you have been abroad with United it becomes a drug to keep on going, the problem is, with a wife and two children it becomes expensive, but he keeps managing to convince the wife and long may this continue.

The main highlight of the run to Rotterdam was a mad March trip to the south of France. Here are Chally's recollections of that memorable springtime foray.

The trip began early Sunday morning - 17th March - in North Wales (I am not Welsh and proud of it!). There were five of us in my Escort van travelling towards Dover to catch the 16.00 ferry to Calais. The journey down was quite uneventful, just a few cans of beer, Phil's dreadful rock tapes and a long delay in the Dartford tunnel - these were the days before the Dartford Bridge had been opened unfortunately! We arrived in Dover with just half an hour to park up and catch the ferry. When we finally parked, in the middle of Dover, time became very precious as we had just ten minutes to catch the ferry. This ferry had been pre-booked due to it connecting up with the night train to the south of France. With due respect to Phil, he may be fat, but his little chubby legs got him there, whilst I coughed up my lungs and had to be carried the final two hundred yards to the terminal - the relief when we boarded the ferry was immense.

The trip was now really under way - straight to the bar - then a quick detour to the duty free to stock up for the night ahead. Once docked in France the train was waiting alongside the ferry port, with a sleeper booked for four and two French girls mighty relieved to find we originally entered the wrong compartment!

The train left Calais with a number of Reds on board and many gallons of beer which was being drunk at a considerable pace. This continued into the night with my last memory being a visit to the loo (there are photographs available to show where I slept that night), my next memory is being woken early in the morning by someone wanting to use the toilet.

The worst part of the trip was about to happen. 6am Monday, at Avignon station with a Stella Artois hangover waiting for a connection to Montpellier. Once on the train everyone took up sleeping positions; on seats, floors and luggage racks. The French did not see the funny side of this, coupled with the fact that we were unshaven, unshowered and stinking of 12 hours worth of their local brew.

We finally arrived at Montpellier, a town situated about five miles from the sea on the French Riviera. The hotel was booked by two friends who had arrived earlier on a sleeper from Amsterdam. The place looked as if it had not been decorated since the last war and the old lady behind the desk was in a similar condition, but all we required was a bed and a shower and this is just what we got.

By mid morning the Stella hangover had began to recede and breakfast was taken by some of the less seasoned connoisseurs at McDonalds - that famous French restaurant chain!

The centre of the town was beautifully laid out, with the main cafes and shops located around an L shaped paved area with fountains at one end, and a large statue at the other. Along the full length of this stunning shopping area there were flag poles both sides making a very picturesque setting for a few days away in the sun drinking lots of beer and watching United play.

Later on in the day we decided to locate the stadium via a long bus trip which wound its way through some nice suburbs, past stunning hotels until it got close to the stadium where the surroundings changed to run down estates full of Arab immigrants.

The stadium was in the middle of re-building, half had been modernised and the other half would have reminded City fans of a typical away match. There was no security and we found one of the gates open, so we spent a little time taking in the condition of the pitch and the seating arrangements whilst making the most of the photo opportunities. After leaving we found a local bar in readiness for the following evening. It was a little run down but I have drunk and slept in far worse, i.e; a whore house in Turin! The locals appeared to be friendly but were keen to point out that Utd were in for a rough time come match day!

The first evening began as most do in Europe, meeting up in bars with other Reds. After a visit from the local plod it was time to quickly move on and this led us to a small bar down a back street which was full of locals who at first appeared to be hostile. This atmosphere soon changed as they discovered we were United fans.

One by one we were introduced to most in the bar and all wanted to talk about football. The bar owner made himself known and was introduced as Rene, at this four of us fell to the floor in laughter, it then took quite a while to explain our reaction. As it turned out the bar owner was quite a celebrity in his own right, as he was a former goalkeeper for Montpellier. With his previous involvement with the club he had pictures of himself with the French version of the FA Cup, of which he was very proud of and insisted that his guests (namely the drunks from Britain) take the photographs as a memento of our visit.

The only problem was that the bar closed early (12.30am) but as one or two of the locals had attached themselves to us we allowed them to show us the way to the next bar. This became a bit of a problem due to a few English idiots who wanted a rumble with the riot police.

Finally they got us to a bar that was open, on entering it became apparent why they had befriended the English drunks as most of their friends had limp wrists. What the hell, a drink is a drink.

After several more and offers to barbecues the following evening it was finally time to return to our time machine (the hotel). On route Phil met a couple of Brummie Reds he knew who hadn't got a hotel so as a good samaritan he offered the floor of our room so they could rest their weary legs.

Unfortunately during the night one person in the room couldn't decide the location of the toilet and used the bed in which I was sleeping instead. Two lads in another room had a strange visit in the night when the key was put into the lock, the door opened and a body went rushing past - very strange indeed!

The day of the game was stunning and very warm. We had settled ourselves early on the sunny-side of the square outside one of the many cafes/bars. As the day went on more Reds arrived in the town and gathered around the statue at the top of the square in front of the town hall, getting drunk, playing a massive game of football and having a superb session.

By mid afternoon there were flags draped from many buildings up and down the centre. Enter George the famous flag of the Blackpool Reds and the more infamous Mick who tried several times over a half hour period to scale one of the many flag poles that straddled both sides of the square. After watching him struggle, beer and stupidity got the better of me, I took the flag and began to climb. It was only when I got to the top and hung out on one of the arms of the structure to remove a local flag that I realised the height.

As I looked down every person in the square had noticed, even the local French television company had a camera pointing at me. When the flag I had carried to the top was finally draped from the pole it was back down to earth to great applause from the watching Reds. Mick came up to me and said: "Reward that man for his efforts" as his flag proudly flew in another European Red haven - I was rewarded with plenty of drinks!

The time had come to make our way to the bar by the ground. On arrival there were a few Reds, French fans and local residents from the area. Whilst standing outside the bar we suddenly saw a United fan lying on the floor with a number of people shouting for assistance. He'd been stabbed whilst walking through the very dodgy nearby housing estate. The usual camera appeared from the British press, but this was quickly shoved back into his face and then told to walk away in short jerking movements, which he promptly did! From the time of the incident it took the riot police 20 minutes to organise an assault on the flats - in the interim period there were clashes between waiting Reds and the housing estate locals.

As kick off time approached many Reds who had made their way to the South of France still did not have tickets, and as most Europeans leave for the game early the bar emptied, leaving just the four of us and a few locals. It was time for a top shelf attack; four double vodkas and two bottles of coke. The bill came to 200 Francs (approx. £20), and Phil was just handing the money over when he realised the cost and in one move he had snatched both the cash and two glasses of vodka before the bar man could even think.

An argument developed regarding the drink that we wanted and the cash that he wanted. The commotion had attracted the attention of the locals who were playing pool, who stood staring with pool cues in hand, outnumbering us two to one. As Phil continued to argue the remaining three prepared for imminent battle. The locals sensed this and turned away to carry on with their game!

With five minutes to kick off we made our way towards the stadium. The police had sealed off the ground to ensure that no Reds got in without tickets. Once through the police barriers we set off to find our entrance. All the gates were closed, the police kept on telling us to go to the next gate, how many times have we heard that since from the police?

We finally got in following a lot of pressure and were forced to stand in a temporary stand erected for the unofficial United contingent, a set of dodgy wooden benches which rocked forwards and backwards, many of which buckled under the weight. A number sat down blaming the unstable floor, not the ten hours drinking! It was a sobering thought to think that this was the exact type of stand used a short time later in a Marseilles game played in Corsica which saw the loss of so many lives.

The game was - at that time - one of the best away performances and results that United had produced for many years. The one player who really became a hero of the night and a legend with the fans was Steve Bruce. A great Blackmore free-kick and some excellent defending saw a win to put us through to the Semi Finals of a European competition again. The unofficial 2,000 Reds at the corner of the stadium (about 4,000 United fans in total) certainly celebrated the victory to full effect, a brilliant atmosphere as: "Always Look On The Bright Side Of Life" suddenly became the United anthem.

After the game we soon discovered that there were no buses or taxis to transport the few hundred Reds who needed to get back to the town centre, which seemed hilarious to some of the police. This resulted in a two hour walk back to the limp wrist bar where we knew that a pint could be guaranteed (Phil the lucky beggar arrived an hour and a half earlier having hitched a lift!). The next few hours were bliss, plenty of beer and a paddle in one of the fountains, apart from Butty who decided that a full swim was in order. The paradise hotel was reached at the early hour of 3am - if anyone had a drink after the game they were doing very well as the police had done their best to dampen any celebrations.

The journey home should have been straight forward, the TGV to Paris, and change there for Calais. What we didn't anticipate was a French rail strike. As the seats had been booked on the 9am two days previously - and it arrived on time - we were unaware of the strike until we found several French people asleep in our seats. They moved quite quickly with little 'French resistance'. The journey to Paris was a pleasure, travelling on one of the fastest trains in the world through some beautiful scenery.

Once in Paris, the pleasure of the first half of the journey became a nightmare, as there was only one train from Paris to Calais that evening. A few Reds obviously thought 'sod this' and instead sampled the delights of an unexpected Parisian night, but after waiting three hours we finally boarded a train with standing room only. As departure time grew closer the amount of people in each carriage became unbearable. It felt worse than the standing area at the 1985 Cup Final against Everton when there were about 10,000 extra people in the Utd end!

This packed train must have been the French way of getting back at the drunken English football fans from three days earlier!

Due to the strike the French had arranged transport from Calais central station to the ferry which had been held back to enable 150 Reds to return to England. This was very impressive and much appreciated, the same can not be said for British Rail who did not have any transport to return back North until the next day.

It was here that we suddenly picked up another Red, local to us. This meant six lads, six bags and a £36 toy cat in an escort van for five hours return trip, not the most comfortable way to travel after three days of continual drinking.

The trip will always be classed as one of the best by the five lads who travelled; Phil, Gary the postman, Darren, myself and a lad whose name escapes me, has not been seen since and could still be out in Montpellier - no one would blame him!

FERGIE'S RED ARMY LAUNCHES OFFENSIVE INTO WARSAW

Legia Warsaw 1 - Manchester United 3
European Cup Winners Cup Semi-final, 1st Leg
April 10th 1991, Wojska Polskiego Stadium.
Sealey, Irwin, Blackmore, Bruce, Phelan, Pallister,
Webb, Ince, McClair, Hughes, Sharpe.
Sub Used: Donaghy
Scorers: McClair, Hughes, Bruce
Attendance: 20,000

Ari

Ari, 35, is a rail signaller (and no, he's not responsible for the delays...honest!) and resides in mid-Cheshire. He has supported United all his life (his first game at home to Everton in 78-79) and an early indication of how this would disrupt his life was on a visit to Fulham in the late 70's for an FA Cup tie. On arriving at the ground he found that the game had been postponed, so having spent the rest of the day in London, he eventually arrived back in Manchester catching the last train home, only for the guard to wake him up and turf him off at the end of the line. To his horror it happened to be Rochdale and with only a couple of quid left he had to walk a good 12 miles home in the freezing snow...

Well here we are. With a little over five weeks of the season remaining and with it a mixed bag of fortunes to boot. Although the rotten condition of our pitch left a lot to be desired, our league form has again been disappointing, lacking the consistency necessary to challenge for that elusive Championship.

However hope is not lost for it's in the Cup competitions where the Boys have shown their true strength and character, and although the defence of the FA Cup was relinquished at Norwich (not one of our happy hunting grounds) it was our only defeat in 22 Cup ties. Amongst that sequence of games was the Rumbelows League Cup campaign, where (amongst others) Liverpool, Arsenal and Leeds were sent packing on the way to the final, where we will meet Sheffield Wednesday later in the month.

Liverpool (league leaders at the time) were beaten 3-1 at Old Trafford, inflicting their first defeat of the season amidst scenes of delight. But the best was yet to come - it was at Highbury that the headlines were being made. Arsenal, also undefeated all season having conceded only two goals at the time, were comprehensively taken apart as United ran riot and trounced them 6-2, condemning Arsenal to their worst home defeat since the war.

By now progress was also being made on another front. After a five year absence from Europe, English clubs were again invited to compete in European competitions again for the 1990/91 season. During the ban United missed competing in the 1985/86 European Cup Winners Cup, the 1986/87 and 1988/89 UEFA Cup campaigns. However in 1990 UEFA decided to lift the ban and as a result of us winning the FA Cup in 1990, United were given the go ahead to take part in the 1990/91 European Cup Winners Cup, with Aston Villa entering the UEFA Cup. As Liverpool had won the league in 1990, but were still serving their ban, England had no representatives in the European Cup.

It was fitting that United, the first English club to enter Europe back in 1956 (it was in 1955 that a new competition in Europe began and to qualify you had to be the Champions of your league) should be amongst the English clubs allowed to compete again. Sir Matt Busby had gone across Europe to see that new competition in progress and knew immediately that this was the kind of stage that United should be aiming for.

He reported back to his Directors, who gave him their approval, however when he approached the FA, they refused permission, and so in 1956 United entered the competition despite the protestations of the FA (nothing changes).

As European competition wore on, Villa were knocked out of the UEFA Cup campaign in the 2nd Round and United were left to fly the flag and become England's sole representatives for a second time. Here was a chance for the team to show how they could perform and for the fans it presented an opportunity to show how they conduct themselves abroad.

Having despatched of Pecsi Munkas (what a coincidence that our last game on foreign soil before the game was Videoton of Hungary and the first after was also in the same country) and Wrexham, United met Montpellier in the Quarter-Finals.

The French side (which had included a young Eric Cantona in its previous seasons Cup Winning side) were highly rated in some quarters and had already disposed of PSV Eindhoven and Steaua Bucharest.

The first leg took place at Old Trafford and United got off to a brilliant start with McClair scoring in the first minute, yet a few minutes later the crowd was brought back down to earth when Lee Martin (whose winning goal in the Cup Final Replay took us into Europe) put through his own goal leaving the French side to sneak away with a 1-1 draw. In the return match in France, United, unfazed by Montpellier's formidable home record (and Valderrama - the bloke with that stupid hair cut) capitalised on the home sides indecisiveness and goals from Blackmore and Bruce gave us a 2-0 win on the night and, at last, through to the Semi-Finals.

At the age of 28 the game in Montpellier was the first time I'd ventured abroad - ever! So with the sun, sea and delightful French totty beckoning, me and my mate Keith decided to take the plunge and head for the South of France. We took a TGV from Paris and couldn't believe our luck as a lad was on it selling a couple of tickets for the game.

In the town square the sight before us was out of this world. Under blistering sunshine was a sea of Red, White and Black, Every building, statue and flagpole - and the odd local - were bedecked with banners and flags. This was the mother of all parties. I'd never seen anything like it and judging by the bemused locals faces neither had they. I was stunned and immediately cursed about not having gone on previous European jaunts.

All in all my first had been a superb trip and the experience engraved in me a burning desire for more European United travel. Having now notched up seventeen the hunger is stronger than ever and as each season draws to a close I hope and pray that we at least qualify for Europe. The whole experience from planning a trip, the travelling itself, the camaraderie whilst there, combined with watching United is simply unbeatable.

The draw for the Semi's was now fast approaching and anxious eyes were now focusing on which team we would play. Barcelona or Juventus were favoured by most for the crack with a few hardy souls positively salivating at the thought of a trip to play in Warsaw.

The draw was duly made and a trip to play Legia Warsaw beckoned and although we had avoided the glamour sides, the two legged Semi had a degree of trickiness attached as Legia - an unknown quantity to many Reds - had beaten the favourites (Sampdoria).

The trip was to severely test my resolve of not missing any further Euro aways. The more I heard about the place the more depressing and uninviting it sounded. For the culture vultures out there, Poland has had a rough old time, being invaded countless times by power mad and land-hungry neighbours to such an extent that the country ceased to exist from 1875 to 1920. The advent of World War Two didn't come as much relief either as the German army swept through the country destroying everything and everyone in its wake.

Warsaw - whose motto is "Contemnire Procellis" (to defy the storms) - suffered the most as three-quarters of the population died and some 90% of the city was destroyed. Communism took control after the War and after years of living under the stranglehold of this strict regime, the people in 1989 decided on a clean sweep and elected its first non-Communist leader since the war - enter capitalism.

Whilst trying to get used to this Western style system the Poles have continued to spiral into an abyss. Food shortages/rationing/queuing are ever present, a welcome relief for our band of merry drinkers whom will delight in the vast range of cheap vodka available.

The place is full of shabby shops that have little or nothing in them (one 'off-license' contained just twenty-four beers in it), definitely no bargains here for the designer set yet an old bill that take a great delight in fining you at every opportunity, boosting their vodka funds. A flourishing black market with whom the jibbers can pit their wits.

The route from the airport into the town contains rows and rows of what was first thought as tiny badly designed glass green houses but on closer inspection were actually home to large Polish families.

No need to worry about the currency as the Zloty has about as much value as toilet paper, Dollars and Deutsch Marks being the order of the day. One Red who had travelled a few years ago with England reckoned we'd struggle to spend £50 in three days yet with the nightlife (or lack of it) it would be as exciting as a visit to a monastery so a solemn trip looked on the horizon.

The lads who I go to home games with decided to go on the one day club trip and a few were going on the four day jaunt organised by various tour operators. It was estimated that about 1,500 United fans would be making the trip and with the fall of the Berlin wall in November 1989 a bit of time there appealed so I decided on an overland trip.

The visitor's passport obtained for Montpellier was swiftly changed for a full ten year one on the Friday before the Warsaw game and all the necessary travel details booked. The Villa game came and went with most of the gossip centred around the forthcoming trip and final arrangements for meeting up over there were made.

I set off on the Monday morning, the first port of call being the Polish Embassy where I met a lad called John who was also going to the game. Having obtained our visas we paired up and caught the overnight ferry from Harwich to Holland.

We arrived in the morning blissed up and bleary eyed, staggering with a couple of crates of Grolsch. We clambered aboard the train to Berlin where we would arrive some ten hours later.

No real time for sight-seeing as we took a quick ride from Berlin Zoo Station on the S-Bhan to Hauptbahnhoff - the main station in East Berlin - from where we would take an overnight train to Warsaw. The travelling stopped temporarily as we had a few hours to kill round the station, an old working class district that had been bombed to oblivion during the War and hurriedly rebuilt by the East Germans. It is here that part of the Berlin Wall has been preserved and is officially classed as the 'East Side Gallery', being brightly painted with political and satirical images.

It does its best to brighten up this corner of the city but as darkness descended the bright lights of the West seemed a million miles away. We spent the next couple of hours in the only bar that we could find and then returned to the station dodging and weaving amongst numerous skinheads and punks, accompanied by even uglier looking dogs and boarded the train for the eight hour journey to the destination of the game.

We were joined in the compartment by Jan and Jozef, two Polish guys on their way to Wroclaw, and for the next four hours we were quizzed about life in the West. About an hour into the journey we were held up at the border for the standard Eastern European custom officer search which - as usual - involved a thorough search virtually stripping our compartment in the process.

Even the top and underneath exteriors of the train were searched. We finally made a move as our new companions explained that the searches are always that vigorous as we were on one of the main black market routes from East to West.

They then produced a picnic of cold meats, cheeses, fruit and bread (a tremendous gesture considering that they earlier stated that they only earn about £100 per month) which we all washed down with the aid of our now last remaining crate of Grosich, whilst we regaled them with stories of United's past and taught them some songs

At Poznan Jan and Jozef said their farewells and we caught up with some much needed sleep. We arrived in Warsaw (match day) at 7.30am, some thirty-six hours after leaving England. We ventured into the station buffet which resembled nothing more than a soup kitchen, the only food on offer being boiled eggs and bread. We opted for coffee, which was nothing more than a brown liquid with grit in it.

Outside the bleak and dreary weather complemented the dull and characterless surroundings and we headed for the Hotel Warszawa. On route I stopped at a bookstall where, whilst in the process of trying to purchase a Polish Dictionary, a tramp for some unknown bloody reason made a lunge towards me with a pen knife. This bizarre situation got even stranger as the bookseller tackled him and threw him down the road. He was so apologetic with what had just gone on that I got a book for free!

We arrived at the hotel around 9.30am where a number of United's drunkards were living up to their name. Even at this incredibly early hour they were downing their weekly recommended alcohol intake of beer, wine and vodka - all in an hour! Everyone seemed in good form, even Sean who was recovering from being bitten by a dog the previous night in an area known for rabies, who 24 hours earlier was in despair when the hospital was unable to treat him due to a severe lack of medicines, and finally had to get treated at the Embassy.

Those who had been here a few days all painted the same boring picture of local entertainment. Bars were few and far between, empty and closed ridiculously early due to saving electricity. Many thought it as the worst Euro destination in a long while and some Reds - of the more misbehaving sort it has to be said - decided to tip several cars over on the road of a bar that had just shut at 10pm. The police were soon called and the night they spent in the cells - they claimed - was more enjoyable than the previous two nights!

One pisshead, Mackie, who stands resplendent in his unique hand knitted red, white and black barred cardigan which he wears for every European trip was serenading a few locals and several others were comfortably holding their own against two Polish guys who had challenged them to a vodka drinking session. It was make your most of the surroundings time and things livened up as the two Polish guys collapsed with the downing of yet another vodka short which in fact resembled a full bottle.

By now the hotel bar was virtually dry so having sorted out a match ticket and the local monopoly money (16-18,000 Zlotys to £1) we went in search of another of the lads hotels. When we got there we discovered it was the place where the official trip was, bringing the day trippers to be wined and dined before the game. If you had any designs on a meal - tough. Unless you had travelled officially the United suits wouldn't allow you into the restaurant!

However the bar was open and what a gem it proved to be as Poland's official sole supplier of Beck's lager. Yet the United fans inside had drunk the bloody lot so for the first time in its three years of opening the bar had to revert back to selling just local beer.

Some Reds had just returned from a shopping spree in the old town and had bought suits (as you do) for what they thought were £6 each, yet when all the noughts had been translated turned out to be £60. Mick in an effort to restore some colour to his cheeks - after spending the whole flight being sick to such an extent that the steward enquired if he suffered from terrible travel sickness (no just alcohol) - had purchased a snazzy (not) little orange outfit, and although the jacket was double breasted it still didn't meet in the middle.

Talking of characters, a Romanian by the name of Emanuel entered proceedings, claiming to be an artist who had fled from the poverty of his homeland. He explained that he was trying to abscond to the West to make his fortune as the next Picasso and was convinced we could smuggle him out of the country. He spent the entire day asking each and everyone to help him as a stowaway!

The bar began to fill up with everyone enjoying a vodka or two as tales were swapped from people's travels so far. One group of Reds had been charged £70 for a bottle of wine in the old town and another Red had gone off with a lady of the night, who took him miles out of the city to her home.

When they reached her apartment it was on the tenth floor of a grim tenement block with every door protected by a steel outer door. On reaching her flat she told him to take a bath "to cleanse himself" and a bit later he climbs out and lies on the bed. She asks him for money and he suddenly realises that it's all in his jacket back in the bar, to which she goes absolutely mental, unleashing her dog and chases him out into the street and through a huge Bronx like council estate. He finally manages to return to the bar (and wallet), some three hours later and two stone lighter.

We decide it's high time to locate a local bar as near to the ground as possible. We jump into a clapped out Lada with a kamikaze driver and spend the journey ashen face with stomachs in mouths meandering (if that's what you can call hurtling down side streets knocking into anything in our way) down little pedestrian walkways.

Finally we notice a large queue by a building and seeing our chance of survival and dispensing of Nigel Mansell's services, we ask him to stop. It's then that we discover we've arrived at the opening of Poland's first ever sex shop, the owner of which is delighted as 200 Poles fight each other for one of the six vibrators and rubber dolls.

We head to a bar across the road, blackcurrant vodka ridiculously cheap at 25p a go and after a big sing-song to a bemused bunch of locals we suddenly remember the 5pm kick off and pile into taxi's for another hair-raising ride.

We arrive at the ground with minutes to spare and once inside soon realised that it was no showpiece. Built in 1930 it has three sides of shallow terracing covered in rotten wooden benches and the one terrace covered by a stand is one of the few buildings in Warsaw that survived the war.

The capacity of the ground is a little under 22,000 and although the Poles take first blood during the game United dominate the 'unknown' quantity such that McClair, Hughes and Bruce all score in our biggest European game in decades. 3 goals away in Europe, in a semi...

With twenty minutes to go the Legia fans left en masse (only to protest outside and look bewilderingly at all the United fans leaving on coaches) leaving behind their flags and banners and a massive celebration by the Red Army.

The United fans in their end join us (a few getting into scraps being heavily outnumbered) and at the end of the game the players come over to applaud us and after a detention of 30 minutes we were allowed to leave, some to the airport and some of us back into town.

We venture into the first bar we come across to start the celebrations and after a short conversation with a young Miss called Mazuur (I can even remember her name!) I give her my zippo lighter, much to the chagrin of mad Pole No.2 who lurches over towards us and attempts to grapple me until he is swiftly pole-axed by the barman. What is it about this place?

I'm invited back to her place (perhaps it isn't that bad) but realising that a smile is probably the only thing I can raise I politely decline (!) and promise at her insistence to take up her invitation on my next visit to Warsaw.

Lack of atmosphere spurred us on to pastures new, so with the scope for a drink in this dull town looking decidedly limited (these daytrippers had the right idea) we end up back at the Hotel Forum, where by this time, Emanuel - our budding Picasso - is crawling around on his hands and knees begging and pleading with everyone and anyone to take him to the West.

Several hours and beers later the expected tacky hotel disco has failed to materialise and so with our artist still trying to secure passage West we move to another disco near our hotel. We take a table amongst several women of ill repute, a large group of the local militia and 60 very drunk United fans - what a mix!

Spotlights illuminate a stage signalling the start of a floorshow, where the haggard girls go through their routine until Tommy decides we have all been abused enough so far this trip and leaps onto the stage, grabs the microphone and bursts into song, to huge applause from not only the mass of Reds but the militia as well.

We continue drinking until the early hours, but after a serious vodka session (minus the mixers) with a local, my last memory is tipping back in my chair and I collapse into a state of oblivion. I awake some unidentified time later in Dave's room. He (about half the size of me and twice as drunk) has carried me single handedly into his room, an event nothing short of a miracle.

I venture into the bar where conversation is centred around two drunken Spiderman who wouldn't let go of the side of any of the buildings they passed - prompting vague recollections of me and Dave feeling our way along the walls of said buildings for fear of falling down as we walked home!

A few of us mercifully opt for an hour or two off the beer and go for a final look at the stadium. We find out that's it part of a sport complex, complete with Olympic sized swimming pool filled with stagnant brown water and a dozen or so tennis courts, barely recognisable due to huge craters in them. Inside the stadium the locals still haven't returned to collect their flags and banners that are tied up to the perimeter fence. Why are we here again?

Back at Victory Parade Square, the biggest in Europe (surpassing even that of Moscow) we catch up with more Reds drinking in earnest. The square is dominated by the Palace of Culture, a seventy storey, 240 metre monstrosity built by the Russians and shunned by the Poles.

Someone who travelled on the club trip said that when they passed it whilst on the sightseeing tour the tour guide made no reference to it whatsoever, despite repeated requests. With the sun sizzling us we spend the time relaxing in the square and as darkness looms we bode farewell to another delighted and now rich bar owner and head off to the station where after several drinks in a stand up soup kitchen we are ready for the torturous overnight train to Berlin.

After plenty of songs we doze off and at last arrive at civilisation after the dreary Warsaw. We grab something to eat in a nearby cafe and arrive in a football mecca, covered - walls and ceilings - in football memorabilia. Soon loads of German fans converge, unmistakeable by their denim jackets plastered with sew on badges, moustaches and enough scarves and hats to fill United's Megastore.

They are in fact Borussia Munchengladbach fans and tell us that they are playing BSC Berlin later that night in the Olympic Stadium.

A five hour session of stories and songs of our respective teams and countries follow with copious amounts of schnapps causing a rousing rendition of the "PRIDE OF ALL EUROPE", to huge applause from the Germans.

As other Reds departed for the airport four of us headed to the match. The Olympic Stadium was built for the 1936 games and despite the stigma attached to that event, is very impressive. It's a huge complex and a quick bar crawl of the many that accompany the forecourt and we take in many sights, including the original Olympic bell (transported from Potsdam in 1936) with its engraved Swastikas still visible.

To the west of the Stadium clock towers is where the medal winners are listed, amongst them Jessie Owens, the American athlete who stood up to it all and won four gold medals. From there you can see the huge Maifield about the size of a dozen football pitches and beyond that stands a 20,000 seater amphi-theatre now used for rock concerts. Throw in the ubiquitous swimming pool on the North side and you have the complete Olympic village.

Tickets for the game were only a fiver and once inside the stadium dropped away below ground level to reveal an 80,000 all seater monolith. The game got under way watched by a dismal 20,000 crowd and with no atmosphere and a dismal game it was, with relief, that we dodged pockets of frustrated fans to head back to the Zoo station.

After a couple of drinks it was time to go - a trip that felt like a lifetime, mission accomplished but in bleak surroundings - and an overnight train to port for a Saturday night arrival back home. Well worth it, particularly the result - but never Warsaw again please.

THE ROAD TO ROTTERDAM

Manchester United 2- Barcelona 1
European Cup Winners Cup Final
May 15th 1991, Feyenoord Stadium, Rotterdam.
Sealey, Irwin, Blackmore, Bruce, Phelan, Pallister,
Robson, Ince, McClair, Hughes, Sharpe.
Scorers: Hughes 2
Attendance: 50,000

Dr.Edward Martins
Dr.Edward Martins is old enough to know better and lives in South Manchester. He is employed as a Social Worker and spends Monday to Friday trying to stop young criminals being naughty. The fact that he also chooses to spend Saturday afternoons with criminals is perhaps taking dedication a little too far. He has supported United since birth and is a regular contributor to the United fanzine 'Red News'. He has never had his hair cut by anyone other than a die hard Red.

Rotterdam 1991 will be a happy memory for many United fans with the circumstances of the occasion ensuring its unique place in the history of great European excursions. Oh, and we won the European Cup Winners' Cup as well.

The 1990-91 season saw the return of English clubs to European competitions after five years of unsplendid isolation following the deaths of thirty-nine Juventus supporters before their game against those loveable rogues from the wrong end of the East Lancs Road. Consequently, many of those following United on this particular season's 'European Tour' were virginal in terms of previous continental experience. Few had witnessed the sole Mancunian success in Europe some twenty-three years earlier and absolutely no-one had ever seen us win anything worthwhile on European soil.

This was also the tail end of the 'Madchester' era, a happy time before Skinner, Mellor and the Gallaghers became interested in the beautiful game. Football had yet to become sickeningly fashionable, except with those who mattered. Celebrity fans kept a low profile and Old Trafford had three singing ends. 'Lads' hadn't yet been invented by Oasis' management company and scallies ruled the terraces with blissed-up all knowing expressions in the most overtly drug orientated era in English football history. On an away trip indeed! Even if every Scouser still had a moustache. In this context, therefore, it was entirely appropriate that the 1991 final of the European Cup Winners' Cup should be played in Holland, in Rotterdam. For Rotterdam read Amsterdam.

I'd been to Amsterdam many times before as I was fortunate to have a mate with the best job in the world, lecturing at Amsterdam University, but I wasn't aware that Rotterdam was only half an hour away. Why would anyone know that? Why would anyone leave Amsterdam to visit Rotterdam? There's not really any point is there? However, very early in the preliminary planning of the trip it became clear that it would be eminently possible to travel to Amsterdam, celebrate, jib down to Rotterdam for the match, jib back to Amsterdam and celebrate, etc, etc, etc... That was the good news. The bad news was that we were given only 12,500 tickets and United were being particularly difficult with them. In spite of the fact that there had been a complete lack of trouble at every leg during this campaign this was still the first year back after the ban and both United and the F.A. were twitchy to say the least. So it was 'official' trips only, take 'em or leave 'em. Compare this with the vast range and number of independent trips available for Porto away in the 1997 European Champions League and it underlines just how bad things were. In addition to the closed shop ticket and travel arrangements the Ferry companies also decided to get difficult and imposed a blanket ban on "football fans" travelling to Holland. This was without doubt a diabolical (civil) liberty and probably illegal but it happened nonetheless. Fortunately, everyone in Manchester has a mate who made one too many visits to the 'Cannabis Connoisseurs' Club' and never came back from an Amsterdam trip. Consequently there were a thousand avenues open to clued up Mancs for alternative ticket distribution.

Basic research revealed that the Stadion Feijenoord had a capacity of 50,000. We were to receive 12,500 behind one goal and Barcelona the same number behind the other goal with the rest designated for neutrals and virtually going on open sale in Rotterdam. This was too good an opportunity to miss. Every exiled Manc in Amsterdam jibbed down to Rotterdam and bought a dozen for his mates back home. Every Swag Man took the cheap Friday flight over and bought a hundred. One way or another almost all of the two neutral sections along the sides fell into friendly Red hands. Absolutely fucking brilliant. A masterpiece of organisation. Power to the people. And the best part was that no-one seemed to know what was going down, except the people who know, if you know what I mean. Even knowledgeable Reds, though, couldn't have predicted just how successful the operation had been. We knew we'd got our hands on quite a respectable percentage of the neutral allocation but...

The authorities, the media and, as you'd expect, United didn't have a clue what was happening. In fact, the Manchester Evening News printed scare stories about United fans possibly being outnumbered at the final due to Barca selling their allocation in two hours and United struggling to sell their's due to the ridiculous requirements for ticket eligibility (this last bit wasn't mentioned of course). In reality we even had some of the Barca end and were in for quite a surprise upon entry into the stadium.

So with tickets guaranteed courtesy of Vincent Vega Enterprises Ltd (our Manc in Amsterdam) only the travel arrangements needed to be sorted out. All my previous trips to Amsterdam had been via the Harwich ferry but if the ferry companies were going to be silly then things could be made very difficult. A decision was made to check out flights direct from Manchester to Schipol. These proved to be more expensive than expected (with some cynics claiming that prices had been increased for that particular week alone - surely not) but still much cheaper than the 'official' club flights. In addition most of us happened to be working at that time and for once money wasn't too tight to mention. So the flights

Athens 1991: the training session (more exciting than the match!)

Montpellier 1991: temporary stand for Utd. fans which nearly buckled

Turin 1996: Albert and Joel Cantona with a few fans

Turin 1984: where flares never went out of fashion

Athens 1991: mad dogs and English footballers...

Warsaw 1991: handy sign for Utd. fans (bottom bit translates as "Polish Olympic brick throwing practice this way")

ENTRANCE FOR BRITISH FANS

WEJŚCIE DLA KIBICÓW ANGIELSKICH

Raba Vasas 1984: You ordered *how* many beers??!

Raba Vasas 1984: Bored players... "God, I wish we could get pissed!"

Videoton 1985: the ski-hat firm is here!

Videoton 1985: the players gutted after penalties

Pecsi 1990: Santa Claus is coming to town!

Raba Vasa 1984: there's a dog on the pitch!

Prague 1983: ...or is it Halifax?

Raba Vasas 1984: Reds!

Eindhoven 1984: Albiston's playing cards again!

Barcelona 1994: great ground, shit result

Galatasaray 1994: and this is seven hours before kick-off!

Galatasaray 1993: all fezzed up and nowhere to go
- a doomed attempt to blend in with the locals!

Madrid 1991: Yes, Drunken Dave's in town!

Pecsi 1990: the Red Army has descended

Warsaw 1991: lovely uniforms!

Porto 1997: 10,000 Reds, shame about the police

were booked in advance. Days off work were booked. All available dosh was directed into the fund and decisions made about what to wear.

The best thing about booking the time off work legitimately rather than going on the sick was that I was able to tell everyone where I was going and brag like mad about it to the one Blue and numerous Reds at work who weren't "All Going To Rotterdam". Trying to change sterling into guilders before setting off proved to be quite difficult and we quickly realised that we'd been beaten to the draw by others more organised and that Manchester was becoming a guilder free zone. However, the good wishes of those unable to provide the Dutch currency sweetened the pill as, clearly, most cashiers had sussed what was occurring.

The club coach trips set off on Tuesday but our flight was scheduled for first thing Wednesday morning which meant that a diabolically early start was avoided - not that anyone got any sleep the night before. Manchester Airport was exceedingly Red that morning although the vast majority were travelling on the eleven official flights. Airport prices were paid for beer but in spite of that a fine atmosphere was created and the foundations were laid for an excellent adventure. The unmistakeable smell of draw wafting through an area crawling with Customs Officers and Dibble was enough to make you smile even without participating in such wicked activities. Just before boarding the big silver bird we spotted the alleged comedian Stan Boardman and, of course, acknowledged him with the traditional Mancunian greeting reserved for Scouse bastards everywhere. And so on to the plane. The majority of passengers appeared to be businessmen but we weren't the only Reds on the flight as we recognised at least two other mobs from the sing-song in the airport bar. I'd guess that the air hostess who wished the Boys luck over the mike was probably one of us as well.

The flight to Amsterdam is so short that you barely get time to eat the meal and we landed at Schipol by late morning. Next stop Dam Square to make the Amsterdam connection and collect the tickets. Having accomplished this it was now time to sample the legendary Dutch hospitality and we were buzzing when we realised that the bars around Dam Square and the appropriately named Red Light District were full of blissed up Reds. Many had travelled over earlier in the week by ferry and told tales of all English east coast ferry ports having countless small groups of suspicious looking scallywags with a total absence of colours standing around trying not to look like United fans.

Amsterdam was kicking. The Ajax boys that crossed our path seemed O.K. as did the sizeable Den Haag contingent. However, when we got down to Rotterdam we were to find that the Feyenoorders had a very different attitude. We were informed by the aforementioned Ajax heads that the authorities had organised some kind of 'concert' in Rotterdam to entertain fans which they added would probably be crap. Anyway, it couldn't have been as good as an all day bender in down town Amsterdam so not much time was spent worrying about it. They also told us about a number of events planned for after the match and distributed leaflets advertising clubs, etc, which we thought was above and beyond the call of duty. Numbers continued to swell throughout the course of the afternoon with those who'd arrived a couple of days earlier being joined by those who'd arrived a couple of years earlier. Bier upon bier was defrothed and the aroma of what made Amsterdam famous filled the air.

That afternoon could have lasted forever but eventually the time came to get the train down to Rotterdam. The weather was changeable with that fine rain that wets you never really disappearing for too long. The train journey to Rotterdam seemed to take about thirty minutes but I could be wrong. I remember seeing a couple of Barca flags draped from apartment windows on the journey which was a little disconcerting but, as would be discovered later, we needn't have worried. The local Rotterdammers (mainly Feyenoord boys) were, however, much less friendly than the top boys in Amsterdam and it was clear that had they not been outnumbered about 500:1 the potential for trouble would have been considerable. Rotterdam itself is a dump, a run down dis-used port living on past glories and full of idiots. Remind you of anywhere? Not that it mattered much as the itinerary didn't include spending much time with the Dutch Scousers. The plan was simple: watch the match, watch Robbo lift the Cup and then straight back up to Amsterdam.

We did have a look at the 'concert' which proved to be nothing special and basically involved thousands of stoned and bladdered Reds hanging around in the drizzle. Home from home really. Rumours were rife that Ian Brown, Manny and John Squire were there. We didn't get to see them (no day could be that perfect) but it subsequently turned out they were actually there. So you CAN believe some of the stories that circulate during pre-match European piss-ups. It was also rumoured that Mick (Barca) Hucknall was also knocking about. This also proved to be true but you can't win 'em all. We did meet some genuine Milan Reds though who were absolute top geezers with a totally cool banner hung up in the park. We also met the famous Maltese Reds with their huge banner (this, remember, was in the days before huge banners caught on in England). The weather was still pretty unpleasant so we didn't stay for long, just long enough to sample a few biers donated from the enormous supermarket stash over by the speakers.

And so it was time to go to the stadium passing hordes of Reds and quite a few Barca on the way, so it was difficult to assess who had the upper hand (unlike at the 'concert'). Hordes of Dutch Dibble were also evident but it was clear that this was a police operation to which a considerable amount of thought had been given. For example, there were loads of police taking on the community policing role who were prepared to talk, joke, mess around and generally have a laugh with the visitors to their country. On the other hand there were also vans full of riot police strategically positioned down most side streets just in case. We saw the coaches carrying the United official flight victims arriving at the stadium about an hour before kick off with no time for a look around Rotterdam let alone Amsterdam. Tales were told back in Manchester of poor souls on the official flights who'd changed dosh into guilders before setting off and never got the opportunity to spend any due to the rigid plane-coach-stadium-coach-plane schedule.

The stadium looked O.K. from the outside but perhaps a little old. While queuing to get in we could see Reds climbing steps up the outside of the stadium to the upper tier and shouting down to their mates below: "It's fucking brilliant". Being naturally inquisitive (especially about anything involving United) I couldn't help wondering what was so "fucking brilliant". All would shortly be revealed. As we passed through the turnstiles and security the stadium on closer inspection looked even older and less impressive, but as we climbed the steps an unforgettable sight awaited. Coming out on to the terracing we looked upon a stadium with three sides occupied by Reds. Unbelievable. This was a truly mighty turn out against one of the handful of European clubs who can seriously consider themselves our rivals. Like Old Trafford on F.A Cup day with the visitors in K Stand and us having the rest of the stadium. Everyone you spoke to was amazed at the size of our following especially given the scare mongering of the media and the obstacles that had been placed in the way of independent travellers. This wasn't a Wimbledon away type support either as everyone appeared totally up for it and therefore created a fantastic atmosphere. This was a genuine gathering of the clans with groups of Reds from all corners of the globe. A truly international assembly which no other club could command. Forget the A.B.U vitriol. We're right and they're wrong. They don't understand because they're not meant to. This was special. This was for us and us alone. We weren't representing England or Britain we were representing Manchester United and no-one else.

The Feyenoord Stadium had only one side covered and we weren't in it but even the incessant drizzle couldn't dampen the pre-match atmosphere. The in-house D.J's concession to Madchester was James' 'Sit Down' and the players saluted the fans after their warm up which was unusual but added to the growing feeling among the Red multitude that something special was in the air.

The teams came out to a deafening Red Roar and as the game progressed we began to believe that something special was indeed happening and that we could win this one. United fans kept turning up the volume and Barca boys sulked silently. It must have came as a great shock to them as it can't be very often that they're outnumbered 3:1 in a European Final. Their team seemed to be sulking as well while United led by the magnificent Robson, an inspired Hughes and an heroic Bruce went from strength to strength. Then the goals went in. Cue chaos. Wild celebrations took place all over the stadium with even a handful of Reds in the Barca end. The Dutch equivalent of M.C.Fane fought a losing battle with his continual tannoy announcements in English urging those at the front of the covered stand to be seated (sounds familiar). This was supposedly a neutral area reserved for V.I.P's press, etc, but was actually full of blissed up Reds giving it some. At 2-0 the game was safe, then Koeman scored and we had to endure a torrid last fifteen minutes with Sunbed to thank for the coolest of goal-line clearances. After about an hour of injury time the whistle was blown and Barca were beaten. Talk about celebrations. Robbo lifted the Cup and it was the best moment of our lives for most of us - remember this was 1991 and few of us had seen United win the league let alone a European trophy. The team took a lap of honour to a deafening 'Glory Glory Man United' and Dutch police around the perimeter fencing were wearing United scarves. Even Dutch police dogs were wearing United scarves, it was that kind of night.

We had no intention of spending any more time than was absolutely necessary in Rotterdam so the first available train to Amsterdam was duly jibbed in order for the real celebrations to begin. Like earlier in the day Amsterdam was full of Reds none of whom were going home that night, some of whom probably didn't go home at all. The locals were even more accommodating than before the match and many joined in the madness. In the obvious haunts around the Red Light songs were sung and biers downed. I was surprised how many of the locals seemed to know the words to our songs but following the afternoon session they'll probably be engraved on their memories forever.

I've always thought that Dutch babes were the best in the world, casually gorgeous without even trying, classy but not unapproachable like most French totty. Well, they were particularly friendly on this night of nights. Many seemed quite knowledgable about United and Manchester and had a thirst for whatever inside information they could get. They obviously weren't knowledgeable enough though otherwise they'd have realised they weren't shagging Ian Brown, Shaun Ryder or Mark Burgess but some barely employed nonentities from Stretford, Fallowfield and Gorton. Any tiny white lies that were told were most certainly only told to improve relations with the (female) citizens of a fellow European state. Fuck you Euro-sceptics!

Very little trouble was seen or reported. We witnessed one minor skirmish which was over almost as soon as it had started. Everyone you spoke to seemed to have something planned for 'later' either organised or heard of by exiled Mancs so there was plenty to do after the pubs which didn't close anyway so there wasn't a problem however hard you tried to find one. I must say though that some bars actually stayed closed fearing mayhem and madness which for Amsterdam was a little surprising. This wasn't too much of a hassle as there were plenty who opened and were quite prepared to take drunken Englishmen's money from them. We went on to a club with a forgettable name, usual scenario, no admission charge but overpriced drinks. There were very few Reds in there and even less action so a return to the bar tour appeared attractive. The pace was duly upped until some bastard claimed that United were staying in a hotel in the city centre and that, of course, was that. Being in possession of such privileged information meant we were duty bound to act on it. The plan was to find the hotel in question, blag our way in and celebrate with the boys at the party to end all parties. Simple eh? Well, no not really and we must have been fucking simple to have even considered it. The reality was that United weren't in Amsterdam at all and we wasted an hour and a half's drinking time wandering around in the drizzle looking for a hotel we didn't even know the name of. I won't even use the excuse that it seemed like a good idea at the time because it didn't.

By the time we'd abandoned Mission Impossible it must have been about 5.00am and we had trouble finding a bar to continue the session. This being Amsterdam though one was eventually found and a few more biers were drowned before fatigue and hunger began to take their toll. We knew we were only staying one night because our flight was booked for Thursday morning so we hadn't bothered about hotels, etc, as the intention was always to drink the night away and see if Amsterdam really was a 24 hour city. However, by about 6.30am all of us were totally shattered and drastic action needed to be taken. Rescue arrived in the form of a vegetarian breakfast bar (only in Amsterdam!) that opened early and had, wait for it, a shower that could be used for a couple of guilders. The owner told us it was a regular haunt of vegetarian truck drivers and who were we to disbelieve him. This was paradise, pure and simple. Fantastic food, countless coffees and a life-saving shower combined to save the day and by the time we left there was only enough time for a quick look round the shops before getting off to Schipol.

At the airport we caught a plane and we got on it (as someone once said) which enabled us to crash out for half an hour before that most beautiful of sights, Ringway, came into view.

Aviation is a wonderful thing. We were back home and still in time to see the boys parade the trophy along Deansgate on Thursday night. Holland in general and Amsterdam in particular have many happy memories for me but I never thought that Rotterdam and the little matter of European glory would take pride of place among them.

"We're too sexy for your truncheons"

PAE Athinaikos 0 - Manchester United 0
(aggregate 0-0, 0-2 after extra time in the 2nd leg)
European Cup Winners Cup, Round One, 1st Leg
September 18th 1991, Apostolos Nikolaidis Stadium.
Schmeichel, Phelan, Irwin, Bruce, Webb, Pallister, Robins,
Ince, McClair, Hughes, Beardsmore.
Sub used: Wallace
Attendance: 5,400

Stefanos Tsichrintzis

Stefanos Tsichrintzis (Steve The Greek), 21, is the poor mug who always gets hassle at passport control because of his Greek passport and unpronounceable surname. He can be often found arguing for the return of the Elgin marbles, moaning about the lack of good Ouzo or gloating about the manner in which Athens won their Olympic bid well after closing time in bars of whichever European town United are playing in. In an attempt to lead a semi-normal life, for about three days a week, he attends a course at the London School Of Economics, where he is studying Sociology, and going to more football matches than lectures.

What could be a better cure from our European Cup Winners Cup hangover than a trip to sunny Greece and Athinaikos? Many maps of all the Greek islands and visits to the local travel agent came in handy to the 1000 or so Reds who planed, boated or trained it to different parts of Greece. With the thermometer pointing at 32c, that the ale would be flowing in excess and that the team would arse about on the pitch were two events totally predictable. This, however, is the story of unpredictable rather than predictable events...

At the tender age of fifteen (it is for what you've experienced) this was my first European away trip. Or maybe not, because being a travelling Greek Red and living just five minutes away from the Athinaikos ground, for me this was probably the only 'home' game that I'll ever go to.

I had only attended my first game in England at Everton two weeks before, where some clued up Reds had saved me from the potential dangers of Merseyside hospitality. In recognition of their noble deeds, I arranged to meet them out in Athens and sort them out for match tickets on the Monday night before the game. The normal 'situation' had arisen whereby the club were charging £15 compared to £6 that Athinaikos were charging their own fans. While obtaining tickets for this match from the home club was quite easy, this has not been the case in most other countries.

Before meeting my mates there was time to celebrate the homecoming of my heroes at the airport. On arrival, with the police security suggesting the visit of President Clinton rather than that of Michael Phelan, meeting the players initially seemed improbable. Nevertheless, where there is a will there is always a little avenue and this materialised when my eye caught an airport worker pushing trolleys through a hole in the wall and out through the other side - the baggage reclaim area. Minutes later, when said worker went round chasing more trolleys, three trolleys and a curled up Red miraculously pushed themselves through the hole in the wall and, hey presto, the whole United team were suddenly at my mercy for autographs and photos in what seemed the most exciting five minutes of my life. With hindsight, hassling Danny Wallace over an autograph in a stifling airport is not my idea of excitement, it is probably something one grows out of.

Also in the baggage reclaim area was Marios, a United die-hard from Salonika who, at the age of twenty seven, had certainly still not grown out of this type of pastime. This man had not forgotten to send Bryan Robson a birthday card, along with a pricey little gift, for the last fourteen years. He told me the story of how he once bribed workers at his local post-office into sending off a box containing little liqueurs to his United hero, something not normally allowed through the Greek postal system. Ain't life sad, eh?

On exit the players got besieged by reporters, whom we very generously directed towards Mr. Robson and Mr. McClair - Neil Whitworth and Clayton Blackmore in fact - as we escorted our thankful heroes to their coach. It would not be the first time that these reporters would fail to sustain any level of accuracy in their reports. Whereas this time their inaccuracy would be inconsequential, other reports, most notably the one straight after the draw that quoted Ken Merrett as saying that United would bring over 16,000 fans, carried a much greater significance for the way the Greek fans perceived their visitors. This portrayal of an overstated army of fans invading, served rather as a self-fulfilling prophecy, as events proved on the night before the game and also during the match.

With a very angry porter looking to kill someone for stealing three airport trolleys and the reporters slowly sussing out that Blackmore didn't sound Scottish, me and Marios decided to head quickly towards the training session the team had arranged for the early evening. Quick taxi to the ground, where we found out that the police were stupidly allowing the 200 fans there, many of them Greek, into one stand only.

As we approached the press entrance, Marios quickly produced a press pass, slung his bag over my shoulder as I mumbled "helper" and it was onto the track around the pitch. All this hassle to watch Robbo have a lie down on the pitch along with the physio and Bruce repetitively ask the reporters to: "Move off the pitch now please". At around 8pm and as the sun was setting, Fergie decided that since his face and Peter's nose were getting dangerously red under the sun they'd better call it a day. The team were applauded off the pitch, Clayton the last off, desperately trying to catch the last glimpses of sunshine for his infamous tan.

Enough running around, it was time for a drink. Off to the Jason Hotel where Tommy G's party of fifteen drunks had adopted the little square in front of the hotel as their drinking base (many didn't/couldn't move until five minutes into the match). The more sensible ones were lured into having a meal, as the friendly waiter serving us had decided to take us to a nice taverna.

When we got back the night had deteriorated as most had either crawled back to their bed or gone seeking pleasure in the dodgier parts of town, notably the Red Light area of Filis Street. Special mention here has to go to Steve K, who puts a great amount of energy into conducting a tour of European brothels alongside that of European football grounds. Earlier he had been explaining how it costs £30 to buy a girlfriend a meal in a restaurant before you go back to her's, whereas you can "cut the bullshit" and get sex for a tenner cheaper in most European cities. For a person of such twisted morals to subsequently miss out on Filis Street is quite an alarming matter (still moaning about it six years on), to settle for a hand-job off a transvestite after giving up hope of anything better, whilst anything better was actually taking place only two streets away, however, is really taking the piss. Furthermore, what in my estimation absolutely takes the piss is that said character has recently been missing games because a little 'lovebird' has been figuring dominantly in his life.

It had been a long day, so my decision at around 1.30am was to catch a bus back to my unsuspecting Mum who thought I'd been at school the whole day (throughout this trip I had the burden of carrying about my school-bag). The bravest of the brave gave up the ghost at around 6am when their renditions of "Robin Hood" were met with jugs of water and police call threats by the locals. Little did we realise that the police invite themselves whether it comes to it or not.

On Tuesday morning our party split in many directions. Having all done their homework on Ancient Greece, everyone headed towards a healthy development of mind and soul in full respect of the cultural emphasis placed on it by the ancients. The signs of cultural metamorphosis were clearly visible on their return from this sightseeing. Mick was philosophising whilst standing on a table in the middle of the square with nothing on but the hotel bed-sheet wrapped around his waist. Whether Aristophane's satirical plays would attract so much laughter out of his little audience 2,500 years back is questionable. The audience, obviously consuming enormous quantities of wine in honour of Dionysus, the God of Wine, were nearing the point of ecstasy, and as far as the orgies go, well, that had been sorted the night before. Concerning the cultivation of the body - though many had a long way to go towards emulating the athleticism of Adonis - most looked quite refreshed after their swimming exercise in the sea of Vouliagmeni. All this rounded off by an afternoon siesta - certainly a case of when in Athens, do what the Athenians do.

In the evening we again gathered in the square. At some point four lads who had wandered off up the road looking for a bar came running back being chased by a gang of local youths throwing flares and stones. What followed can only be described as all hell breaking loose. While it all went off most Reds scattered about, many caught on their own and given a kicking. Things worsened when the police arrived on the scene, as if sent by Aris the God of War. They wielded batons on the United fans throwing tear gas towards the in no way replying English. Some Reds gave chase only to get arrested up the road. This looked like a set-up.

Noah, an ex-miner, got done over far worse than anyone else. They handcuffed him to a tree as they threw punches and kicks at him, shouting "die, English pig" to the point that they broke his arm. Nevertheless Noah, like all of us in Athens, just out to enjoy ourselves, somehow managed to see a funny side to it, as he lay there battered and bruised and began singing: "I'm too sexy for your truncheons, too sexy by far!", along to the theme of the then chart-topping song. Sadly the police did not share his sense of humour - whack! whack! Casualties included a little Scottish guy who had to be taken to hospital and missed the match.

When we got together again, it was noticeable that we were missing Pete, a man of small build. As we ran back to get him, we could see sod all due to the smoke from the flares and the situation began to get worrying. Suddenly who should emerge like Gary Glitter in concert, singing "Do you wanna be in my gang!", but Pete, unharmed and so drunk not even realising what had gone on.

Teresa, a grandmother, hid in a broom cupboard behind a big fridge in the hotel, where she saw the police battering everyone in sight. From there she could also see the Bobby Charlton look-a-like behind reception, who was pointing out the 'troublemakers', as far as his wildest stretch of imagination could visualize them that is. Remember Greeks have traditionally been good in telling myths; it needs no telling that the next day Bobby was OFF duty.

The police eventually came round and apologised on the Thursday morning - "it was all a mistake". The question that inevitably arises from this experience is why would Greek boys be out in town looking for a ruck, and similarly the police. The only reason is the media creating folk devils and moral panics through its misinterpretation of Reds as hooligans; both thought they were taking on Europe's finest. Finest drinkers maybe, but not hooligans.

The rest of the night was spent having a quiet drink in the safety of the hotel lobby. A real shame that the Tuesday night - traditionally the best on a Euro away - had been marred by these events.

On match day (another day off school) a battered and bruised party gathered around in the square for breakfast, which for some consisted of bottles of Ouzo. A few drinks and the previous nights events were Ancient Greek mythology. Most tried to make up drink-wise for the night before and proceeded to a session of epic proportions. A major reason why people hadn't moved from the square during their stay was that Athens is one hard place to get hold of a taxi, particularly during peak hours. This problem manifested itself as a valuable hours drinking time was wasted trying to get taxis to the ground.

Our next port of call was a little bar - of the many - outside the ground. Initially the barman didn't want to serve us but when he saw what we were like and what we drank, he became our 'best mate', naturally enough inviting us back after the game. My most vivid memory is of one Red being physically unable to move, begging his mates to sell his ticket as they tried to carry him to the ground.

The match was the worst goalless draw I have ever watched in my life. Burning your bum sitting on a stone all-seater terrace did not contribute towards enjoyment either. Quite surprisingly, the game had been switched here from a ground that was even worse. The ground Athinaikos normally use for league games is surrounded by hills populated by billy goats, which, much annoyed by intruders to their privacy, readily stick their horns up the backside of any mug that tries to retrieve the ball when it goes over the fence. After running out of balls - and having no floodlights - Athinaikos appealed to UEFA who switched the game to the old Panathinaikos stadium and the billy goats were now substituted with Panathinaikos bullies, milling around their old territory.

Funny how a ground that Panathinaikos have abandoned for their domestic games for nearly ten years qualifies as fit to hold a European tie. Even funnier that it will take the media about six years more, until the Porto game, to realise and kick up a fuss about the not-up-to standard stadia and inadequate policing that exists. In the meantime we have been risking our lives on several occasions in the "stands" of the likes of Montpellier and Pesci Muncas and been chased about by illiterate thugs that have been trained as riot police (Istanbul) even though we had legitimate tickets for a segregated section.

Since the players were not producing anything of interest on the pitch, attention began to be focused on events in the stands. The goings-on in the away end were completely baffling the locals. Five minutes into the game three drunks, one of which was blowing a bagpipe, stumbled into the ground singing: "We are the Busby Boys", and Harry, full story below, was fast asleep on a railing, having a drunken snooze under the afternoon sun. Phil was too drunk to realise he was throwing up over what John would have to wear for the next 48 hours, the only pair of shorts he had brought with him!

A queue of Reds were anxiously waiting for suncream to be rubbed onto their faces by their mate who had generously offered to grease up his hands, and they all then proceeded to sunbathe lying down on their Union Jacks. Quite obviously the time of kick-off (afternoon) for television purposes had to account for this level of aposynthesis, on and off the pitch.

Apart from the proportion of the Greek end that were studying our antics, the rest were getting bored as well. Towards the middle of the second half, a bunch of 30 Panathinaikos fans in the stand to our right started chanting the uniquely intellectual chant of "Fuck You Manchester, Manchester Fuck You". One of the reasons for this was the fact that the Reds had taken over the bars behind the ground, which Panathinaikos fans have claimed as their territory since they used to play here before moving to the Olympic Stadium. The stand to our right was Gate 13 - the apparently notorious stand these fans named themselves after - calling their gang, "Cockneys-Gate-Thirteen". The etymological explanation of their name clearly demonstrates their terminal sadness; seriously believing that Cockneys are the purest race in England (as if), and thinking that they are the "purest" among Athenians, they found it most appropriate to name themselves as such. What is not so clear however, is the way Panathinaikos fans manage to hear the Bow Bells in Athens. I've tried asking, it gets them confused.

These cowards, who obviously had attacked us the night before as their main supporters club was just around the corner from the hotel, proceeded to single out lone Reds in their end, one at a time of course, kick them and nick whatever flag or scarf they were carrying. Like most European pretend hooligans, with orange bomber jackets and sad English names, once they know you are aware of them, around the ground after the match for example, are they about? No, they've fucking disappeared.

While most were half-heartedly clapping the team off the pitch we were busier with taking the piss out of some of our mates who didn't have any option but to go on the official trip and were leaving straight way. One such person's wife, Phil, had given birth the day before, yet he still managed to arrange some visits for her and made the match - thus rescuing his post-1969 European away record. What a happy Dad in every sense! Customers on this one day trip had to rush back to their flight having spent only an hour and a half in Athens apart from match-time. All this for the bargain cost of £329, compared to £169 with two nights stay which some unofficial travellers had paid.

Our next gathering took place in the hotel lobby, as the situation again looked dodgy in the square. Our company had the good fortune of being lightened up by Harry, who had set off by train the Saturday before from our game in Southampton but only made it for the Wednesday morning. His late arrival was due to the fact that he fell asleep and got off the train in Trieste instead of Milan. Not surprising from a man that can't stretch his left arm because he once slept whilst driving a motorbike on the motorway.

Harry, being the train time-table buff that he is, worked out that the only way he had time to make the match by avoiding the Yugoslav war was via Budapest. He finally arrived in Athens with £1.50 to his name, borrowed another £20 off the Embassy and made do by putting his two watches and a camera in a hat and swapping the lot for a match-ticket. After crossing no-go war zones, six countries, travelling 3,000 kilometres each way and also spending his last dime to get to the match, Harry opted to enjoy the afternoon sleeping under the sun, rather than watch the game. This was ludicrous even by the standards of the locals and they had only spent twenty pence and ten minutes on the bus!

Most stayed in the hotel bar for the rest of the night, although the more energetic ones wandered off, quite bravely, on a bar crawl. The modest price of 80 pence for a bottle of Heineken was a major motive for staying. The session was soon accompanied by the customary sing-song and a good crack was had by all. At around 1am, having had six hours sleep in the previous two days, I decided to go back to my unsuspecting Mum and complain about the homework overload at school.

The next morning there was still time for a quick drink in the square. That Mediterranean people gesticulate emphatically during speech is a well known fact, but there was something different with the people in the square. They waved fists at each other - but not at us - and we at first thought it was to our loud voices or as general abuse. At closer inspection we realised that they were members of a deaf and dumb society, getting pissed alongside us and having the crack in sign language. Happy that we hadn't offended the regulars off we went to the coaches waiting to take everyone back to the airport.

At this stage I wished my mates a good trip back, since the prospect of joining them in what I knew would be a three hour long delayed trip on a crappy charter flight didn't seem at all attractive.

I had my own mountains to climb, as my headmaster sent an absence sheet to my Mum - and United embarrassed me to all my classmates by needing extra-time in the second leg in order to beat the Manchester City of Greece (small club, feel at home in the Second Division).

Madrid '91: (Gordons) Gin-gered-Up

Atletico Madrid 3 - Manchester United 0
(aggregate 4-1)
European Cup Winners' Cup, Round Two, 1st Leg
October 23rd 1991, Vicente Calderon Stadium.
Schmeichel, Parker, Irwin, Bruce, Webb, Pallister, Robson,
Ince, McClair, Hughes, Phelan. Subs used: Martin, Beardsmore.
Attendance: 40,000

Nigel Swinbank, The Ginger Prince

Most K-Standers will know Nigel Swinbank as the annoying (balding) ginger-haired fool who arrives ten minutes into each half of every home match to cries of 'sit down'. Chorley-born, Preston-bred, Altrincham-based, Nigel is yet another Southerner thru-and-thru not in the 98%, who makes it to the odd game or two. There is no truth in the rumour that Nige wants to emigrate to Istanbul one day, nor that he is a role model for tee-totallers.

Onwards to Spain. Hughesy had put an end to mind-numbing boredom against the apathetic Greeks of Atheniakos after a game lasting three days at OT and immediately thoughts had turned to what the second round would bring. Atletico Madrid was the answer. Fully sombreroed-up. Game on.

As was the custom of the day, Rob was in charge. Rob tours of Preston (predecessor to the mighty M&B Travel) had taken us all to Rotterdam - a full week of Amsterdam, Delft, Eurdi-guerdi-ngen- left us with little choice but to request more cheap lunacy, frivolity and debauchery for Spain. British Airways scheduled flight whatever on the Monday morning from Manchester, booked joyously cheaply at the student travel agency (I'm still one at 30) and off we flew. Rob, myself and Webby. A man who was so named due to an uncanny resemblance to the pie-filled midfielder of the day which gained him much kudos with the female sex prior to the offending oaf signing for United, and has rendered him an object of much derision ever since.

Usual shenanigans at Ringway. Compulsory pre-flight consumption of half a dozen pints of Boddies before taking to the skies. A journey which is of little note but for the meeting of Ronald Andom (name lost in the mists of time), a geezer sat on the row in front who listened to our non-stop United bollocks banter before introducing himself as wife-and-kidless for the week. As well as friendless. But a man to be of high importance in the next couple of days.

Arrival - a total blur. Then, and definitely now, six years on. Off to the centre of the city - muppets that we were, we were totally unsorted on the accommodation front. We wandered down to the centre of Madrid, and indeed the geographic

centre of Spain (bollocks irrelevant fact number 1), the Plaza du Sol and ques-
tioned a couple of fellow Reds for clues on where to stop and were directed up
shady alleys and a vertical hill. A subsequent visit to Madrid has told me that we
walked up to Grand Via and found deluxe (not) digs near there. Well, to be exact,
two cheap and grotty twin rooms in the middle of the red light area.

Madrid is quite a sizeable place. So off we wandered to explore, starting off back
down towards the Plaza du Sol, around which bars galore and a few arriving Reds
could be found. We soon found our rhythm on the 'cagnas' - local draught beer
- as ,incidentally, did my arse the next day after drinking the impure shite. 'Tres
cagnas' was mastered and beers were consumed along with countless crappy
white fishy things which seemed to get served up with them - these apparently are
tapas - a nice welcoming gesture, but bloody horrible.

The night progressed to another local speciality - sangria - ludicrously potent red
concoctions which blow your head, make you vomit and give you monstrous
hangovers. Served in atrocious shaped jugs with flowers all over them. I blame this
fluid for getting myself and Rob thrown out of the downstairs bar we plotted up in
- for leaning respectively out of the male and female toilet windows singing -
incoherently, loudly and obnoxiously (as you do) - several verses of the complex
lyrics which comprise the song 'One Bryan Robson'. Always a good one when
leathered. We jibbed the bar due to their lack of hospitality and inability to sing
along. Walk outside; head breathes air; fall over; taken to bed.

Tuesday and other Reds were arriving in town. Quite a few independents like
ourselves had sorted their own flights out and were already in town. We ventured
up and down Gran Via and eventually saw a Red or two frequenting a bar just off
the main drag. Notorious Reds galore were demolishing beers by the barrel. The
Nantwich Godfrey mafia, Phil Holt, Vidal-Sassooned-up as ever with trademark
goatee beard, Welsh people, but across the road lay our mecca - The Brindisi Bar.

Across the road we wandered to the establishment which was to become our
home - and a base for many Reds - over the next two days. The place was small
and dark as you like, but before you know it, full on Madchester days were in swing
- The Stone Roses, Mondays, James (Andy Godfrey proudly playing tunemaster of
the day - probably!) - all blarin' at top volume, beer flowing and on tour we were.
Reds would come and go from this gaff over the next few days, knowing that you
could always wander back and find a group you'd know.

It was in a corner of said bar that Veg, leathered, told us all about how one day
we'd be in Tokyo watching us win the World Club Championship. Jesus Shit, we
hadn't won the league for 25 years. Shut up, Chris. And I've been proved right. It'll
never happen. But in Rio in '99, you watch us.

Red soul mates were made in that bar which remain today. Staunch and
seaworthy chaps. Andy MacGarrie and Phil App - on his 21st birthday tour - boys
we'd seen with the Holmes Chapel posse in Sammy Platts (did I really used to drink
there?) post-Atheniakos. No sign of those heavily-bronzed Heywood boys in Spain,
though (part time, eh Nell?). A bunch of young chaps dragged us outside for Union
Flag photograph action, a youthful and enthusiastic bunch led by a certain
Andrew Mitten - a genuinely sound chap and a star in the making - a young man
I still hold very high in my esteem (I'll see you for payment on this compliment when
you've really made it, Andy - and not just on Soccer Poxy Extra with that Torquay

tart).

The bar, I am informed, was also the scene of some typical touring exploits. My own personal claims to stupidity consist of spending fifteen minutes in mock sexual action with a door (caused by the fact there was some kind of stained glass figure of a female on it!!) and also the legendary Gin farce. Mid afternoon had arrived and quite evidently ALL of the bar's gin supply had been consumed. So our ever present host tootled off to replace it from the local off-license. Back he returned with some form of ludicrous Spanish named nonsense. I wouldn't have any of it and flared up big-time, gesturing and pointing the guy back out of the bar. Following quite a sizeable scene involving major gesturing, raised voices, multi-lingual obscenities (and apparently a bit of goose-stepping - obviously forgot which country I was in), neatly avoiding a diplomatic incident, off popped Manuel to return sometime later looking somewhat pissed off but carrying a very large bottle of Gordon's finest. Rapturous applause followed from the whole bar.

It was in this bar that we were to spend the whole of match day. I awoke to the obligatory hangover. Absolute shed collapse. And to news that my life had been saved in the night. My memory of the previous evening ends with Webby escorting me on a treacherous 10 yard journey to the taxi outside the famous Brindisi. I recall handing over a hotel card, a blurred 15-20 minute journey back to our hotel. I handed over huge amounts of pesetas to the heroic Spanish cabbie. (Heroic I thought, until two days later when drinking outside the same bar, and requesting a cab to the hotel, the cabbie broke down in hysterics and got out of his cab to point approximately 100 yards up the road to our residence. Evidently Manuel on Tuesday had taken me on a circular tour of the Madrid Ring Road on the first occasion).

On my return to the hotel I had been carted up to my room and dispatched unconscious on my bed. There ends my memory of the day. However, there did not end my activity. For apparently, in a gin-induced sleepwalking fiasco, I had decided in the middle of the night to try and relieve myself of several litres of the aforementioned liquid resting in my gut. I turned right out of bed, opened the patio window and walked straight out onto the balcony of our ninth floor hotel room. I was in the process of clambering over to plunge to my death when Ronald (Mr Andom, remember him?), who had the dubious pleasure of sharing my room, awoke and stopped me from climbing over the railings and led me back to the safety of the room. See, I said he was to be important. He saved my bloody life. To this day I am indebted to him but cannot remember his name. You know who you are.

Match day. A little fresh air first thing in the morning slightly eased the queasiness. We wandered down to the main square where the t-shirts announced it was the 'Invasion of the Vicente Calderon' - as in the later invasions of Porto, Vienna, Barcelona, etc, etc. (I don't know to this day how I ended up possessing one of these shambolic pieces of attire). A couple of cheeky cagnas were forced down and we had a wander down to some massive garden - bigger, even than John Godfrey's, which is, after all, known as 'Cheshire', eh John? More sun, more beer, and more banter with many of the usual faces who were in town.

A little hair-of-the-dog gin (Gordon's, obviously) was consumed and we felt ready to venture towards the ground. Phil and Andy from the bar were both with us and we were all recounting with untold hysterics the tales of the day before. Phil, birthday-ed up, was in a right 808 state (although not as bad as four years later in a Barcelona pizza gaff). Phil is a man who carries hangovers worse than anyone you have ever met before. Andy was leathered, because he's Andy...plus ca change (I think. I hate French now because it reminds me of Eric. And that makes me sad. Things will never be the same). Anyway, I digress. We walked down from Bar HQ and Reds galore were milling round the Sol Plaza ready for action. We wandered up to the hotel where Scottie and his UF crowd were staying for a couple of quick ones and, after several hundred pesetas of negotiation with the man, onto the coach we went and out to the stadium.

An unescorted trip through the suburbs followed. My lasting memory being a ten minute rendition by Reds hanging out of windows blasting:

"We are not, we're not really here, We are not, we're not really here, Just like the shadow of the invisible man, We're not really here".

A favourite of the days when we were banned from travelling in Europe and never a truer song in the case of my head, which certainly didn't feel on my shoulders.

Spaniards stared incredulously as we approached the ground. The coach pulled up just short of the stadium and off we spilled, posturing and strutting straight into the bar by the ground packed by Spaniards having their own pre-match drink. Police swarmed around, sirens blared, and there were more horses than the Grand National but I'll confess to not seeing, receiving or throwing a punch in anger (no surprise at the last two, I'd have fallen flat over even at the thought). Thousands of Spaniards surrounded us, and before long we decided the best tactical option at this stage would be to stumble over to the ground. Astoundingly, it was before kick off, a habit I've always struggled to get into (and still do, to this day).

So to the game. Shit, the game - am I supposed to write about the game? I guess all loyal and true Reds will know that 95% of any away game - even more true for a European away - is about the journey, the crack, the laughs, the lads and the mischief and only 5% the game. But I'll try and recount what little I remember.

The stadium was typically Spanish. No surprise there. Reminiscent of the Bernebau or Nou Camp, but not as large or impressive. We were situated opposite the main stand on some open terracing pretty much on the half-way line. I recall the main stand having some form of transportation running under it - road, I think, my memory tells me it was more peripherique at the Parc des Prince than the line to the sidings at Bloomfield Road. It was a big open bowl of a stadium, with three two-tiered sides having this open terraced top tier, with the cantilever main stand opposite. The ground filled quickly approaching kick off, I'd say we had about 2,000 of the 40,000 crowd which filled the Vicente Calderon. A good and vocal following, all in positive spirits. We'd started the league season well, sitting on top after a dozen games, and after all, this was OUR trophy to retain.

The team was read out. Parker was back from injury which meant no Phelan at right-back, but the European rules of the day meant that Giggs was sacrificed on the wing for the flying ex-Claret (a man who will always have a special place in my heart - I did name my cat after him - and not because it was crap!). At least the absence of Giggs would enable us to prepare for unexplained and lengthy absences in the years to come. The outfit sounded solid and experienced, though

- Robbo, Ince, Hughes, McClair (even Brian was good back then) and our companion, the slab of lard himself, Mr. Webb. And a back five which was arguably the best we've ever had - Schmeics, Parker, Irwin, Bruce and Pally. Not bad at all. Who did they have? Schuster - a German, England's football nemesis in the side - he was distinctive but surely getting pasty after being traded around Spain's top sides - granted winning the league with Barca and Real -for years. And the talented Paolo Futre as captain (wasn't he at West Ham in later life? OK, scrap the talented). Abel, Tomas, Manolo all in the side - Spanish internationals galore. It was a tough test, but we were effervescent with confidence, our first season back in Europe had generated an air of invincibility with our victory the previous year. A great dawn - but one of utter naivety - little did we know the five or so years to come would yield so little similar success. We thought, in Madrid however, that we were the finest in Europe. Surely we would cruise through, even against this class.

The match started off with the Reds in confident form. We played well, competing and indeed having at least half of the game until the half hour. We had our chances. But they took one of theirs. Futre scored after about 35 minutes and we looked a little rattled. But even after that, we fought our corner - Incey had a goal disallowed and I remember Neil Webb flinging himself at a header, to the shock of all of us on the terraces (and to tremors for a fifty mile radius when he landed!), which went literally only inches wide. Half time arrived, with us still in decent spirits, our invincibility convincing us that we would be able to pull something back in the second half. But the half time entertainment was one of the highlights of the trip. Not on the pitch, but on the terraces.

Andy MacGarrie, as anybody who witnessed it will agree, performed the coup-de-grace. Andy was perched, throughout the first half, somewhat precariously on the edge of a step of what was pretty deep crumbling terracing (3ft deep, 5ft of terrace). He then managed to perform one of the most acrobatic forward flick, half-sulko with tuck manoeuvres of all time. Starting in the seated position, the somewhat inebriated gymnast in question toppled effortlessly forward commencing a descent of twists, turns and flicks of Olga Korbut standards before coming to rest about six steps and ten yards beneath us. Sorry if this is situation comedy, but if you were there, believe me, it was one of the funniest things you've ever seen. Utterly ludicrous. The Red jury was unanimous in its marks of 6.0 for technical ability. Artistic impression was, however, somewhat less emphatic. Proud of you to this day, Andy. Perhaps a future career for young Lauren?

The second half was one of frustration. The reds, Robson supreme, holding their own, yet not able to get the crucial away goal. Then, disaster struck, and the defence of our trophy was over. Two goals in the last five minutes - a second from Futre and then a killer third and the game's up. Phil App was in tears. I adopted what was to become annual "we fucked up in Europe" head-in-hands pose. Also to be demonstrated by yours truly in years to come in Istanbul, Barcelona, Gothenburg, Dortmund. But Madrid was a shock. We thought the team were clued-up enough to take all-comers, but it wasn't to be. The Cup Winners Cup success of the previous year was to prove the exception to the European rule. And not the norm we were expecting. It was to be until 1997, six long seasons later, that anything approaching success in Europe would be ours again.

Emotions in the half hour after the game were mixed. We were held back on the terraces to allow the celebrating red and white hoards to be noisy as you like and taunt us mercilessly whilst we were held back by hundreds of uniformed police. Emotions from subdued disappointment of the masses to the bounce up-and-down "let's get at 'em" attitude of a certain infamous resident of St.Albans. We were held for some time inside the ground prior to being released outside into a heavily surrounded police presence which cordoned us all in. Missiles were flying to and fro - there were plenty of Spaniards still around and apparently up for it. We were eventually released and they scattered - we were bundled back onto the coach and headed back to the centre of Madrid under a far more substantial escort than the one we had (not) arrived under.

All the way back into Madrid and the police sirens were blaring - announcing the arrival of a defeated Red Army. I remember the disappointment being huge back then...how pragmatic we all are now about such set backs, we know a lot more, and have far more realistic expectations. Or do we? I can see Eric making a come back, winning us the European Cup and letting me live out that fantasy in Rio de Janiero as the Reds triumph in the World Club Championships. See you there, Chris.

We can all dream...but a word of advice, do not sleepwalk in your dreams after litres of gin, particularly on the ninth floor of a Madrid hotel. It could all end in tears. Mr X, whoever you are, thanks again. I'd never have seen Eric without you.

From Russia with love

**Torpedo Moscow 0 - Manchester United 0
(aggregate 0-0, lost on bloody penalties)
UEFA Cup, Round One, 2nd Leg
September 29th 1992, Torpedo Stadium.
Schmeichel, Irwin, Phelan, Bruce, Webb, Pallister, Wallace,
Ince, McClair, Hughes, Giggs.
Subs used: Parker, Robson
Attendance: 11,357**

Phil Williams

*Phil, 31, is a Civil Servant, working five days a week to feed his United addiction.
He lives in North Wales and has supported Utd for as long as he can remember.
He attends every United game , home and away, and in Europe and has done
so for many years - and hopes to for many years to come.
Supporting United according to Phil is not merely a hobby but a way of life - a
religion - and one which he finds impossible to give up.
Phil has written his article on one which most people have probably forgotten
about, as not a single goal was scored in 210 minutes of football. The off field
activities were slightly more interesting...*

Everybody probably has an impression of what they think Russia and Russian life
is like. For many years I had wondered what a trip behind the old 'Iron Curtain'
would be like. The impressions I had formed were mainly from what I'd read in the
newspapers and seen on the television and when I heard the draw I saw this trip
as one with great potential.

The draw for the UEFA Cup First Round match took place over two months before
the game so there was plenty of time to sort out the travel plans. With no direct
flight available from Manchester to Moscow it was with reluctance that a group
of us booked a flight with Aeroflot from London Heathrow. The match was to be
played on the Tuesday so with that in mind we elected for flying out on the
Monday, returning on the Thursday.

Booking the flight was the easy part, we also had to sort out travel visas and hotels.
Anyone who has ever had to arrange for a Russian visa will know it is not an easy
mission, so we entrusted our visa applications to INTOURIST Ltd of London - the
specialist Russian travel agent. Unfortunately to get a visa from them you also had
to book your hotel with them, at their prices!

They had a fair range of hotels on offer but all of them at scandalous prices
considering the general standard of living in Russia. The cost of a twin room, full
board, was £40 per person, per night, this took the total cost of the trip to around
£380, including insurance. I was hoping it was going to be money well spent!

In the weeks leading up to the trip, much research was done into what to expect in Moscow. According to a paper report the week before departure, there were on average 19 murders per week, which was on a par with Los Angeles. Moscow in general had a soaring crime rate so we knew we had to be careful. There was also a special ITN news report on a newly opened club in Moscow called *THE REDZONE*, in which naked ladies danced about in cages high above the dancefloor - one to look out for!

The first leg two weeks before had been a dull affair, ending in a 0-0 stalemate in front of Old Trafford's smallest ever competitive European crowd of just under 20,000. The previous Saturday we had another 0-0 bore draw, this time against Queens Park Rangers at Old Trafford, so it was not with great optimism that we ventured beyond the 'Iron Curtain'.

The late morning flight from Heathrow meant a very early start from up North on a very foggy Monday morning. The airport was awash with businessmen going about their daily routine, but also a group of about 40 or so hardy souls heading for the Aeroflot check in desk. Due to overbooking by the airline, they were offering a later flight with compensation but with everybody determined to stick together, nobody took up their generous offer.

Now 'Aeroflop', sorry Aeroflot, has a reputation, and I can tell you it's not a very generous one. The plane we were to fly on was old with paint peeling off every surface. The stewardesses were akin to their Olympic shot putting team and the food was poor, something we had to get used to. In fact the only plus point was the massive amount of free vodka they had on board which I think the pilot had started on judging by his take-off! The flight was pretty boring as in-flight entertainment had not yet reached the Aeroflot itinerary. We finally arrived in the gloomy city, late afternoon after a four hour flight.

Once we were through the strict customs check we were greeted in the arrival area by a posse of souvenir hunters/sellers and the Russian equivalent of ticket touts. As no tickets were obtained at the rip-off price of £7 direct from the club back home before we left, I decided to invest some dollars with these touts and obtained six tickets for the princely sum of 50p each, quite a profit for the touts as the face value was a mere 9 pence each!

We boarded our coach for the half hour journey to the Hotel Belgrade in central Moscow. Although decent it was clearly not worth the money we had paid for it. The first thing we noticed when we arrived were the amount of people hanging around in the hotel lobby, mainly very shady looking blokes flashing wads of Roubles! As we thought we needed Roubles to exchange for beer before the nights drinking started we decided to change some of our Dollars with these shady characters as they appeared to offer a generous exchange rate - 600 Roubles=£1. However we quickly realised that it was going to be very difficult to spend these Roubles as virtually everywhere we went they would only accept Dollars. Apparently inflation was running at a percentage higher than the local temperature, and as usual the poor were getting poorer and the rich were getting richer.

The meeting place that night was to be the hotel bar followed by the Arbat Irish Bar, that's one guarantee wherever you go, the Irish bar! It was strangely enough situated on one of Moscow's main streets, Arbat Street. We were to quickly find out why the rich were getting richer as the price of a pint in the bar was approximately

£2.50. There was no local crap, just imported beers - you go all the way to Moscow and drink the same thing you drink back home, great isn't it! The price of the ale didn't put off any of the 100 or so Utd fans in the bar from getting it down their necks and by throwing out time most people were worse for wear and in the time we'd been in there, every United song in history had been aired, including a heart felt rendition of *The Flowers Of Manchester* sung by the legendary Mallet from Brighton to an otherwise quiet audience. The roar of approval when he completed this most emotional song was quite deafening to say the least.

The bar was eventually cleared at around 1am and most Reds headed back to their hotels. Not one to be defeated by 'early' closing, a few of us purchased more alcohol supplies from one of the many 24 hour kiosks which appear on every street. The prices at these kiosks were more like the prices we wanted to pay, ridiculously cheap beer at 20p per can, vodka £1 per bottle and the local 'Champanski' champagne at 75p per bottle. Some rations were taken back to the hotel cellar bar and drinking and singing continued long into the night. Due to one of the lads bringing an Elton John type wig with him we were afforded some great photo opportunities!

On the first day, apparently none of the group had eaten in the hotel, however many had tried the newly opened McDonalds off Red Square with burgers at 40p each and it was touted as the best fare in Moscow. Due to the previous nights alcohol abuse and lack of sleep most of us missed breakfast and from what I heard we were the lucky ones.

It was matchday and the weather was miserable and wet, in fact it was pissing down and it was not to stop for the rest of the day and long into the night. The plan of attack for the day was basically to sample a bit of the local ale and then board a pre-arranged coach for the hour long journey to the ground. Despite the weather the mood was bright and spirits were high, mind you, that may have had something to do with the local Vodka prices. Once again the vocal chords were tested and any Russians within earshot were warned that there was only one Red Army! Many Champanski bottles were opened with the resulting corks flying all round the bar including one hitting a very pissed off barman.

The match was due to kick off late afternoon, so the coach was booked for an hour and a half before. Previous reports had suggested that there were no bars near the ground so there was no point in arriving any earlier. When we did eventually arrive it was still pissing down. There were quite a few Reds milling about around the stadium, taking a chance to buy dodgy Lenin pennants and anything else the locals could sell you. There were also some great photos taken, especially when Andrei arrived as he was obviously more than happy to pose in his home-land.

The ground was basic to say the least - scoreboards behind both goals and open stands along both sides with a capacity of approximately 18,000. Utd had been allocated a small corner along one of the sides. Believe it or not we had to queue to get in with the police not having a clue on how to control and organise a crowd - something we have experienced several times on the Continent since!

When we eventually got in we soon realised our part of the ground had no toilet facilities. Having been on a coach for an hour I was bursting for a piss so I went in the nearest available place - behind an electricity power box - unfortunately the local gestapo got wind of this and very generously beat me around the legs with a baton, and needless to say I finished off quickly!

The game kicked off under floodlit gloom with the ITV commentary team, including Denis Law, situated in a 60 year old yellow bus alongside one side of the pitch, 'Luxury, bloody luxury', I remember saying at the time. Somehow the scoreline had an air of inevitability about it, no goals at Old Trafford and you couldn't see anyone scoring here either. Even Captain Marvel, getting on for his first game in five months couldn't change it. Neil Webb came closest to breaking the deadlock when he hit the post but when five minutes later Mark Hughes was sent off for his second bookable offence we knew penalties could be our best option.

Eventually, after 120 minutes of tedium in deteriorating conditions, it did come down to the dreaded penalty shoot out. Our previous UEFA Cup adventure had ended seven years earlier by the same method - oh what an optimist I am! This was to change as we charged into a 2-0 lead, surely we can't blow this one...WRONG! Misses from Bruce, McClair and then Pallister ensured a miserable day should end with an even more miserable exit. There is no truth in the rumour that McClair's woeful penalty passed us in the plane coming home on the Thursday!

After the match, despite their victory, some Russians wanted to have a pop at the 600 strong travelling Red Army and got just about what they deserved. During the game I had swapped a Utd scarf for some natty Russian head gear in order to keep my head dry. I also used his umbrella during the game and at the end he was under the impression that I was going to give him $5 as well. As I left the ground he followed me to our awaiting coach and because I wouldn't give him any money demanded the hat back in exchange for the scarf. One of our merry band didn't realise our previous arrangement and hit the Russian thinking he had stolen my scarf and promptly took the scarf back, the poor Russian ended up losing his hat, the scarf and had a punch on the nose for his trouble!

The coach trip back was not a happy one, we arrived back at the hotel in time for the evening meal - whoopee! Yet again it was meat, cabbage and rice with various other items, which ended up being used as ammunition in a massive food fight by the 80 odd Reds in the hotel restaurant. The staff were obviously not best pleased but the amount of dollars we were spending on Champanski soon cheered them up.

As it was still pissing down outside, venturing too far was not very tempting as we had all been soaked wet through at the game and had only just dried off. A few of us decided to have a few beers in the hotel across the road from ours as apparently it was a little more interesting than ours. We realised why when we got there, there were tarts everywhere charging top rates for anything that took your fancy. One of the crew, Kev, a legend when it comes to taking off his clothes in public and not versed in Russian explained what service he wanted by stripping naked in the bar and gesticulating wildly. They said 'NO!, Not at any price!'. Poor old Kev!

Yet again the drinking went on late into the night with bed eventually reached around 4am. Now it had been a bad day with the result, but things were to get worse, a number of the hotel's bedrooms had been broken into and not only valuables were stolen, anything and everything else too, including towels, shampoo, toothpaste, razors, you name it, it was stolen! The strange thing about it was that none of the doors had been forced open. Apparently duplicate keys were suspected of being used, our suspicions naturally turned to the shady characters hanging around in the hotel lobby. Prior to the trip it had also been in the papers that some Western hotels in Moscow were actually run by the Mafia - we were now beginning to believe what we read in the papers!

The Wednesday morning was taken up with people making statements for the police about what had been stolen, our beautiful Intourist Rep Enya was certainly now earning her Roubles.

To say the previous two days had been interesting is an understatement, but Wednesday was to be the real eye opener. It was sightseeing day, as I thought you couldn't go all that way without seeing some of the culture and heritage of this ancient city. We started our tour by walking from the hotel down to Gorky Park via a street market. In the market the poverty stricken locals were selling anything and everything they could to raise enough money to live on in this inflation-hit city. Saleable items included fruit &veg, stamp albums, Russian dolls and any household possession. One of the group paid $5 for a stamp album which on return to England found it to be worth at least £500! There was also an elderly lady who was selling just two strange looking vegetables on an overturned orange crate! Very sad.

When we eventually arrived at Gorky Park it was deserted. We walked through the main gates only to be called back by a lady - we hadn't paid the 10 Rouble (2 pence!) entrance fee. After wandering around for an hour we decided to move on as there was bugger all to see! We then headed off along the banks of the Moskva River to Red Square which incorporates the Kremlin and Lenin's tomb, this was more like it. Plenty of film was used in the camera as the photo opportunities were amazing. There was also a posse of dodgy salesman trying to sell Russian army gear. The ugly spectre of begging reared its head also, with young girls with kids grateful for as little as 1 Rouble (1/6th of a penny!), however once you gave one, the rest flocked around.

After about an hour or so we got pissed off with all the hassle so decided to head back to the hotel for an evening meal. We used the very useful Moscow taxi service - basically every car in Moscow is either a Merc or a Lada and everyone of them at sometime has been a taxi. We flagged down a passing Lada with this in mind, who was more than happy to take us anywhere for $5, again a standard charge wherever you wanted to go. On passing the street market again the old lady with the overturned orange crate was still there so we threw her some Roubles, she packed up and returned home - poor old cow!

That evening instead of another solid 10 hour drinking binge we decided to go and watch another match, this time at the Lenin Stadium for the European Cup First Round match between CSKA Moscow and Viking Stavanger of Norway. We headed off to the ground after yet another meat and cabbage special in the hotel restaurant, this time the mode of transport was to be the famous Moscow underground, an extremely grand mode of transport believe it or not, costing just 1 pence per journey. Each station had chandeliers hanging from the ceiling, an amazing sight.

Despite the population of Moscow its football teams are not well supported. The

Lenin Stadium with a capacity in the past of 100,000 had barely 15,000 hardy souls in it. As we arrived late at the ground we decided again to use the touting system to obtain tickets as there was a large queue at the ticket office. This time we paid 20p for a 10 p ticket (Oh to pay Russian prices every week!). The game ended 4-2 to the home team, the four of us sat high up in the Main Stand amongst a group of very unemotional locals.

We decided to leave 5 minutes before the end to beat the rush for the local transport back into the centre of the city - the only problem was there was no transport! The four of us walked for half an hour or so until we managed to get a lift. An extremely large blacked out limousine stopped and a very tall smartly dressed chap got out, opened the back door and asked us to get in the car! Desperation had set in so we got in, the doors were closed and we were on our way with the Russian equivalent of the funeral march blaring out of the sound system! The four of us just sat in the back shitting ourselves, not uttering a single word, just looking at each other as if to say: 'What the fuck have we done?'.

About 15 minutes later - it seemed an eternity I can tell you - the car pulled up outside, amazingly, our hotel, to much relief from its occupants. The "chauffeur" opened the doors and let us out but did not want any money - SPOOKY! Needless to say we emptied our pockets in appreciation of his efforts!

Back in the hotel some of the lads had been doing their best to boost the bar takings to record levels. Noah, a drinking goliath, not having mastered the opening of champagne bottles just smashed the bottle on the edge of a table and drank out of the broken bottle - amazingly he came to no harm!

With the hotel bar closing at 1am a couple of us decided to venture to a kiosk in a nearby street to purchase some supplies for the rest of the night. Unfortunately I was caught short whilst out so I nipped behind one of the kiosks for a piss only to be caught by an irate Moscow bobby - they're every bloody where! This copper started shouting and balling at me, obviously making very little sense. He then held up his baton to my face, at this time I needed to go for a Number Two! However, instead of arresting me the cheeky bastard dipped my pocket and ran off with my $60 - did I not like that!

I immediately alerted Darren, who was with me, to what had happened and we gave chase, eventually catching up with him down a dark alley. Now luckily Darren is bigger than the average human and along with my efforts we 'persuaded' the nice Mr.Policeman to return my $60. Darren didn't realise this Russian was in fact a copper so asked him for his money as well - we ended up with more than I had lost - serves the robbing bastard right anyway!

When we eventually returned to the hotel we both realised what had happened and appreciated how lucky we had been. What sort of place were we in? We had learned nearly to our cost in just a few days.

At the hotel a few of us decided to stay up all night and polish off a couple of bottles of vintage Lemon Vodka - top gear. The flight was early morning so there was little point in going to bed, especially as there was a chance of some dodgy Russian jumping in with you!

There was time enough in the morning to sample a Russian breakfast for what it was worth and then it was off to the airport for the Aeroflop flight home. As nothing else had gone particularly smoothly there was no reason to expect the flight home to be any different and naturally enough there was a three hour delay, not what you need when you haven't slept and a serious hangover is looming.

The flight home was fairly uneventful apart from actually spotting that Brian McClair penalty just above the cloud level. We landed at Heathrow mid afternoon completely exhausted. It was then that I realised I still had £10 worth of Roubles left which were realistically worthless - mind you, the busker on the Underground I deposited them to was more than grateful and thought it was Christmas!

Home sweet home was eventually reached late evening, the mind still going over what had happened in just a short space of time. I brought home many souvenirs, from football pennants to Russian Dolls and army hats. Also four bottles of Vodka and two bottles of the vintage 'Champanski', one bottle of which I vowed to save until we won the football league. I didn't think I could wait that long to open it, however, it was used to great effect the following May on the way down to Wimbledon for the 1993 Championship celebration party.

Once I was safely back in Blighty I took great interest in Moscow affairs and still do as it is quite an amazing place. In fact a week after we returned somebody was shot on Arbat Street leaving a bar - 'There but for the grace of God go I'.

I vowed never to return to this crazy country but as usual, the temptation of watching the Reds wherever they should play was too much and I returned once again to Mother Russia for the UEFA Cup tie against Rotor Volgograd in September 1995 - this again turned out to be another trip full of great stories!

I WAS A TEENAGE ARMCHAIR HONVED FAN

Kispest-Honved 2 - Manchester United 3
(aggregate 3-5)
European Cup, Round One, 1st Leg
September 15th 1993, Jozsef Bozsik Stadium.
Schmeichel, Parker, Irwin, Bruce, Sharpe, Pallister, Robson,
Ince, Cantona, Keane, Giggs.
Sub used: Phelan
Scorers: Keane 2, Cantona
Attendance: 9,000

Pete Boyle

"Love him or loathe him, if there were more Pete Boyle's at Old Trafford, it would be a better place. It would certainly be a noisier one" (United We Stand - March 1994).

Pete, 27, is an office worker and part-time DJ! Looking much older than his 27 years, Boyle's father first took him to Old Trafford in the 2nd Division season. By the tender age of seven he had amassed 2 Wembley trips under his Snake belt. During the 1979 Semi-final at Maine Road, Boyle and his father were concentrating that much on the Reds kicking Scouse arse after Dalglish scored, that they actually missed Jordan's equaliser. In recent times Boyle has become renowned for penning dozens of songs heard at Utd games nationwide and has released several tapes & CD's respectively. The legendary 'John Taylor' one of the original Utd songsters recently declared Boyle as "The Most Famous Utd Fan!". Not all will agree but Pete is on this occasion not arsed!

A trip down to Chelsea was always a laugh but this one proved to be a warm up to something special. Ten thousand Reds descended on Stamford Bridge with hundreds being led from the notorious Shed itself. A game which we lost 1-0 but will always be remembered for Eric's shot from the halfway line just 60 seconds before their goal and which led to Motson's immortal: "who needs Pele" line. To many Reds Chelsea was a side show, for the real fun would start in 48 hours. United were Europe bound, Budapest was beckoning for our first Champions Cup game for 24 years.

We arrived in the Hungarian capital on Monday afternoon - me and my loyal drinking buddies from Denton, the Bruvvers Earley (Tony and John). At the airport security quickly pulled us over and made us wait whilst they recruited more colleagues. After a couple of minutes they returned and asked: "Are you Manchester United fans?". We nervously but nevertheless politely answered "Yes". "Ah, Bobby

Charlton, George Best, Eric Cantona, Ryan Giggs, Micky Phelan (Ahem)" they enthusiastically announced, sailing through Customs was now a formality.

When catching a taxi to the accommodation we had secured at the airport, we realised we were staying as far as Altrincham to Manchester but weren't too worried as the £5 between 3 was hardly steep for a cab fare. We were greeted at our apartment by a local pest (Buda, of course) called Nemeth J Attila, who assured us his name was actually Steve? The accommodation was fantastic for a mere £8 per night although admitting it was irritating whenever you needed a crap as the master's dog barked furiously whenever your buttocks touched the throne.

For the Reds staying a few days "The Fregget Pub" proved to be a popular watering hole. Reds from Manchester, Yorkshire, London and East Anglia converged into this city centre inn. Songs good, bad and completely outrageous were bellowed out at regular intervals. What was memorable for myself was this pub saw the birth (or reincarnation) of the Denis Law classic terrace song: "...We'll drink, a drink...".

It also gave way for two other songs not in the same class but very special and poignant for the trip. The first "Drinking in the Fregget", this song clearly influenced by "Frigging in the Rigginn" and going something like this:

'We were drinking in the Fregget,
Standing by the bar,
Jumping up and singing songs,
Ohh Ahh Cantona,
Drinking in the Fregget,
Drinking in the Fregget,
Drinking in the Fregget cos the beers so fucking cheap.

Each day was quite similar,
We did things quite familiar,
Drank more beer,
Sang more songs,
Like we hate Scouse, Leeds, Villa,
We once went for a pizza,
My God it was so cheap there,
They didn't mind us,
Thought we were great,
For we are CHAMPIOGANA*'

Bizarre I know * (champiogana) being a play on Hungarian translation of mushrooms. Yet not at all strange in comparison to the "Bright Eyes" song which was accidentally invented like so:

After several hours drinking in the Fregget it became noticeable that one of the barmen had an uncanny resemblance to David Gower and Art Garfunkle. I and the Yorkshire contingent amongst others broke out into:

"Bright Eyes burning like fire, My God you look like David Gower".

At first there was just a handful of us, but within a couple of hours the whole pub broke into this ridiculous song. The poor lookalike's presence nearby was usually the instigating factor, but to this day I swear he was oblivious to his connection with the song. For the remaining days in the Fregget it was without doubt our anthem. Meanwhile around the corner at the tiny "Amstel Bar" we became regulars when the Fregget was closing. The barmen here looked ever so slightly like Michael Atherton but no such silly songs were forthcoming. On our first visit here we were charged the equivalent of £1.50 for a tiny cheese sandwich which was reduced as visits became more frequent. Eventually we were only charged 50p for the same sandwich. A week in one of Europe's finest cities and all we eat is cheese bastard sandwiches.

The night before the game a strange occurrence happened in the tiny Amstel Bar. An impeccably dressed local (posh suit/full monty) befriended us and two Reds from Reading. "Come with me I show you something good?". We surprisingly took him up on his offer.

He led us literally a hundred yards from the bar and up some steps into an important looking building, as he nodded and blagged security we did likewise. Up in the lift a few floors, left, right and hey presto! we were here, where? The Hungarian Parliament/House of Commons. Looking extremely pleased with himself he informed us no photographs could be taken. He finally relented, we took some, but what's more when we got outside and said goodbye, the Reading lads had gone and swiped the Prime Minister's bell. Shit. Fortunately a national security alert was averted but that poor bastard who took us there probably got executed.

On match day we not surprisingly converged on the square in the city centre. Tourists were amazed by our drunken songs and Americans were most stunned. "What are you? Some sort of political organisation?" one asked, "Are you a religion" asked another. Of some sort we bemusingly answered. That's why they got the World Cup I thought intrigued!

Onto the ground, little battle and tear gas later we won 3-2 and Micky Phelan hit the bar with a rasping header. Our section of the ground spent the match baiting Lee Sharpe about his alleged drug stories. He amusingly nodded and shook his head in an attempt to communicate with us whilst assuming his wide left wing role.

After the game it was back to the respective drinking establishments for the usual bout of rowdiness via one of the many strip show bars. How can one East Anglian Red justify paying £50 to have a woman sit on your lap all night! OK she was French and gorgeous but that sad git had to buy her drinks all night as well! - I just don't know?

The reckless taxi journey home had ended when we actually ended in the garden wall at our accommodation (gnomes and all). Our bemused host informed us on our next daily departure that we had made a mockery of his rockery (honest).

The next day we arrived at the airport where the security were equally as vigilant as on our arrival. This time the brothers Earley were persuaded to swap their United shirts for green Hungarian security jackets (well and truly done boys). Passport control grabbed us all into the cubical and insisted we drink their whisky straight from the bottle. We obliged, and duly waved goodbye to one of our best ever excursions. A truly great trip watching the truly greatest team in a truly great city. The birth of Eric The King, all together now: "...We'll...".

We Shall Overcome

Galatasaray 0 - Manchester United 0
(aggregate 3-3, knocked out on away goals)
European Cup, Round Two, 2nd Leg
November 3rd 1993, Ali Sami Yen Stadium.
Schmeichel, Parker, Irwin, Bruce, Sharpe, Phelan, Robson, Ince,
Cantona, Keane, Giggs. Subs used: Dublin, G.Neville
Attendance: 40,000

Mr.Anon

Anon, wishes to remain that way as he is currently still involved in a case for compensation over the treatment he received in Istanbul where he just went to watch a game of football.
He would like to tell you that he is a dedicated Red, gets to some - but not all - Euro aways - is in his thirties and has a job where the only fun comes from goading Bitter Blues. He's Manchester born and bred and has promised his family never to step foot in Turkey ever again.

After the delights of Budapest, a draw pitting us against Galatasaray of Istanbul was a welcome one. A new country to add to the list, and from all reports Turkey was a stunning, if rundown, place. That they had a terrible human rights record surely wouldn't affect a few thousand football fans staying for a few days, would it? We weren't Kurds after all, but citizens of the European Community, and the ancient city of Istanbul should provide some wonderful stories of another eventful trip. How right we were, but for all the wrong reasons.

Perhaps I should have listened more carefully to those Irish supporters who'd complained that the stand they were allocated for a recent World Cup qualifier was set alight by the Turkish fans, some of whom are the most fanatical in the world. If Irish supporters, hardly the most troublesome, had problems then it now, looking back with hindsight, seems silly to think that we wouldn't. Add the fact that England fans in Izmir had a terrible time, with a complete lack of security resulting in Mark Raven (who is still awaiting compensation) being blinded in one eye after being struck by a coin, and its clear to see my naivety cost me dear.

Turkish fans have been involved in several serious incidents, from attacking linesman during games to rampaging through the streets after defeats, and with the local newspapers whipping up the support in a frenzy about our arrival it was when we arrived at the airport and saw headlines that really did say: "Welcome To Hell" that the first indication of local hostility was upon us.

The press blamed the English media for portraying the Turkish people as stupid and went one better by declaring nothing short of a hate campaign on their visitors, which resulted in some very chaotic scenes as the United team arrived in Turkey, defending a 3-3 home draw, to be greeted by a barrage of abuse.

So from all this we quickly discovered that the lead up to the game could be, how shall I put it, highly volatile and that there could be trouble by the ground. But this was a massive city, there must be loads of people who hate football and with so many teams based in Istanbul none of this would affect having a good night out...would it?

So it all started normally enough. After the captain had told us to: "stay out of trouble" we departed the airport and headed to our modern, and quite decent, hotel, The Hotel Tamsa (how those words now brings a shudder down my spine).

After some expensive drinks in the hotel bar we headed out for a good night. Bars were hard to find but eventually one was converged on and we began to enjoy the night. Some songs were aired and a few lads headed off into the night, either to find other Reds or to go to the Ajax-Besiktas game being played elsewhere in the city on the Tuesday night. A sign of things to come was that all the gates were locked at the ground.

After a few beers a few of us went a bit further away from the hotel and had a good time with some Fenerbahce fans, wishing us well against the hated Galatasaray tomorrow. This illusion of a grand time was quickly shattered as we headed back to the hotel at about 11.30pm to get some money before we headed off clubbing. The nightmare had begun.

There was a very, very large group of Turks massed outside the hotel throwing bricks, stones and rocks at the hotel foyer, entrance and at the windows where United fans were barricading themselves in. Windows were being smashed everywhere. Chairs were used as shields to get United fans in, and this temporarily stopped some Turks, but the raining down of missiles soon continued. A Turk even tried to climb into the hotel from the side. These lot were maniacs, who reacted to Utd fans whose only crime had been to drink in a bar and walk back to their hotel. They'd come in large numbers out of nowhere, and a few years on its quite easy to realise that the whole thing must have been a set-up, planned during that evening.

The police arrived - what relief. This didn't last long as some of them joined their countrymen in throwing stones as well! The crowd grew in size, as did their misplaced anger and to our repeated anger and surprise over the next hour or so the police continued to do nothing to stop the melee, with some repeatedly encouraging the perpetrators and getting television crews to film Utd fans. I was really beginning to get worried. From fear to absolutely shitting myself, and I make no excuse for it - those who ere there will ever know how scary it was.

It seemed to go on for ages like this, with Utd fans showing the greatest of restraint (what could they have done?) but with the police clearing some of the locals a lull finally arrived and by about 3am the hotel was quiet. The Reds who'd stayed in their rooms during the trouble now asleep, some worried - and rightly so - about what was going to happen next. A chilling 'We Shall Overcome' was aired for a few verses.

The police were begining to amass outside and at about 4am all 150+ Reds staying in the hotel were roughly awoken, their rooms full of police, most of whom were heavily armed. The old, young, women, children, it didn't matter to them, as they roughly treated everyone, clearing our room and asking us to immediately go outside where we would be taken to another hotel. I had my doubts.

Those who didn't wake up quickly had a variety of methods used to get them up, among them a punch in the mouth, battening, pistol whipping and in one case a deodorant being sprayed into someone's eyes. Under these circumstances it's obvious to go along with what someone with a big fuck off gun is telling you to do, but United fans showed great restraint during the whole appalling catalogue of events. In fact, just as they have done in places like Porto, Juventus, and anywhere else the Red Army has travelled to.

As predicted, the 'other hotel' in fact turned out to be a mini-bus ride away to a police station. Here the most bizarre event of the whole trip took place (and that's saying something in this night of David Lynch style events), we were all breathalysed. Just what for? All of us in this police station passed the test and small groups were put in a tiny cell, where we were kept together for the rest of our 'stay'.

We were repeatedly told that we were being moved to another hotel, but by this time we all knew what was going on and we were moved from police station to station, and into yet worse cells. One was tiny enough for just a cat, with the stench of urine hanging in the air. We couldn't sit down at the same time so took it in turns, in another cell we could hear one of the older women on the trip begging to be allowed to contact someone in authority. That fell on deaf ears.

Those staying in the Tamsa now had a variety of different methods used on them before the inevitable deportation came. Some were kept in their cells for a horrendous 17 hours without being let out, others moved to offices where they had to confess to being drunk and one young lad had the indignity of being touched up as the Reds with him all agreed that they wouldn't leave him alone no matter what the consequences for them all. And still the thought that went round was that we are British citizens and passport holders who have travelled all over the world safely, in a supposed civilised country (the more I read about Turkish human rights violations now, the more I can relate to them), with our only crime wanting to see a bloody football match. It would be comical if it wasn't so frightening.

A group of Reds from Brighton got talking to one policeman who could speak English and when they asked what would happen to them he replied: Ah, I think now that you live in a prison..ha..ha..ha". They also had a young guard continually uncap the bolt of his rifle and point it at them. Some practical joke.

Everyone seemed to be told we would eventually get to the game with our valid match tickets, our that we would be able to contact the British consulate. These were all lies. We were charged money to have our passports photocopied and one cell had two Turks inside it who had been inside for seven days without any sign of a defence lawyer, and only two loaves of bread and a bottle of water to survive. The police back home are angles compared to this lot.

A translator finally arrived and we were promised that our departure would be: "soon...very soon". Our passports were confiscated and no-one out of our group knew what was going to happen next. Someone finally managed to speak to the British Consulate but their attitude was a disgraceful 'there's nothing we can do', 'why did you misbehave' tack. Thanks a bundle.

We were finally allowed our bags and got into another van as locals crowded round and tried to get at us. We knew by then that the airport was our destination, but still they'd drive us around Istanbul, heading for the airport and then turning off and leaving us parked in the middle of nowhere, surrounded by locals as the guards had a quick fag. We went to a number of police stations, seemingly just for the entertainment of some new guards to treat us like shit and another group went to four different police stations only to end up in their original one. Other Reds in smaller groups were beaten up in their cells - knowing they couldn't retaliate.

At long last we were finally driven to the airport and found ourselves with the rest of our party, all who'd been looking forward to this country just a short time ago. The old people on the trip were still being treated like garbage in front of us but there was nothing we could do. The Captain of the plane was great though. He told us he'd break every aviation rule and not leave until every English person was safely inside the aircraft and not detained. People didn't have their flight tickets as they'd been confiscated as had some passports and people were standing in the aisles. All we wanted now was just to get out of this 'hell', the game now seemed inconsequential. Some lads were booked on another flight but didn't want to get off for obvious reasons and the Captain asked for all those with wrong tickets to come forward, giving his word that they wouldn't be thrown off. A lot of people were still scared and six of our group were still missing, as they found themselves in an even worse situation. For us the trip to hell was finally over.

Yet these six were chosen as ringleaders (of what?) and in a mockery of a trial sentenced to jail. It seems unbelievable now that they were imprisoned in that terrible Midnight Express prison for doing nothing, but they did, and - despite receiving better treatment in prison than in the police cells - it took a full two months for them to be freed, and, like us, they all received the 'deportee' on their passport stamp. You can't imagine how they must have felt.

Even those not on our trip suffered, and I shudder to think what would have happened if we'd actually won the game (with Galatasaray fans arriving at the ground at 9.30am in the morning!). The players had their own bust-up after the goalless draw (you'll understand that it would be a bit ridiculous for me to comment on the actual game, but I'm told we didn't play positively enough!) knocked us out and saw first hand how the police behave in Turkey.

Many Reds arrived at the away 'section' a short time before kick-off with their legitimate tickets only to find the gates locked. They were pushed into a queue on the pavement, more police arrived yet not one person in authority who spoke English (a useful idea). Turkish fans began to queue with the 100 Utd fans locked out as their end had also closed and as kick-off started the police - for yet another unknown reason (as there was space in the Utd end for these ticket holders) - began pushing the Utd fans up a hill to get them away from the ground. They then used truncheons to clear them (some women) away, including a Turk in a wheelchair. They also had guns and many Utd fans just realised how dangerous the situation was and departed with their health intact, as there was no way the section was going to be re-opened.

Those who did get into the game saw their coaches attacked and one smashed to pieces (again women on board), including a boulder that was thrown through the window that was about the size of a human head. How lucky nobody was seriously injured.

UEFA gave out a token fine, but we saw a year later that - although there was no trouble - Galatasaray were still able to compete in European competition. The media, on the large, brushed the whole affair under the carpet and perhaps the most disgraceful treatment meted out to football fans was brushed under the carpet apart from by those who were involved in this horrific catalogue of events. We went for a football match, but can you imagine any other section of society, or group being treated so abysmally?

European football is about money and the Turks provide plenty of that, which could give quite a good indication of why their teams remain in competition, despite a catalogue of misdemeanours. Every Red who has been to any of the three games we've played over there in recent years will vouch that their people are of a completely different mentality. The English were hated for our visit, for a variety of reasons, yet our treatment was at first put down as a 'English hooligans rampage' on the British TV news, without any checking of events.

We're quick to be identified as culprits but when this surely isn't the case why don't we receive the attention that our terrible treatment deserves? An old woman was spat at in the face by the police for God's sake.

I have to admit that the whole affair took a lot out of me and has made me seriously think about which matches to attend in the future. You can safely say I'll never visit Turkey again, but also that I won't let our treatment be ignored.

At the time we were told we had no redress, the Consulate, the FA, UEFA and the Government basically ignoring our pleas for help. The club finally supported us (although Martin Edwards did say: "The least said the better"), particularly Fergie, and David Mellor on his radio show highlighted some of our group's treatment.

But I wanted more. We were visiting a country that has close ties with our own and I don't want to think that any other group of people (whoever they support/for whatever reason they are there for) will suffer like we did. That's why I am still, to this day, pursuing the matter through the courts, and why I will not rest until all of us who suffered, whether it be in the Tamsa or outside the ground, have the redress that is our basic right.

RETURN TO HELL...
AND BACK!

Galatasaray 0 - Manchester United 0
European Cup Champions League, 2nd group match
September 28th 1994, Ali Sami Yen Stadium.
Schmeichel, May, Sharpe, Bruce, Butt, Pallister, Kanchelskis, Ince,
Keane, Hughes, Giggs. Sub used: Parker
Attendance: 28,605

Wayne Iball
Wayne is 33 and is an accountant working in Local Government. His first visit to Old Trafford was in 1967 when 2 years of age, and has "had the bug" ever since. He first held an LMTB in K Stand in the 1974/75 season and has subsequently watched the Reds from all parts of the ground, currently resident in J Stand. He has not missed a home game since 1976, despite the inconvenience of his brother's wedding clashing with the QPR home game in 1984 - the match was fitted in between attending the service and the evening do, with the reception having to be sacrificed! He now attends every game at home and away, has been to every European game since 1990, and is one of the small number who have been on each of United's three Turkish excursions, although on the first occasion was one of the many who did not get to see the game.

Supporters of small clubs often make the criticism that supporting United is easy. I would beg to differ!

Following United in Europe is never easy, but the glory and the crack make it all worthwhile. My first such experience was perhaps a foretaste of things to come. In the dark days of 1984 when away European travel was banned, United played P.S.V Eindhoven, a trip which I was determined to make - so I did! Our coach reached the stadium in good time to pick up the tickets promised by our tour operator, yet needless to say we never saw any tickets. Without even getting off the coach we were to be escorted back to the border.

Several excellent trips followed however, culminating in the unforgettable Rotterdam 1991. The next major problem to befall me was the infamous Galatasaray Hell of November '93. I had a ticket on this occasion and it's still fully intact. The chaos at the ground meant that it was never going to be of any use. Despite this, I still consider myself lucky when relating this to the grief suffered by so many on that trip.

It was the 20th July 1994, barely eight months on from the nightmare of Galatasaray the previous season, the day the incompetent administrators at U.E.F.A were to make the draw for the new style Champions League groupings. Normally this would be a tense but exciting day, anxiously awaiting the news of who we would be playing, followed by the usual preliminary planning for the independent travel to the away ties.

However this time it was different, the news filtered through as usual at about lunchtime and a dark cloud loomed on the horizon. Our only definite opponents in Group A were to be Barcelona, which was fine although they would perhaps be formidable opposition, but what a cracking trip it would be (I was right on both counts - but wish it would have been the latter only!).

The other two teams we would meet were to be the winners of each of 2 preliminary round ties. One of these wasn't a problem, Sparta Prague vs IFK Gothenburg - any of those two would do. Our final likely group stage opponents did not meet with the approval of either myself or for that matter any Red I know of. Subject to their overcoming of the "mighty" Avenir Beggen of Luxembourg, the scene was set for an uncanny return to the Hell of Galatasaray of Istanbul. A couple of weeks later the inevitable happened, the Turks won the away leg 5-1, so barring a miracle in the second leg, the nightmare scenario was effectively confirmed. It was time for the soul-searching to start, with the question being that posed in the song by The Clash - "Should I Stay Or Should I Go".

Having had a good trip the previous November, that is until reaching the ground and facing up to the chaos that ensued there, there was an initial temptation to opt for the same sort of two night stay independent option. It was never going to be as simple as that though. I had vowed never to set foot in Turkey again, yet here I was merely 9 months later mulling over not so much whether to go back as how I intended to travel. When it came to decision time, head ruled heart I'm afraid - I opted to go with the official club trip with the priority being to actually get in to see the game this time. A small number would be travelling independently and all credit to them for doing so.

Driving to the airport in the early part of Tuesday evening with Welsh Phil, Cheshire Nige and little Pete as my travelling companions, the air of anticipation at the start of any European trip was understandably slightly different. The mood was relaxed, but at the back of the mind there was perhaps the odd tinge of concern at what may be about to follow the next day. Having parked up on the long-stay at the airport, we took a taxi into town to embark on an extremely early pre-match drinking session - even by our own very high standards in this respect.

An arrangement had been made with an accommodating city centre landlord for a private party of a fashion - who knows it could have been our very own latter day equivalent of the Last Supper. The usual highly efficient grapevine had ensured that a healthy proportion of those on the trip were aware of the extended facilities at this particular hostelry and a good evening was had by all, including a few friends and acquaintances who weren't actually making the trip.

Anyway, a drink or two later and the atmosphere was building as more of our number arrived from all corners of the country. How could we fail to enjoy the all too pleasant sight of the Blackburn pie-eaters being humbled out of the U.E.F.A Cup by a bunch of Swedish architects, postmen and quantity-surveyors. By way of contrast to the inept performance of a certain "greedy bastard" in this game, we watched later in the evening on Eurosport as Ravanelli scored all five goals for Juventus as they beat C.S.K.A Sofia 5-1.

The beer was flowing well by now, and the opportunity was taken to have a game of pool. In order to enable all those who were interested in having a game to play, it was decided to have a game of "Killer", which seemed entirely appropriate bearing in mind where we were preparing to depart to! This was followed by our bar-meals which were much appreciated as it was likely to be the last decent food any of us would see for a while.

Eventually, in the middle of the night, we made our way back to the airport, but first we had to make a slight detour. A young female student friend of Phil's had joined us for the evening and was in need of a lift home. Our lift back to the airport (who shall remain nameless) was only too happy to oblige. Unfortunately, young Jane wasn't absolutely sure of her bearings as we struggled to find the right road. Our driver, who let's just say had drunk more than a couple of shandies, was distressed to hear her utter the immortal words as she recognised a local landmark: "It's not much further from here now - it's just down this road and past the police station!".

On arrival at the airport we completed the formalities, which of course included a visit to the bar - just to be sure of getting a decent kip on the flight you understand. This went according to plan and we touched down in Istanbul about four hours later after an uneventful flight. The ridiculous rigmarole of queuing up to pay £5 for an entry visa for the right to enter this "delightful" country was endured, only for the half-wit passport control official to proceed to stamp once again over the previous years Visa, before grunting an obscenity and correcting his handiwork.

Having finally passed through this shambles, we boarded coaches to take us to the first port of call on our itinerary. We were taken to a restaurant in the centre of Istanbul for a "meal". Whilst the positive side of this exercise was that beer would once again be available, which was of course most welcome and duly accepted, there always has to be a negative, and of course this was provided by the "meal". Those with iron stomachs picked at their food with all the enthusiasm of a bulimic. I chose to err on the side of caution, on the basis that what doesn't go in doesn't have to come out.

This charade was followed by a display of clog-dancing, although I'm not sure if the dancers were either locals or Blackburn fans who'd somehow managed to get lost on the way to Sweden - let's face it they're hardly experienced European travellers now are they? The belly dancers that followed them seemed far more likely to be full of Eastern promise.

The predictable U.K media presence circulated and did an interview here and there, prompting choruses of the usual repertoire of United songs from the lads. I don't personally have much time for media types, but I suppose that on such occasions they are perhaps a necessary evil, to be tolerated rather than welcomed.

They are of course generally selective in what they choose to report and decided to look the other way when a shameful decision was taken as the coaches were about to leave the restaurant. There were two well-known female Reds who had travelled to Istanbul independently, and having met up with the official party at the airport, were hoping to be allowed to stay with the party in order to ensure safe access to the stadium. Needless to say, somebody in their "wisdom" decided otherwise, and despite reasoned appeals being made by others on their behalf, the coaches departed leaving the two women alone in central Istanbul. This decision concerning which numerous people subsequently tried to "pass the buck" was made all the more bewildering by the fact that other male independent travellers in the same predicament were allowed to stay with the group.

Our next port of call was the tourist area of Istanbul which featured the famous Topkapi Palace and Blue Mosque. We soon arrived and were told by our tour guides for the day - the "suits" - that we had three-quarters of an hour free time to explore the area. Eager to make the most of this opportunity we hurriedly disembarked and headed straight to the nearest bar. On our way, Phil and Nige took time to reminisce at the scene of a "great escape" the previous November. They had been phoning home to check in after the game from a street telephone kiosk, when a tribe of marauding Turks came charging down the street towards them. Luckily enough they had clocked this quickly enough and hastily departed leaving the receiver dangling with one of their nearest and dearest at the other end wondering what the Hell had happened and whether they would still be alive.

Conveniently enough we had been drinking in this area the previous year and were welcomed back with open arms by the bar owner who was most pleased to see us again, as he had thought that we would not be coming. The bar where we had literally been dancing on the tables nine months previously had been tastefully re-decorated and fitted out with new red and black furniture. It somehow seemed entirely appropriate, bearing in mind that it was probably paid for out of the profits from our previous visit.

All good things come to an end, and this one did all too quickly, as we headed back to the coaches for the next exciting instalment in our hectic schedule. Whoopee! It was to be a pleasure boat cruise down the Bosphorus. A few of our number wisely decided against this option and took taxis to our next destination in order to maximise the available drinking time.

We piled onto two boats and set sail, quickly discovering that the boat was "wet" and not just underneath! Another lucky winner we thought, we could have a leisurely can of EFES Pils as we cruised along the Bosphorus admiring the scenery in the mid-afternoon sun. As we did, a radio reporter was recording interviews with a few of the lads - they just never know when to stop these media types, except when it suits them.

There was much good natured banter between the lads on the respective boats as we passed by the teams palatial hotel and later under a bridge which had a rather large banner hanging from it, presumably for our perusal. The boats moored and we had a quick stop in Asia-Minor before re-boarding the coaches which were to take us to the ground. As we set off towards the stadium the suits informed us that we wouldn't be allowed to take any coins into the ground, so they would all be collected and put into little bank bags with our names on to be re-distributed after the game. What a nice touch that was when you consider that the Turks would most likely once again be free to take all sorts of weaponry and fireworks inside with them.

So it was here we go again to the Ali Sami Yen, only this time I thought to myself we should at least all get in even if it is going to be a bit hairy. Darkness had by now fallen and after about an hour we were nearing the stadium. It seemed all too familiar, the surrounding streets dimly lit with only a few locals making their way towards the ground gesturing at us as the coaches gradually neared the entrances. The main masses of Turks were of course already inside by now and had probably been there for hours already, whipping themselves up into a frenzy. There were still a fair number hanging around where the coaches were about to drop us off, and as we arrived they seemed to be getting a little excitable. One of their favourite little tricks in their perverse approach to psychological warfare was to run their index finger along their throat as if to say "you will get your throat cut". Such charming people. Thankfully though, there was also quite a heavy police presence, although there didn't seem to be the same sort of army personnel who had caused so much of the trouble outside the ground on our previous visit.

An attempt was made to clear a path for us to negotiate the short distance from the coaches to the turnstiles and as people made their way to the gates there was quite a bit of chanting from the Turks still hanging around which we naturally responded to by giving them back some of our own. Despite everything, it wasn't really that heavy but after a short while queuing in the narrow passageway that led to the turnstiles, it was something of a relief to be finally inside the stadium. I thought once inside - as the Turks might say - "Welcome To Hell".

The facilities inside our section seemed reasonably comfortable and secure, unlike those on the opposite side of the ground where the United fans had been the previous year from what I've been told. But, considering we were being ripped off for £50 for the privilege, so they bloody well should be!

The toilets were as clean as you're ever likely to get in Turkey, which of course isn't all that clean. Refreshments were available for those whose appetites outweighed their fear of food poisoning, although alcohol was not available so I didn't have to bother troubling the sales staff. I did take the opportunity of grabbing a few of the free programmes that were on offer - there's always likely to be someone who'll appreciate them.

There was now a lengthy two hours to kill before the kick-off, part of which was made more bearable by the novelty of being able to watch the players during their pre-match warm up routines, as I'm not accustomed to this being something of a habitual last minute arrival at most games. The Turks behind the goal to our left who had already become a little over excited at our arrival in the ground were getting themselves more worked up again as the United players started appearing up the steps and on to the pitch.

I found myself thinking: "What's wrong with these people?'. It's all very well getting excited at key moments during games and at the end of the game when you've just had a good result but honestly, this was unreal. The saddest comparison I could relate this to in a domestic game involving United was the pathetic sight of Swindon Town fans cheering wildly at the award of a throw-in in their favour as though they had just won the World Cup.

The atmosphere continued to build with the constant chant of 'Cim Bom Bom' reverberating around the stadium. When the teams emerged they were greeted by an incredible blast of noise and smoke. If they kept up that sort of atmosphere and their players responded to it, it would need a hell of a performance from the lads to take something out of the game.

The Galatasaray side was somewhat different to that which played in our previous games, with five different players, but still included the dangerous strikers Hakan and Turkyilmaz. United were once again hamstrung by the ludicrous limit on the number of foreign players. Only U.E.F.A could dream up a system to effectively apply restraint of trade in a European football tournament.

Denis Irwin was to be the unfortunate victim on this occasion as the Boss had to once again juggle the pack as best he could. It was pleasing however to see Peter Schmeichel back in the line-up after having missed the previous game at Ipswich. Less pleasing though was the knowledge that David May was playing at right-back.

It was a determined workmanlike performance with young Nicky Butt in midfield displaying a maturity beyond his years with a composed performance in a difficult and hostile environment. United seemed to be content with a draw which may well have appeared to be a good result, but with our next two group matches against Barcelona, the extra point might have been invaluable. Sadly, this did in fact turn out to be the case, as one more point would have edged us ahead of Barcelona and progression into the Quarter Finals.

The crowd kept up their racket throughout most of the game, but towards the end even their enthusiasm waned as the inevitability of a goalless draw drew closer. It was frustrating though to have played two matches here now without being able to muster a goal.

The players came across to acknowledge the small gathering of about 150 Reds, which went down well. They could have been forgiven had they not bothered, because having played in that sort of atmosphere and keeping their concentration focused on the job can't have been easy and it must have been tempting to get out of the place as quickly as possible.

We were to be locked in for about half an hour which no-one seemed to be too distressed to hear. When we were eventually let out we discovered that the coaches hadn't arrived and we had a further wait of about ten minutes or so before they turned up. As we moved away from the ground and headed for the airport, one or two people were nervously looking out of the windows, anticipating some bricks to come heading our way but thankfully nothing materialised, unlike the previous year when several of the coaches had been showered with bricks.

All in all it was reasonably peaceful, despite all the pre-trip concern about how rough it might get. I wonder though how much it had to do with the fact that the Turks still had to come to Manchester in December. Even they must have realised that anyone coming to that game would be due a hot reception after everything they had put us through on our first visit.

The players were at the airport and seemed pleased to be finally getting out of the place. They also seemed pleased enough with the result, I suppose they saw it as a job well done and were confident enough of scrambling enough points to qualify from the remaining fixtures. The four hour flight back to Manchester passed quickly enough with most people taking the opportunity to catch up on their sleep. We arrived back in Manchester at about 5am.

After dropping the other lads off I stopped for a paper before going home. In the shop was a Liverpool fan I knew a little who asked me if I'd watched the match last night and saying that it had been like watching paint dry. I considered telling him that I'd been and had just got back but thought better of it. The likes of him watch their football from the comfort of their own living room and just wouldn't understand what watching your team in Europe was all about. They're not worth responding to, so I just got my paper and went home to get ready for work.

BARCELONA BY COACH?!

Barcelona 4 - Manchester United 0
European Cup Champions League, 4th group match
November 2nd 1994, Camp Nou, Barcelona.
Walsh, Parker, Irwin, Bruce, Butt, Pallister, Kanchelskis, Ince,
Keane, Hughes, Giggs. Sub used: Scholes
Attendance: 114,273 -
The highest at the ground since the 1982 World Cup... *'Only come to see Utd!'*

Paul Woosnam
*Paul, an engineer, is 31 years of age and has been a United fan for all his life.
He has been travelling to games now for some 15 years. His first trip abroad to
see United was in 1986, a 'friendly' in Amsterdam - just the beginning of many
great trips. Barcelona was one of his better trips because of the traditions of the
club and people. But, by far, the biggest thrill for him on a Euro away is the
pornography. A trip without porn would be unthinkable.*

'Leave it with me' he said.
'I'll get something sorted'.
But with only a matter of days to go, my mate still hadn't anything booked. When
he finally came up with a flight, it was no good to an old bugger like me. £150 for
the Under-26's or £400 for the seniles. With time running out, I decided I had one last
option, the dreaded coach.
The coach leaves Victoria, London at 10am Mondays, arriving in Barca at 9.30am
Tuesday - a whole bloody day, an endurance test before the drinking has even
started. But at £120 return, I had no alternative. I arrived at Victoria to find a handful
of Reds waiting for the coach. Among them a nutter well known to travelling Reds.
The last time I had travelled away with him was to Holland in 1986 on the now
infamous ferry. Only then, the ferry got half way to Holland before turning around
and returning to Harwich. I prayed at this point that the coach would arrive in
Barcelona without incident.
The thought of one day on a coach was uncomfortable to say the least, but two
days was totally numbing. We set off without incident and most of the Reds sat at
the back chatting. It was only about a third full, which was a great relief as I'd visions
of a packed coach and having to survive the journey sitting next to a twenty stone
Senorita with incredibly sweaty armpits.
We arrived at Dover in what seemed a very short time - 'this isn't too bad' I thought
to myself. Customs boarded the coach for our passports, which, incidentally, the
nutter didn't have. To his credit he achieved a jib, quite how to this day I'm not sure.
I remember passing through Reims, thinking once more: 'this isn't as bad as what
I had thought'. We stopped at services and stocked up on plonk and everything
felt great.

But by the time we arrived in Montpellier I was hallucinating looking out of the window. I saw French legionnaires waltzing with Spanish Bulls on a bed of Zarzuela de Mariscos. I was sweating uncontrollably. I now knew why the coach was the last resort.

It was a real relief to arrive in Gerona for breakfast - Spain at last. By this time I was feeling really grimy and looking forward to a shower (and good piss up). By the time I fell off the coach in Barca, I was mixed up and in serious need of a psychiatrist. No chance of finding one in Barca, so a fucking good drink was in order. I somehow found my way to the hotel where everyone was staying and was relieved to find everyone there. I jibbed in my mates room and headed down to the bar. After the marathon of a journey I was going to let my hair down, although for the rest of my weeks stay the return journey would always be at the back of my mind.

Tuesday night was superb. All our crowd followed our self appointed 'tour guide' with his Rough Guide to some of the best bars I have ever been to. We did about 10 bars including one simply called "VELVET" which was inspired by David Lynch. All the chairs had a phallic appearance (leave that one to your imagination!) with some of the weirdest decor being reserved for the toilets. The bars all seemed to have a strange pride in their bogs, with each different bars toilets stranger and more ridiculous than the previous. As you entered the gents in "VELVET" you immediately felt as though you were in the world of TWIN PEAKS, with dark lighting and strange gothic designs across the walls. As you approached the toilet itself you activated a tile on the floor which set off a series of strobe lights which not only made it look as though you were pissing crystals, but that you entered the toilets of Dr.Who's TARDIS in the middle of take off. Weird - but what a city!

Headed down to the Marina in the city where many Reds were drinking. It was smart and trendy and plenty of space to sit outside. The police presence became a bit heavy so we decided to go back to our hotel and drink.

One of the blokes staying in our hotel bore an uncanny resemblance to Alan Brazil and received much abuse from John, a man never afraid to speak his mind, about his bald plate and heavy beard.

"If you want to lose the Alan Brazil tag once and for all, there's only one thing you can do - turn your head upside down".

Finally it was a stagger back to the hotel at 6am feeling ever so slightly worse for wear.

Awoke early Wednesday cold and shivering on the floor, with only a clean pair of curtains which I had found in the wardrobe covering me. I felt a little stirring from underneath the curtains and realised that I hadn't masturbated since I left home. I was soon in full mode and climaxed into the curtains. I folded the curtains and returned them to the wardrobe. The maid will certainly get a surprise when she goes to hang them. But at least the plain old boring curtains will now be a sort of flowered pattern!

Worried about the game (of much importance to our chances in the rest of the competition) we decided to meet up early, enabling us to get to the stadium for kick-off - something we have great difficulty in doing at Old Trafford and then headed to a friends hotel. Met someone who was sharing a room with a bloke with terrible foot odour. Last night his feet smelt so badly across the room that he couldn't sleep. It got so bad that to take the smell away he took off the blokes sweaty socks, and soaked the feet with spray on deodorant. With the stench gone he put the socks back on!

You could tell there was a tension that you don't usually see at United Euro aways. Even those who've been going years, seen it all, looked nervous. One person who looked as unconcerned as ever (or should that be as drunk as ever) was Drunken Dave, a legendary Utd imbiber who is a cert for every Euro away. At a restaurant he came in, headed to our table and proceeded to pick up slices of bread and describes each one as: "pure sex". Yeah, quite. He then moved his attention to a Catalonian lady sitting opposite. As she finished eating, he turned to her and - most diplomatically - said: "Do you know what love, I've never seen a woman eat so fucking much in all my life". The disgusted look she gave back I'll never forget.

We decided to take in some sights (which were actually disused buildings and uninspiring housing estates - some eyesores considering the architectural bliss that Barcelona generally is) and walked to the ground, a journey that took some 40 minutes. Arrived in a bar where the others had been in on Monday to buy up plenty of tickets for us off of touts. Met up with a few mates who still hadn't got tickets. By now there was no chance of obtaining a ticket, the jib was impossible, and many headed back into town to find somewhere with a good atmosphere to watch the game. There were a number of people milling around, but not in the numbers I'd thought. It's hard to put a guess on how many didn't get in - but no more than a few hundred.

We entered our section, passing the first of three stringent ticket checks, and met up with a lad who couldn't get in. He'd been so worried about losing his ticket that he kept hold of it all day in his pocket. Unfortunately, he'd sweated so much that he'd washed the bar-code off the ticket and the computer was unable to read it (he specifically bought a wallet to prevent the same accident next game!). He kept trying, but couldn't and didn't get in. Some people did have better luck though and several clever jibs into the stadium were successful.

One Red managed to get in the official section and hide in the toilets for over an hour before dashing up the stairs when the attendant had disappeared. Another Euro veteran, Tommy, easily got in claiming that hooligans had robbed him of his ticket whilst his wife stood next to him crying her eyes out. Drunken Dave, who else? got in being held up by three people as he wore a Cantona Cup Final wig but we think was too pissed to notice. All said there was no-one/nobody who was going to stop them missing IT. And what a ground it was.

We were in their section (ridiculous official ticket stipulations once more preventing the independent Utd traveller from obtaining the deserved tickets in a proper - and safer - Utd end) and most of the locals were fine - the result obviously helped. Because we didn't score (or have a shot for that bloody matter) you couldn't get a real idea of how many Reds were inside, but I'd say the total (including the official contingent way up in the sky on the third tier of this class stadium) was an excellent 7,000. Oh what a goal would have done, but seeing Schmeichel on the terraces and Walsh in his place perhaps said it all. Goal after goal followed...

The game? We didn't play, it's as simple as that. You could blame players, tactics, etc, but we were humbled and had done to us what we had done just four days earlier to the Geordies, with Stoichkov and Romario in true once-in-a-lifetime 100% peak form, unbelievable to watch. Those sitting behind us reassured us that

Barcelona hadn't played that well in years - it didn't make me feel any better. Nor did seeing their fans at the front, wearing Liverpool and Arsenal scarfs, prancing around without shirts on as the game ended. I left, after seeing their supporters cheer our team off and applaud our supporters. You could still hear the official travellers singing 'Always Look On The Bright Side' as I left the ground dejected and fought an ever losing battle with hundreds and hundreds of departing home fans manically screeching away on scooters. Why do they do this?

No-one put it more clearly than Fergie who glumly said in the press conference after that: "it was a lesson...a humiliating experience". The gap had been shown.

We went on the piss, but it felt hollow. I couldn't face it and left at 3am. The others all carried on, deflated at the result but glad that they had still made the trip. So they drank, sang 'we only lost 4-0', and tried to forget what had happened during those 90 torturous minutes. Most did a good job at it, but, sadly, when I and they woke up...we'd still bloody lost 4-0. Que Sera Sera.

To breakfast (the first all week) where the dining room resembled a scene from a prisoner of war film. Never have I seen so many ill looking and wrecked people collected in one room. Bloodshot eyes, sore heads and aching limbs were compulsory and all looked as though they had, or were on the verge of being sick. Phil, a legend in his own bathtub, had been singing all night in La Ramblas, off his head and half naked. The bar was closing and they wanted to bring the table in on which he was standing - and singing - on. He wouldn't leave despite being asked repeatedly, to which the barman came back and chucked a bucket of cold water over him. Phil, cool as anything (literally) didn't even blink and carried on with the next verse. He then said: "Cheers - it's the first shower I've had all holiday".

After the food was consumed to do battle with the alcohol still floating around my stomach we decided to do a tour of the city. Our roommate was still unconscious so we left him and saw the main sights of this splendid city. Gaudi's unfinished surreal Sagrada Familia was magnificent, likewise the Spanish Arc Del Triomf and the Cathedral.

To capture these I lay on the pavement to get some pictures of these wonderful works of art - and got bloody covered in fresh bird shit! I've smelt dog shit and goat shit but bird shit really is something else!

We then toured the slender and eerie streets of Barri Gotic which was like a 200 year time warp and finished at the Picasso Museum. Pleased that, at last, we'd seen some of the city we headed back. Read some papers, with both the English and Spanish poorly reporting events off the pitch.

The main Barcelona daily accused United fans of abusing their culture and city and of fans drinking, disgracefully, for 24 hours a day. The English press had the usual headlines about trouble and reported on the arrests (minimal). It's a shame that only those out here knew the real score on what a brilliant and good natured trip it had actually been.

There were still a lot of ill faces in the evening - and lemonades were out in force, albeit for a short time. We headed off to a crappy club where they fulfilled the obligatory Spanish nightclub record selection, and we were repeatedly ser-enaded with the awful Boney M and the crowd pleasing 99 Red Balloons. Well, the city couldn't get everything spot on could it? I was fully ready for A Day Trip to Bangor when suddenly the host of video screens lit up and began showing the goals from the game. The record that all their fans had sang before kick-off suddenly blasted out of the speakers and the whole club joined in with a massive chorus of "Barca". I couldn't quite picture this same scene in any English club without a deluge of confrontations, and to say we were pissed off was an understatement. Enough was enough, so at the end of the song a few of us lifted ourselves up onto the highest stage and let rip with a loud chorus of: "Ooh Ahh Eric Cantona". We sang and sang - watched by a mystified group of locals - and satisfied at my sad attempt at revenge departed in a real 'barney'.

Back at the hotel and my mate said: "No wonder so many go to football, it's the only way they can enjoy themselves. They don't get drunk and they listen to crap music...all they've got is football". "Mate", I said: "That's all we've got".

Up surprisingly early and off to a 5-star hotel to meet some friends who were being put up for free due to a 24 hour lightning strike by Iberia the day before. Shocked by the luxury. It usually costs £115 a night for the single but there were at least 50 Reds being entertained for free, including vast quantities of alcohol.

The last dedicated few were left in the bar before departure and they gave us a spare voucher which entitled us to a free lunch. Considering the food (or lack of it) we'd eaten all trip, this was an oasis. We went to the food like bloodhounds at a fox hunt. I ended up feeling, and looking, like that obese bloke in Monty Python's Meaning Of Life. I had the lot, washed down nicely of course, all courtesy of those tremendous people from Iberia...who none of us had ever travelled with before in our lives!

One of the group having trouble ordering shouted across: "What's French for tomato?", and looked totally bemused when we all fell on the floor laughing. They left - staggering down the hotels steps - and we stayed in the bar all afternoon, just seeing the other half.

With everyone going home I booked into a mighty cesspit in La Ramblas for my last night, the sort of joint where they pay you money to spend the evening. It had been one of the great trips and we wanted to finish it on a high - wrecked again. We ordered three drinks in the main square and they were served to us in what looked like goldfish bowls, they were that big. We just sat there laughing and joking at the mammoth task ahead, and were unable to finish such a daunting drink. The waiter brought the bill over with a big smile on his face - £25 - and as he departed with his own laugh he must have seen us coming! It was perhaps not much of a surprise that we decided to head for another bar in La Ramblas, and after chatting to a few local girls they asked if we fancied going with them to a local rave.

As we supped the last of our drinks one of the most amazing scenes took place. Roughly chronicled, it went like this - a) a biker with full gear has massive argument with barmaid who is obviously girlfriend, b) he becomes violent towards her and is pushed out of the bar by the barmen, c) he repeatedly rushes at the door trying to smash it down, d) The staff pull down the iron shutters and close the bar, e) Everytime they open the shutters to let someone out the biker, now wearing his helmet as a weapon, comes charging across from about 100 yards away and smashes his head either into the door or into the shutters if they've been pulled down in time, f) this process is repeated at least 20 times until the police arrive and now arrest a blubbering biker with a severely disfigured helmet...

Just another night on our European travels I guess.

After all this action it was onto a lengthy cab journey to the outskirts of the town and arrival at a club in a massive warehouse. It was mightily impressive, and we'd missed an early career BLUR concert by just one week. This was obviously where the clued up Barca youth frequented. Loads of people, cheap beer, puffing, and a great chilled out atmosphere, supported by loads of locals offering us free drinks to cheer us up after the result. If only all the other countries where we've been stuffed had followed suit! By this time - after a week of constant alcohol abuse - minor details, like music, are a non runner on the memory stakes, but I do remember dancing as if my life depended on it whilst being watched by the locals as if I'd come from another planet...

It ended and we crossed the dance floor which was covered in a layer of broken glass, as everybody just smashed their drinks onto the floor when they'd finished with them. A novel revision of the recycling idea I suppose. My two mates caught a taxi quite sharpish to go back to their hotel about 10 miles away and collect their bags for a flight that left in about 20 minutes and I headed back to the now appealing cesspit totally hammered.

I woke up on the Saturday, a full three days after the game had bloody finished, not knowing where I was, nor who I was for that matter. More worrying was that there were two dirty books and a handful of tissues on my chest as well! I didn't even know if I had or hadn't (so I made sure).

My coach wasn't until 5.30pm so I made the most of my day with some more sightseeing. I got the tube to Espanol's ground, the area surrounding it fairly affluent but the ground itself very much in the shadow - in all senses of the word - of Camp Nou. Apparently Espanol are the working class club in the city. Stadiums turn me on, so I couldn't leave this wonderful city without taking in the 1992 Olympic Arena. It was a mighty fine place, high up in a stunning part of the city with great views across the whole of Barcelona.

On this particular day the stadium was holding a S.E.A.T Car Festival with lots of different Seat's, old and new around the running track. Most uninteresting.

I'd been trying to put it off but it was time to start heading back to the coach. Still feeling rough from the past week I thought the only way to take my mind off my hangover before the dreaded journey home would be to visit one of my favourite little booths down Las Ramblas. It worked, for three minutes anyway.

Just as I was boarding the coach for the most mental of trips - a full 24 hour coach journey, with nobody to talk to and work immediately on return - I suddenly realised it was my birthday. Now how could I possibly have a dull journey back!

Despite promising never to use a coach to a European away fixture again, Paul has travelled to both Vienna and Dortmund on them. Some people never learn.

Look right-back in anger...

IFK Gothenburg 3 - Manchester United 1
European Cup Champions League, 5th group match
November 23rd 1994, Ullevi Stadium.
Walsh, May, Irwin, Bruce, Kanchelskis, Pallister, Cantona, Ince,
McClair, Hughes, Davies. Subs used: Neville.G, Butt
Scorer: Hughes
Attendance: 36,350

Rob Pattinson
Rob, 24, is a computer technician from Urmston who has been travelling to Utd
games for the last fifteen seasons. The best thing about United for him is the
European away and pre-season trips, which are one of the few times when
everyone gets together now. The worst thing is the cost of this habit which has
kept so many lads his age away from the match.

After the euphoria (and immense piss-up) in Barcelona at the beginning of
November, the lads faced their second Euro away in three weeks with a less
prosperous trip to Sweden. Reports of ale prices had filtered through on to the
typical "foreign trip nightmare" grapevine with rumours of up to £7 a pint scaring
the shit out of most Reds and everyone had already started planning what bottles
they were to buy from Duty Free!

The trips available were pretty expensive, especially as it was so soon after the last
one, but the temptation of yet another mini holiday with all your United supporting
mates was too much, and the thought of leaving the blue quarter sat at home
once again set us on our way.

The ticket allocation for the game had been typically pathetic, with 2,000
Scandinavians in the United section of the stadium, leaving most of the unofficial
travelling Reds struggling to obtain overpriced IFK end tickets.

Whilst half of our regular Euro travellers were watching United against Crystal
Palace at home on the Saturday and planning the week ahead, the other half had
set off in a minibus, as they were skint and determined not to miss what could be
(and turned out to be) our last Euro away for the season. Others were flying to
Copenhagen to meet them, the remainder who couldn't get the time off work (of
which I was one) were to fly directly to Gothenburg on the Wednesday.

The minibus crew had set off with a planned six days to get to Gothenburg, driving
via Dover, through Belgium, Germany into Denmark and then across the border
into Sweden.

They were to take in the Gothenburg match on the Wednesday, see Oasis in
Amsterdam (amongst other things to see and do in Amsterdam) on the Friday,
then return to London on the Saturday for the Arsenal game.

By funding the trip swagging at both the game and at the concert, jibbing accommodation where they could and travelling in the cheapest possible way, the lads, many of whom were students or on the dole, could just about justify going.

Many of the hours travelling were spent drinking, then sleeping off hangovers, before starting again - sharing the back of a minibus with fourteen others what else can you do? The lads eventually reached Copenhagen on Monday night, and decided to stop for a break overnight. By chance they bumped into the group who had flown into Copenhagen, but unable to keep up with the fresh faces, and capacity to drink, they departed for Gothenburg.

My own trip had begun Tuesday lunch-time in Manchester, meeting the lads at Piccadilly with 8 cans of Stella for the long train journey down to Heathrow. Our flight was at 8pm which allowed for a good eight hours of getting pissed to relax those pre-flight nerves!

Eight hours later, finishing our last English pint in the bar at Heathrow airport, we crawled and staggered our way onto the flight. By the time the doors of the plane had shut, the rest of the passengers who were not wearing such fine lager helmets as us, were calling for us to be thrown off the plane. In particular one bloke at the back who pleaded with the Swedish stewardesses: "Please do not let this take off with these 'crazy Eeenglish hooligans' on board!".

After numerous words off the pilot and the stewardesses we eventually calmed down and the plane took off, so we got scandalous again - after all, we are on holiday! The lager helmet then turned into a wine helmet, then into a spirit helmet before we finally landed at Gothenburg airport feeling thoroughly fuelled but ready for a good night out.

We got taxis to the hotel with a shock at the £30 fare, thought about jibbing it, then couldn't be bothered with the hassle after the copious amounts of alcohol would have hindered any chance we had of doing a runner!

The duty free bottles of spirits were cracked open in the foyer and we sat around ordering cokes to dilute the vodka and bacardi! The intention of going out soon went by the wayside and three hours plus two bottles later the other lads arrived back at the hotel after a night at the swinging Auld Dubliner and with no late drinking holes the hotel soon filled up with the biggest pisscans that Sweden had ever seen.

Lads were wading through the man made stream in reception collecting the coins that had been thrown in, others were asleep in the reception, on the stairs, by the bar, in the lift, basically anywhere that they could get their heads down. Singing and shouting rang throughout the lobby amidst pleas from the receptionist for a bit of peace and quiet at 2am - no chance!

My next recollection was waking up on a window sill freezing cold in sub-zero temperatures with Grant and Jay sat holding their heads in bed groaning. The hotel sauna became the breeding ground for stories from the night before. Wednesday morning also saw the arrival of the majority of Reds, and notably the arrival of about 1500 Scandinavian Barmys who proceeded to walk round the centre of Gothenburg dressed in more United gear than the team itself singing "Glory, Glory Man United". How these idiots got tickets in our end I don't know!

Everyone made their way back to the Auld Dubliner chatting up groups of Swedish students and schoolgirls who had skipped lessons to witness the invasion that was to occur!

A typical Euro pub full of Reds singing and dancing pre-match. Upstairs sold glasses of lager in three different levels - each having a different price. As the afternoon went on the singing got louder, a superb afternoon was to be had by all. I remember someone getting up on the table and singing the full version of the Flowers Of Manchester and following it in fine style by saying: "That's what it's all about, one big happy family". That was what Euro was all about, coined in a phrase, brilliant.

Soon it was time to make our way to the ground for the match, an important match if United were to make anything out of this European season. It also promised to be a tricky match against the group leaders. I haven't got a clue how I got from the Auld Dubliner to the ground, but I do know that it wasn't long before I sobered up with the sub-zero temperatures!

The Ullevi stadium is Scandinavia's biggest, with a capacity of 36,000. The biggest stadium, and also the biggest ballache for anyone who has stood behind one of the nets. The running track round the pitch just made it harder to try and see under the influence of drink. Robert from Cov' wore a "Tour Of Duty" outfit behind the nets to the surrounding Swede's disbelief.

There were so many familiar faces in our end (the Swedish one) that you would have thought United had been allocated the section. Unfortunately they had not. It annoyed me immensely that our official end (4,000) had been invaded by 2,000 Scandinavian "Reds" many of whom were watching their first ever game. Real supporters were forced to buy off the black market or jib into the stadium (like the young North Manc lads seem to do at every game!). Even the surrounding IFK fans didn't look like they'd been to too many games before - football clearly isn't a big thing in Sweden (certainly not as big as sauna's or porno's).

However, not being such a big thing with the fans did not mean that the team were no good - far from it. United were played off the park and, although this was partly due to the shit foreigners rule at the time meaning that our Championship winning side could not play in the Champions League, it would be unfair to take anything away from a classy IFK side. Talented youngster Jesper Blonqvist scored the first goal after only 10 minutes, May was absolutely ripped apart in the full-back position and United were giving their typical Euro away performance of the time.

As we shouted out in support and anger at our lack of lustre, Hughesey lifted the spirits with a well taken equaliser. A goal away in Europe. We jumped up onto the fence in both ecstasy and disbelief, after 240 minutes of football on foreign soil during the season, we had finally scored! The goal, however, proved to be a false dawn as the Swedes scored again before we had even got down off the fence to duly end our celebration (and effectively our European season). A third goal added to our misery, then Ince was sent off to thoroughly top things off, then finally our misery turned to disgust and anger as about half the team didn't even have the decency to clap the travelling support, either in our end or in the official "Barmys end".

Thoughts turned back to winning the league again, and to the night ahead back at the Auld Dubliner and an Australian themed bar called, ahem, "Dancing Dingo". Both the bars were packed with Swedish birds out on the pull with the English much to the delight of the travelling lads. Andy, Rob B, Nell, Robbo and Phil, etc, departed to get the train back to Copenhagen so we went on to enjoy the rocking tunes at the local nightclub before we went back to the airport to get the early morning flight home.

When we reached the airport we were gutted to find an official plane about to set off for Manchester - what we would have given to be on that flight. Instead we had to wait 5 hours for a flight to London before getting a train back up to Manchester amid straight back into work at lunch-time. As we tried to get our weary pissed heads down some alcoholic was wandering about the airport singing: "I feel like chicken tonight, like chicken tonight", whilst walking around making chicken impressions as if he was on the advert. More and more Reds turned up at the airport in search of a cheap bed for the night.

Restless hours passed before the flight and we were delirious when it actually arrived. Most of the journey home was spent sleeping, and waking up feeling rough as a bears arse.

On arrival back in Manchester I stacked work with a sicky (it was always on the cards) and went home to recuperate after another tiring but unsuccessful European trip!

Smithy, Danny, Ste and the minibus firm had driven back to Copenhagen on Thursday, and spent most of the night smoking weed in a bar inhabited by Danish hippies. Friday was spent in sex capital Amsterdam where the Oasis concert was to be held at the Paradiso Club.

Luckily the lads were on the guest list because of a Liam/Manchester contact as the concert had totally sold out, so all 14 of them sailed into the back stage area.

The next time I met up with them was at Highbury on Saturday, when I realised just by looking at the state of what Europe can do to your body system, just why I had declined the offer of going on a minibus!

So that was it, another European season was over, I was £1000 down, United were out, but still I wouldn't have missed it for the world!

We'll keep the Red Flag flying here

Rotor Volgograd 0 - Manchester United 0
(aggregate 2-2 - Rotor qualified on away goal rule)
UEFA Cup, Round 1, 1st Leg
September 12th 1995, Central Stadium, Volgograd.
Schmeichel, Neville.G, Irwin, Bruce, Sharpe, Pallister, Beckham,
Butt, Scholes, Keane, Giggs. Subs used: Parker, Davies
Attendance: 33,000

Teresa McDonald

Teresa, a mother of three and grandmother of three, is 61 years of age and has supported United for more years than she'd like to put down in print. She has become something of an institution amongst Utd supporters, rarely missing a game over the last two decades and travelling to twenty three European away games over the past fourteen years. She has had a varied life - rich in content - from running her own specialist jazz bookshop to now, ironically considering the essence of many of the stories in this book, working for an alcohol concern unit. She has a room full of Utd memorabilia but has yet to go the full hog and buy an official club duvet.

In the 1950's I worked as a bookseller for Collet's London bookshop, the notorious bookstockist at 66 Charing Cross Road specialising in communist material. Collet's had a lasting reputation which began in the 1920's when, allegedly, a well-known anarchist - Mr Henderson - owned the premises. His reputation as an anarchist and firebrand earned the shop an unwholesome nickname of the 'Bomb-shop' and speculation always drifted amongst literary circles as to whether or not Henderson manufactured bombs on the site. Well at least it gave us something to discuss a few decades later when the shop lay silent waiting for the next bunch of radicals to enter through the front doors.

History has moved on such that the establishment is now a Lesbian bookshop - the Silver Moon - and I can exclusively reveal in this book, an unlikely outlet you'll agree, that the current owners have a unique work of art hidden inside the shop. Namely a ceiling mural dedicated to Karl Marx and the Russian Revolution, and now hidden by a false ceiling. How's that for a football story...

Whatever, by the 50's when Eva Reckitt, the heiress to Colmans Mustard and Reckitt's Blue Dye used her inheritance to open a chain of communist bookshops in London and for me it was an opportunity to get a job completely different from anything I'd done previously.

For a twenty year old arriving into a hot bed of fervent Marxist customers it was an eye-opener to say the least. I didn't get the job through any political affiliation but as was common in those days, if there was a situation vacant another worker would be approached to elicit if they knew of anyone suitable. My then boyfriend left to work in a jazz record shop (these were swinging times remember!) and I got his job - good old nepotism always did go hand in hand when it came to communism.

What the bloody hell has this all got to do with Manchester United and their visit to Volgograd the reader might justifiably ask. Well, to a political virgin working in a shop where 90% of the staff were card carrying members of the Communist party, and oneself being vaguely Labour in those days, it was another eye opener. My frequent references to that great double act 'Charlie Marx and Freddie Engels' didn't always go down a treat, but when you are young you are oblivious to others finer feelings.

The literature which Collet's sold was supplied in the main by the Foreign Languages Publishing House in Moscow. It was ridiculously cheap, poorly written and badly printed. But the aficionados queued regularly to buy their *Soviet News*, *Soviet Weekly* or *Isvestia*. These magazines caused me much merriment and - in truth - feelings of envy. This propaganda spread tales that everyone in Russia had a house, a job, health packages, technology way head of the US, and a general way of life superior to that of post-war Britain. Remember this was at the height of the 'Cold War' and what we were being fed was dangerous information. I was vaguely impressed by it all, but as a free spirit I never fully embraced any doctrine and the only Red I would ever be was a United supporter.

But an impression remained with me of Russia and deep down I always had a desire to visit Moscow one day and see the Kremlin, Red Square, Lenin's tomb, etc. I also wanted to see at first hand this spectacular success story where women were equal, in all ways of life.

Then the opportunity arose. Man Utd were drawn against Torpedo Moscow in European competition and off to Moscow we went. What a Kafkaesque experience this turned out to be. It was still very old guard communist for that visit. Western influence was just starting to get a grip and I can only recall a Dubliner bar in the centre of Moscow (these Irish bars get everywhere!), which we had a few sessions in, as any form of European investment. And the women were far from being considered equal. But overall my recurring memory of Moscow was a feeling of being trapped and wanting to get out. It rained constantly. It was grey, very grey and very grim. Poverty and wealth were juxtaposed side by side. So you'd see a glamorous blonde in her newly acquired fur walking past a vodka soaked drunk passed out in the gutter - and they were just the United fans!

When we came to leave after being knocked out of yet another European competition we boarded a coach to the airport, and the courier said over the microphone that we all must have our exit leaving passes to depart the country. To say I nearly shat myself is an understatement. A feeling of real panic overwhelmed us. Some of us didn't have any and she read out a list of names who did have a pass, and I think I would have killed someone at that point to obtain one. She then let on that this was in fact a Russian sense of humour joke. No doubt she went through this ritual regularly, waiting to see the green faces as the realisation of possibly being trapped in Moscow hits home It turned out the form they actually wanted at the airport was the entry visa - a declaration of wealth and intent. A certain Mark Hughes' (not that one) form entered the following - *Purpose of visit: Invasion of Russia. Weapons: A Luger.* I still have the form and it was stamped and passed on entry, so much for Russian Intelligence.

When the draw for the UEFA Cup was announced in the Autumn of 1995 and we were drawn against Volgograd (who? where?) my heart sank. Not another Russian trip. The first had cost in the region of £400-500 and my Visa was beginning to feel a little bit pained at the abuse it was taking.

Many Reds had held back from going to Russia then, unable to afford the high price and assuming (and hoping) that we would automatically qualify for the later stages. As per usual with planning like that, it was to be 'Adios Europe' for another year. So those who had gone came back penniless but feeling glad they'd made the effort.

This time round there was a similar reaction - perhaps more so considering Volgograd was even further, the untempting Ben Nevis of European away trips. Wait for the later stages and save the money. Yet again they were to be denied a season in Europe as we crashed out against Volgograd and a fair proportion of Reds won't be making that mistake again, whoever we're drawn against.

However the diehards dreaded going back to Moscow but decided yet again to venture forth into the unknown territory where no Red has gone before. This was to be a journey almost to hell and back and was daunting to say the least. I didn't fancy the 'in and out of the country' official trip - wanting to enjoy the luxuries (and not so) of the cities I visit for a more satisfactory period of time, so I looked into the possibility of the unofficial trips on offer.

Which were sparse to say the least as even the club couldn't rally a plane full of people to make this trip and it was left to Scotty at UF Tours to offer an alternative. If he hadn't have got his act together to organise a trip (proving he could get fans anywhere) I doubt we would have made it, as the few of us like-minded enough to want to have a few days in Russia were met by many pieces of red-tape floating down from every orifice of every enquiry office we encountered.

The authorities (with a little help from those at a certain club) seemed determined for some inexplicable and illogical reason to prevent us from getting out there. We were all having a nightmare obtaining a visa until Scotty intervened, when perhaps you'd have thought they would have been more than happy with some extra addition to their tourist income.

UF Tours (and others) take United - and other - fans on 'unofficial trips' to European games, and Scotty hails from Dundee, the least likely Scot you'd ever likely encounter but hence the nickname. He is the bane of Utd's life but this likeable entrepreneur proved here he can take you to the furthest outpost of European ventures. He dances along to the name 'tour operator' and excelled himself with sorting this all out.

So as the draw was made, arrangements made, changed, made again and changed again we all gave the sigh: 'Not Russia again'. This all too often happens (luck of the draw eh!), being drawn to Hungarian teams four time recently and trips to Istanbul three times. Now why would English clubs keep getting long distance opposition teams? I wonder.

But where the bloody hell was Volgograd? The battered *Times Atlas* was consulted and revealed that Volgograd was in the far South and indeed was what was once called Stalingrad, a scene of terrible devastation during the Second World War where over two million Russians lost their lives.

It seemed a daunting venue to reach. Rumours always circulate before the actual game, will we be allocated tickets?, are the club going to stop us? The club have always been uncooperative to 'unofficial travellers', something to do with the suggestion that they want more people to travel with their own - usually more expensive - official trips. But there is a band of diehard travelling support who like to travel abroad independently of any organisation. In the past there have been 'drunken buses', road trips, rail, and for the further distances flying is the only viable option. Sometimes we don't know up until a few days before departure that the club are handing tickets out to those travelling unofficially, and it can only be welcomed that this policy has softened over recent years. As there has been virtually no trouble by United fans over recent years this makes common sense. Something, it has to be said, usually seen in limited doses when it comes to running a football club.

For Russia there is another problem, that of obtaining a visa. This is where we began to hit snags. We were told that the Russian Embassy offices in London and Manchester - for reasons still unknown - were not going to issue any more. This meant that we had to go through a tour operator who had some savvy and knowledge of what went on behind the scenes. Ironically the reason we did actually obtain the visas in the end was through some Liverpool fans. They were also playing a Russian team in Europe at the same time, had arrived at the same visa obstruction but through Scally resourcefulness found out that if you went to Edinburgh you could get visas from there, no problem.

Perhaps the initial worries on behalf of the authorities had been about the rival supporters clashing. Considering that Liverpool only took a handful to their match and the distances between each venue it was a pretty uneducated suggestion.

The tour cost was very prohibitive (£550) and it had to be considered a 'one-off", but did include a match ticket! (which was most probably 3p in Roubles!). Once again my dear plastic friend came round for a chat and bailed me out.

The trip involved an early morning flight on a Monday direct to Moscow, and from there we had to transfer to a local airport terminal - Domodedova. To say we were unprepared for what lay ahead was an understatement.

We met up at the airport terminal, Howard the great Utd songster the only Red I knew from previous Euro trips, joined a select band of 26 people who'd found the necessary cash to go. The Leicester Reds were here and a good time was had during the flight as we settled back to enjoy the trip. Unlike the previous wet and miserable trip to Russia we anticipated a warmer Southern climate with shorts a pre-requisite of the luggage.

The flight was by Aeroflot (or Euroflop as some refer to it). We also knew this was the airline onto Volgograd so any queasiness in the guts was resolved by downing plenty of the local drink - vodka and a strange sort of orange juice. If you've never had the pleasure of Euroflop, take my advice, don't willingly seek it out. It is a plane journey that invokes genuine panic. The planes are awful, the food crap and the air hostesses all look like retired shot-putters (and probably are). Even sadder is the sight of the other passengers from Eastern Europe who beg and plead with you for all the plastic condiments; salt, pepper, spoons. This illuminates the subtle differences between East and West. After an interminable flight we arrived at Moscow airport, and had planned to visit the Irish bar for some jars before transferring to Domodedova Airport but had overlooked the sullen approach of the average Muscovites working at the airport, still bureaucratic to the core. It took ages to get through immigration. This left no time for partying in the capital, although we were staying there on the return journey.

We all piled onto a bus to the centre ostensibly to catch the metro from there to Domodedovo airport - a two hour journey we learnt in amazement, with no shuttle service. Shock waves hit us as we realised that a) we couldn't locate a metro, b) it was a two hour journey for a flight leaving in, roughly, two hours.

However once the bus pulled into the centre of Moscow, Scotty ingeniously waved a bundle of US dollars at the driver and in a sense performed an act of financial hijacking, as the driver immediately turned the bus around (a bit like back home really), turfed everyone else off and set out of Moscow, away from his planned route and out to the suburbs.

It was an interesting journey, through the Stalinst tower blocks and past the nouveau riche estates being built up on the city outskirts. When we finally arrived at Domodedova, a nightmare scenario greeted us.

It was an indescribable shit-hole, bursting at the seems with thousands of very poor peasants with no proper security as the locals mixed freely with those about to be transported.

Those locals that were travelling also had a worn look, all sadly trundling hefty great bags, heavily bound with masking tape to prevent theft by those very dodgy characters roaming unhindered around the airport.

Russian inefficiency coupled with stern faced bureaucrats at every corner can be pretty daunting, a bit like 1984 meets Percy Sugden. We queued up at a small decrepit waiting to board desk only to be sent round and round in circles before they finally caved in and sent us to the 'Eurodesk' check in section. Charlie and Freddie's sense of humour no doubt.

A useful ex-pat Yank helped us through all the Red tape which in effect meant queuing up several times over to have the same papers authorised. Twelve people doing one persons job, they make queuing for anything an art form and you feel this is perhaps someone's bitter idea of getting revenge on the capitalist system.

When we finally got to the plane on a Tarmac which resembled Stanley Park I nearly threw up at the sight of the plane. It's the first (and I hope last) time I've ever entered a plane through its arsehole, but the steps were in that vulnerable area and up we trudged. What next - when we land we discover we've entered a Russian war-zone as conscripts?

The plane was packed and seemed to be a first come first served free-for-all. My edgy nerves were getting decidedly edgier, not helped when a surge of black smoke started billowing up from the floor area followed by a white nitrogen type smoke. I thought it is so bad that they were fumigating the plane against some plague (and from the sights I'd just seen this was in a sense reassuring). The Brit beside me who was an RAF engineer said it was in fact the air conditioning. Oh yeah, that's all right then!

As we were about to take off people were still boarding and amongst the late arrivals were the SKY tv team with my hero, Kevin Moran. They all looked as though they'd had a skinful (to dull the senses perhaps) and Moran's expression was one of 'shock-horror', and he wisely slept throughout the whole journey. Martin Tyler and Nick Collins (the latter who always looks like a grease-ball prat during his link-ups) chatted amiably and both were quite charming and downed one of our beers with relish. My fears about Euroflop this time were unfounded, if by that it means after a shaky take-off and a rattling landing we arrived in a warm Volgograd at 12.30am.

Stories had been floating around before we'd set off that the city was the most polluted in Russia, a place full of lurking serial killers salivating at the prospect of their first English footie victims, and that our hotel would resemble Norman Bates', but without the mother.

The media had come to the club's aid in their battle to stop unofficial travellers by ridiculously listing all the hazards that would await us (with a typical 'Euro fans in travel peril' pre-match headline) - namely plague, pestilence, famine and war. I jest not, as they linked the war in the nearby region with the poverty in the area and the industrial pollution and came up with the Four Horsemen of the Apocalypse. One even pointed out that Volgograd had more serial killers per square mile than anywhere else in the world and - in general - travelling unofficially could be life threatening (but not going into details). The good old British press eh!

As if you would avoid catching any diseases spreading in that area if you travelled officially instead of unofficially - what would we all be breathing, different air!

Despite all this we got to our destination safely (well!) again. United fans resourcefulness knows no limits, irrespective of the propaganda, whatever the destination. My fears regarding the shortage of food and water in this remote region proved unfounded. I had sadly lugged across Russia two large bottles of Evian, several tins of Sainsbury Mackerel in Curry Sauce (which I left behind to the bemusement of the Soviet cleaning lady), sardines, crackers and biscuits.

Reports that the bedsheets would resemble that Bates Motel, bloodstained and covered in decades of unwanted personal hair also proved fruitless. Our hotel was a mid-thirties old style Commissar resort and displayed a decaying grandeur. The bed linen was spotless and the bath water hot, in a clean bath. I did though get the impression that the toilet paper had been exported straight from Fanny Lee's factory - like City it was rough and uncultured.

Resplendent on my hotel room table were bottles of mineral water. So much for planning ahead. I opted for bed and a bath whilst my other and more vulnerable companions chose a local nightclub to have a grand old time. Breakfast was a mixture of hard-boiled eggs and stale bread with appalling coffee (or scorched earth) and cold herbal teas.

I emerged from the hotel to be greeted with wonderful warm sunshine and a city of unexpected beauty. A quick stroll (bumping into one of my companions, Howard) of the town revealed many shops, well dressed locals and an abundance of goods. The river was breathtaking. Such were its pollutants that it was deadly to swim in it supposedly (remind you of home?), and I reflected on this later as I ate some nice tasting fish and wondered exactly where it had been caught!

Back to the hotel to meet up with the late risers from the night before to be greeted by one wearing just leather boots and a silk dressing gown with the words-'Man Utd - Simply The Best' on it. The reception staff looked on bemused as he demanded soap. We headed for a bar and met up with the familiar Euro faces who'd travelled on the official trip. Pete Chapple in French beret was in good song in the open aired bar and champagne (tasting gorgeous) at 25p a bottle was the order of the day.

A few idiots began singing 'We won the war for you' which was not very apt as it was the week commemorating the two million who had died in Volgograd (then Stalingrad) fighting the Nazis, and it rankled the few locals who were assembled there. In particular the fat female proprietor who'd been happy to accept our collective round of $250 but then called the police, who arrived mob handed and were going to start arresting us when she said she hadn't been paid. That was until it was pointed out that the quite substantial amount of dollars was still in her till.

Despite our protestations the heavily armed police ordered us all out and everyone left apart from Alan from Stockport and Howard, still both singing. Alan folded his arms in protest and demanded to finish his drink up. "Niet, Niet, Go now, Go now" brought back that lovely song by Bessie Banks later immortalised by the Moody Blues. We managed to all leave and once down the road discovered Alan was on the one dayer, had no ticket on him, no idea where the meet was or, in fact, who he was. He'd been on a session since leaving Stockport but did manage to tell us that he'd finished all his gardening before leaving home. We hauled him back to the hotel and as luck would have it the coaches for the one day trippers were packed outside our hotel (one of the two in the city).

Another session took hold inside the hotel. A very drunk Scandinavian lady (aren't they all big pissheads?) of uncertain age who actually lived in Volgograd was our bar attendant. She obviously had some scam on with the cook and she would regularly leave the bar with our money and come back from the kitchen area with some large bottles of excellent ale. We followed her at one juncture and it looked like all the cooks were on the piss with her. Scotty promised her a ticket there and then for the game (she said she was in love with him) but said she would get us a taxi to the ground only if we would come and see her cat first - certainly a novel approach to 'it'. She repeatedly assured us that it was her 'pussy cat' we would all see, we declined the offer and made her order the taxi to the ground. She actually paid for a ticket and then did a runner outside of the ground - another complete loon!

Our tickets were in a very noisy 'home' end and about fifteen of us were surrounded by a protective enclave of massed blue uniforms, all armed and looking absolutely baffled by our constant signing. Vodka bottles were being passed down to us regularly by the locals and this went down particularly well with the Leicester Reds who were slaughtered.

Howard the gent escorted me - with an armed policeman! - to the only toilet in the ground which was under their Director's section. It was yet another European 'shit-hole', literally, the only novelty being that it actually had a large stained bath in the corner. A beautiful young girl was in attendance but she declined Howard's offer to join her for a bath!

The game was very poor and uninspiring and at the end all 150 or so Reds were ordered to stay put for our own safety, although this actually resulted in much mutual hand-shaking, and the usual swapping of faded and old United shirts and scarves. Yet another trouble free trip, our luck was further in when the police gave us a lift back to the hotel in their van. Onto a meal (fish again!) and a good drink. Next morning we boarded another old crate back to the Domodedova cess-pit and eventually back to central Moscow. We had a right result with a five-star hotel but with the usual Russian bureaucracy it took several hours to check-in, via ordering beers in the hotel bar while we waited.

Eventually we got through and headed to the Irish bar. Since last time it had been taken over by Russians and the first thing I noticed was that all the vegetarian dishes previously on the menu (and good) had now been replaced by solitary cheese sandwiches. The Guinness was sub-standard and very pricey, but we joined up with the other Reds and a good crack was had until the wee small hours.

The bar now only accepted Roubles so all our crumpled Dollars were meaningless currency, as redundant as Blackburn's chances in the Champions League as we watched their game on a television with the worst reception I've ever seen. You could see three pictures of every player and a few joked that that was what it was like for them at Old Trafford every game! The Russians in the bar were baffled when we cheered on the Russian team. Solidarity my arse.

Next day we had the usual hassle at the departure gate. There was no logic to the never ending queues and we thought we could be stranded at the airport as take-off drew ever closer. One panicked Red told the police we were the United team and had to get the flight for our next game. The police let us through, then saw my aged bulking figure and said: "Who she?!". I barged through with the others shouting: "I'm their cook", as we gratefully, and finally, entered the plane.

It was now back to home, England the destination and the venue for the whole of the season as elimination came barely two weeks later in the home leg, despite the best efforts of a certain Danish goalkeeper with serious goal scoring instincts. But at least the home record hadn't gone...yet!

But all in all it was a great trip and thanks have to be extended to Scotty for sorting it out, and for finding out that Moscow is under change, no longer the grim and oppressive city I'd first visited. Sorry to sound like a Pseuds corner here but if you haven't seen the sun setting over the Kremlin after a few nips of vodka then you've never Timothy Learyied.

To the furthest corners of Russia with love, via the strangest of avenues. Where next?

We are the
Self Preservation Society

Juventus 1 - Manchester United 0
European Cup Champions League, 1st group match
September 11th 1996, Stadio Delle Alpi.
Schmeichel, Neville.G, Irwin, Poborsky, Johnsen, Pallister,
Cantona, Butt, Cruyff, Beckham, Giggs.
Subs used: Cole, McClair, Solskjaer
Attendance: 54,000

Barney Chilton

Barney, 26, has supported United since birth and has been a LMTB/Season Ticket holder for the past 17 years. He has edited the first ever United fanzine, Red News, for its ten years and is currently undertaking undergraduate studies at the least well known University in the country, on a course entitled: 'BA Hons in selecting lectures that don't coincide with midweek matches'. As with others, he adores European away travel, giving the opportunity for him to combine his two greatest loves - United and travel. He is not a tee-totaller, nor a sex-symbol and definitely not a fitness fanatic, but, give him credit, at least he tries. His greatest wish is to marry into the Cantona family.

The day before travel and I again make the mistake that has blighted several previous European encounters - to go on a session the night before. This is a bizarre piece of logic; that if you depart hung-over your body is better prepared for the drink that's about to happen on your travels. Yeah, and Shergar's alive and well and being ridden by Lord Lucan in the New Forest.

With everything packed - including my map of Turin, which took me ages to find until a helpful assistant pointed out that the city is actually known as Torino - it was on to my local (one of the many) for a 'quick few pints'. This can usually be roughly translated as: "We're here until they chuck us out".

Here we saw the first appearance of Rob's handy Italian phrase sheet. Being an Italian himself, Rob had prepared for us unilingual Reds a vital source of contact between Utd fans and Italians. Such as "Do you want to come back to my hotel room?", and "I can promise you an unforgettable night" - a phrase where he'd obviously mistakenly added the un to forgettable. No prizes for guessing that the phrasebook was as useful in Turin as a coolbox in Alaska.

The last topic of the night turned to the game. We were optimistic after the 4-0 Leeds win. Perhaps a draw was on the cards. Well, at least we'd surely see a goal in bloody Europe again. "And they've only played once competitively all season so they could be unprepared" was the upbeat consensus. One wise sage - who shall remain nameless because it's the only sensible thing he's ever uttered in his life - commented: "It means they'll be even bloody fitter than usual". How prophetic or with our performance should that just be how pathetic.

It's an early rise to Stanstead - my first encounter with the space ship style airport...pretty impressive, although it would be a nice confidence booster if you recognised just one of the airlines that regularly used it. With just a few weeks since the draw there are only 21 on our trip, all having scrimped and saved to get the money together at such short notice.

Customs involved yours truly having the most ridiculous body search possible, such that it was the closest I'd come to any contact with a human being in months and straight through perfume counters, video arcades and those strange looking people who walk around airports with walkie-talkies and into the bar. Many Reds had obviously opted for a quiet night in the pub last night as water was the predominate order.

This didn't stop the dedicated few and Drunken Dave was informing the novices on the trip of his top tips to enjoy air travel. This can be listed as such; Don't get a seat with a window, what is much more useful is to check in and ask for a seat at the very first or last row, that way you get to the drinks trolley first. He also waits until the final call this utilising the airport bar to full potential. "The third call is the final one...you always get three named calls".

The flight to Milan (it's a train from there to Turin - and by the end we're all left feeling 'was this really worth doing' just to save £50 on the fare quoted to Turin) was easy enough. Free drink and the typical sort of cheap airline food which resembles nothing else that you've ever seen on a plate before...apart from on the last flight you've taken. And just why do airline desserts always look like they've just been freshly produced at the local sperm bank?

We get talking to some Italian girls from Milan, who warn us of the unwelcome reception we'd get in Turin: "Everyone in Italy hates the Torino people". They were friendly but a little bit confused after their first holiday in England. They tell us: "All the English men do is...you know that Trainspotting song...Lager, Lager, Lager, Lager, Lager, Lager...but you seem so different". I hadn't the heart to break the illusion.

The quick flight had still managed to take its toll on Mackie, who manages to leave the aircraft as if he has just been fitted with wooden legs and fifteen steps takes about fifteen minutes to navigate.

I headed through customs to get the ritual passport stamp, marking another European destination, where a delighted official turned his 'kiosk open' sign round to show a newly penned sign declaring: "3-0 Juve". Confident, eh?

United fans are arriving on a variety of different flights, with by far the most impressive sight being a large United banner being unfurled and Dave approaching a Hertz rent-a-car booth and dancing wildly as he sings: "Hey hey we're the Monkees". You can safely work out that the Hertz workers had never seen anything like it in their lives.

We head off to get the bus into town which will take us to the train station, leaving hundreds of Reds behind. They must have been thinking: 'Just what are hundreds of Englishmen doing here for a game the next day?' - that wasn't even taking place in their city!

Milan station was stunning. The architecture was on a grandiose scale, and the sort of place where you fully expect either a classical orchestra to be playing in the background or for a Mafia shoot out to be scattering the massive concourse. Just as incredible was the very large old prostitute who, while we were all admiring the sights, had been attracted to Dave like a bee to a flower and was - for some unknown reason - trying to bite him in a wrestling match they had become embroiled in. Ahh, the delights of these European experiences!

The two or so hour train journey to Turin can only be described as mental. Commuters packed on an old crumbling train which made Virgin's fleet seem like the most advanced ever, but quickly departed as they saw what the next few hours had in store. Many of the 21 were now drinking their bottles of Duty Free as if it actually meant 'It is your Duty to drink it all in three minutes' and as the songs got louder suddenly more and more seats became available. You could just imagine hundreds of businessmen returning home (to their wives/mistresses/sheep delete as appropriate) and asking: "So just who is this Cheer Up Kevin Keegan?".

Once in Turin we found the Astoria Hotel and headed to a restaurant across the road. The service was typically Italian - first course takes three hours to arrive and the main meal then comes thirty seconds later, but the food was gorgeous and we spent the hours people watching relaxed in the knowledge that where we were staying was alright and in a safe area - how stupid can you be.

The food settled and we went looking for the Shamrock Bar where all the other Reds were supposed to be (why is it always the Irish bars where everyone ends up abroad?) and ended up in the main posh square - with unfortunately no brightly coloured minis whizzing around - sampling some very expensive drinks but in a spectacular location.

We were now actively seeking all the other Reds (although there were only a few hundred staying in town the night before the game), and after leaving the elder members of the party (who ended up out-drinking us) we head off in what we think is the right direction. And then, naturally, get completely lost.

I heard a group of English voices coming from the direction of eight suited men and - thinking that they were on a business trip - approached one, tapped him on the shoulder and asked if he knew where the Irish bar was.

Imagine the amazement when Our Martin turned around. Startled, I showed my grasp of successfully using the English vocabulary: "My God". I held out my hand and he amiably shook it. Still suffering from a complete lack of saying anything remotely sensible with the man I have wanted to ask so many questions to for so many years, I ask: "Do you know where the Irish bar is then". Peter Snow eat your heart out.

I finally try and obtain some semblance of mental activity and finally stop asking about bloody Irish bars and their location. "Can I compliment you on issuing tickets to all supporters for this trip...I hope it's maintained for Istanbul and Vienna". He replied that each game is considered on merit and I replied that Reds are always on their best behaviour. "Even though you come in from a lot of criticism, you do actually deserve praise for this decision". A silence as he obviously inherits my speech disorder. "Well, you do get a lot of criticism - I'm the Editor of one of the Utd fanzines and we criticise you a hell of a lot". His body language changed immediately and with an added: "Red News is the one I do", he gave a wary look and dashed off!

It seemed as though the Shamrock bar was in the general direction that Edwards and co were walking in, but embarrassed that they might think we were following them we begin waking through a park, not realising that this is the good old square opposite the train station that **EVERYONE** had told us to avoid because of trouble.

Getting to the end of the park we spotted a group of about 20 Italians standing by some cars. At last, we've found some taxis to take us to the bloody bar. Er, wrong. I don't seem to remember cabbies all wearing baseball caps with scarves hiding their faces, and I quickly told our group of five to get ready to do the off.

It was too late and they were on to us. "Engleeish" was the shout and one decked Rob onto the floor - ironically (but no laugh) the only Italian Red and he got twatted. He got up and immediately did the best impression of Forrest Gump you'll ever see in your life (bearing in mind he weighed 17 stone and was off his head) - running past us like Desert Orchid at her finest.

As we ran across a busy road a carload pulled up by us. Our first thought was that the Juve knife carriers also used transport and we were fucked. They pulled us against a walk and showed us their police cards. This was the Italian equivalent of the National Intelligence Unit - they were all clued up, young and smartly dressed - and instead of presuming 'English trouble makers' immediately believed our story. Whilst they were talking to us another group of Reds were attacked by a machete and chaos ensued.

Many of the Italians had done a runner but the police had caught some and we were asked to go into the crowd and pinpoint some of them out. We were comically left standing (just me and Rob) with two plain clothed policemen in the middle of a massive Italian mob as they made friendly gestures about what would happen to our necks. Even more worrying was the ridiculous sight of one of their number wearing a York shirt. Hardly macho and if this was a way of taking the piss out of our League Cup elimination it has to go down as the saddest object since Micky Phelan's moustache.

Getting worried we told the police that they couldn't just leave us here as we'd get battered. "No comprehende" was the police response. "Look you bloody understand this - if you leave us we'll get stabbed". A nervous giggle until some more police arrived who began slagging off the locals.

We were escorted away, leaving Mr. York City being held back, and we began a conversation with the local constabulary about who was having the better start to the season - Ravanelli or Vialli! With the mob still lurking the police followed in cars - well that's what we thought, but in fact they soon got stuck in traffic and we ended up on a very twitchy walk back to the hotel.

Here there were many stories developing about innocent Reds being attacked, stabbed and slashed by the locals - what a bunch of real cowards. The police were shutting bars that Utd fans were in (including that Oasis we never found - the Shamrock bar) rather than clearing away groups of locals, and to those United fans who went to Turin it was no real surprise to see the scenes (incompetent policing) for the England game in Rome, and why we weren't too happy about going back to Turin for the 1997/98 European season.

For Turin the crack was hard to find. A mainly industrial city, bars difficult to locate and clubs non-existent, the xenophobic nature of the locals (geed up by successful local political parties suggesting that everyone outside Turin should be hated) was a real problem, and it seemed that the only pleasant Italians to us were the restaurant and bar workers being given so much money by Utd fans. Perhaps they should start a Turin tourist campaign with the words: "Turin - we like a scrap", and perhaps the worst thing of all was the sixteen year old kid slashed - along with eight other Reds - for no reason. And we've played this lot four times recently!

But European aways are about making the most of your surroundings, and we'd just have to find the crack ourselves, and, like on so many other occasions, anything and everything can happen. And by the time you get back home to whatever normal existence you have, you soon begin to realise that spending several drunken days in a European city watching the Reds (despite playing like they've never seen a football before) can not be beaten by any experience.

And so it was without any breakfast (it's something of an anomaly on these trips) that I found myself hoping to get a better understanding of the city and its culture and see some sights. Well that honestly took about ten minutes and the last port of call was to see the famous Turin Shroud that isn't (you know what I mean).

After more confirmations of incidents the night before (and sightings of a drunken Bryan Robson and Viv Anderson) we decided that maybe a sober lead up to the game would be the best course of action. Yeah, that sounded a great idea.

Rob was looking bad from his injuries (he'd woken up asking: 'Did I fall over last night?'), with plenty of bruises and Drunken Dave had also suffered at the hands of the locals.

They'd mugged him of his money, match ticket and sexy plastic Morrison's bag which had contained just one change of clothes and a toothbrush - what a steal! He'd spent the night in hospital but had no recollection of the attack, I suppose there's a lot to be said about suffering whilst under the influence.

When we reached the Cathedral housing the Shroud we were disappointed to find it locked, even worse that the building was in a terrible state of disrepair, covered in paint bombs. You'd hardly believe you were at the supposed home of Christ's cloth - in the homeland of Catholic religion. It said it all and I wasn't at all surprised to hear nearly a year later that the church had nearly been destroyed in a fire, caused by negligence .

So that and this was Turin. Where now? We headed away looking for food and met up with Martin and crowd. "You're on the way to the Turin shroud?". "Are we fuck - we're looking for a bar". A search for a bar started (how many times did that happen in Turin) and we swapped stories of our respective trips. He'd discovered one of his mates asleep in the hotel lobby last night and woke him up to enquire why he wasn't in his bed. "Because there are hundreds of cockroaches in my room and on my bed and there are none here!". This was not to be the last mention of those indestructible bastards that day...

We found a bar and had some decent lunch, with some bread. This too was nice, until a giant cockroach popped out from under the last piece - as if it had just been woken up by our activity - and began scrambling all over the table. Our disgust was not matched by the waiter who came over with a response that wasn't: "My God there's a cockroach in my restaurant", more a: "Not another one".

A quick departure and we head to the station where every Red and his dog is. One bar holds court for the official and unofficial travellers, where the expensive beer on sale is being replaced by some cheaper stuff brought in from the supermarket across the road.

A big sing-song is developing before Utd fans board buses to the ground and we head to a bar just next door to the hotel. This is, I can safely confess your honour, is where my promise to 'lie low' goes completely out of the window.

Yeah change before the game, yeah have a shower, yeah keep your wits about you, yeah, yeah. Five of us supping cheap beer, became ten, became thirty. And that's where we stayed for the four hours leading up to kick off, in which time;

Rob got locked in the toilet as he discovered, much to the hilarity of the barstaff, that when the door shut you couldn't get back out of the grotesque unisex toilet (or should I call it by its Latin name - aholeintheground). Oh dear what can the matter be - several other Reds got stuck in the lavatory as they drunkenly shut the door just as we all shouted: "NO!". Each prisoner found himself locked in with smells reminiscent of the Isle of Capri for twenty minutes, not helped by a ticketless Steve each time offering words of support such as: "Pass your ticket under the door".

The song of the trip was born: "There may be trouble ahead", and this continued to be voiced - in earnest - for a number of hours - during the whole time we stayed in the bar, (arranging for a late opening for when we got back), during taxis to the ground (oh how the drivers loved us) and finally when we came to the Stadio Delle Alpi, or, to call it by its better name, the spaceship that has landed on a patch of barren land.

Here another song was thought up: "I feel safer here than in Turin", and many a Juve fan must have been baffled by these strange English people dancing lavishly around the concourse in confident mood. The atmosphere seemed safe and relaxed, yet two other Reds were slashed before kick-off, showing that it's a thin line between lucky and bad fate. Many of our group headed to the ground to soak up the experience - the rest of us headed to the nearest bar to soak up yet more beer. There were plenty of Reds inside, plenty of "What a friend we have in Jesus" and banter with home fans - all of whom were predicting a big win for guess who.

Phil, after falling asleep at the side of the river last night, once again showed us his specially concocted queue avoidance technique, ie; get there with one minute to kick off and you are guaranteed to avoid all queues, but we are none too pleased to see the Utd section having a pay-on-the day facility. It's not this that bothers us (but still a total violation of UEFA standard policy) but that they are charging just £10 when we had to pay United £30!

Everyone later commented about the severe body search (all coins bloody confiscated again) but it couldn't have been that good as one Red - so drunk - had accidentally left his razor and toothpaste in his pocket after a quick shave before the game. Don't think he would have been able to explain that one away!

On entry to the stadium, the 3,500 Reds were making a racket, and with the second tier packed we headed for the emptier first passing the usual crap continental facilities down below, where we could sway in comparative peace. The Juve fans were surprisingly quiet and the attendance was pathetic considering it was their first European match since winning the trophy. Even worse was the horrendous racism which Andrew Cole received when warming up. No surprise that the press didn't mention it at all in any of their reports.

The match (was there one), well was typical early 1990's United European fare. How we wished for a goal, how the Italians didn't manage to score more than one. We were overran in the first half, and thankfully the referee disallowed a second

Juve goal (although many Reds thought it was 2-0 at half-time). The second half display was better than the first but it was scant consolation at the time. Europe's best had humbled us, and with hindsight it is immensely pleasing to see that Fergie was fully vindicated at the time when he said we would learn the lessons from this night. We were taught one - but just over a year later the players showed how much they've matured and learnt in Europe by finally conquering Juventus at Old Trafford and gaining full revenge.

Perhaps this 1-0 thumping was the stepping stone needed that will eventually (who knows when) lead to ultimate glory, but as we were kept in the stadium for ages we knew little of how this (96/97) season in Europe would develop and grumbled loudly about bad tactics and how Cruyff and Poborsky just did not perform (nothing new there then). It was disappointing that most of the Utd players did not respond to the Reds who had travelled so far (they apologised the next weekend), but well done to the three (Pallister, Neville and McClair) who realised it's more than about defeat. We're used to European defeats - it doesn't make it any easier for us - but the Reds sang as loudly as they could knowing the inevitable.

We were kept in for more than was reasonable - and with the police adopting an incredibly heavy handed approach and the gates still closed causing a severe crush at the front, clashes occurred that were reminiscent of the 80's. Police indiscriminately used tear gas and batons and they, many trigger happy young conscripts, lost control and all hell broke loose. The crushing got worse and one girl went blue in the face until rescued out of the melee. Once Utd fans were finally let out a battle took place across the forecourt in an uneasy and quiet atmosphere. Tear gas, Reds being battened - and the Italians once again blamed English fans. It all left a bitter taste in the mouth.

With the trouble developing we led Teresa McDonald back into the stadium and Martin cooly commented that Eric's brother, Joel, was in front of us. Low and behold there he was with Albert Cantona and some friends. Yet again heart ruled head and I rushed down and knelt/bowed in front of Cantona senior. After this rather embarrassing behaviour, we had a good chat, took photos and waited for the trouble to clear. It didn't improve and they said: "We stay here by you". Such moments are which dreams are made of...I'm sorry, but this man was the reason for our King!

The police became even more agitated at this point and beckoned us to move quickly with their batons. Cantona senior gave them an Eric style look of distaste, moved past them and just had a piss against the nearest concrete pillar.

Teresa was attempting some appalling French conversation, and yet try as we could (her holding Albert's hand pretending she was scared by the trouble) the police would not allow us to join the mini-escort they'd arranged for the Cantona's - oh if only.

We were finally escorted back to town via buses, which took us all to the wrong station (great planning again). A quick search for taxis as we all dispersed leaving some very confused and impotent Italian police and we returned back to the bar, where the owner was waiting for extra takings, and boy did he get them.

The bar was attracting Reds like a beacon, and we discussed the past few hours events, but definitely didn't do anything resembling singing, as each time the owner would shout: "SSSSHHHH" every time a "Bring on Sunderland and Arsenal was started.

As the night wore on and we got continually louder the bar owner enquired whether - as it was 2am - we would like to leave. "No chance, but if you're tired, you go to bed. Don't worry, we'll look after the bar for you", didn't, for some reason, convince him. When we walked past the bar at 8am he wasn't there - no doubt well into his long haul flight to the Caribbean.

A few bars followed and it is at this stage that I began losing the plot with reality. We discovered the one and only trendy bar in Turin (where the owner told us the locals never came in because it was too decent) and then headed to 'Down By The Riverside', the natural beacon for those of an alcoholic persuasion.

No idea how we got there, but once there a party was in full swing, with a hard-core 100 strong Red turn-out. It developed from here into a memorable night. The bar in a tiny marquee turned into a mini Old Trafford for the night. Singing, dancing, ridiculous behaviour, it was all happening, including Mick chasing a 3 foot, 6 stone transvestite (who was wearing stockings and suspenders) repeatedly during the night for no other reason than that he was a 3 foot, 6 stone transvestite. He finally caught up with him in the very early hours, hit him - and then realised that the prone man in front of him was someone he'd never seen before, and the man hitting Mick back!

There was singing all night (many old classics), people falling down all night and a half-hour rendition of "We all live in a Drunken Dave world". Things were really deteriorating, and as a sign of how bizarre all that was going on was, the barman produced a sign reading: "6am-6.15am. Happy Hour. 2 drinks for the price of one". What was going on here? The tent opposite began to resemble the Viper Room and at around 6am Steve, Veg and Najib headed off running to the train station fifteen minutes away with just five minutes until their train left. Steve was sick twice on the way, but still made it, but just why Najib ran (also vomiting) for the next two miles when he was flying back with us the next day still remains unanswered. We actually drank the marquee out of all its beer and by then (7.30am) it was certainly time to say goodnight Zebedee. Back for one last drink in a nearby hotel (but by now I'd drank so much for so long it could have been old rhino's dribble for all I knew) and we staggered back across the park (no-one would have gone near us with a barge pole at this point) where Rob had been attacked, happily singing a full repertoire of Utd songs. A new day.

There was no point in going to bed, and during the next hour I can only think that I must have been abducted by mischievous aliens and replaced by a clone as I (they told me the next day) walked down the main street with a toothbrush in my hand singing: "This is the sexiest toothbrush in the world". Why, why, why!

Our party re-grouped for departure a few hours later with my body now back in place and my head staging its very own Aerosmith concert. I was not looking forward to a journey back to Milan and then back to Stanstead. In my, er, confused state I'd somehow ended up leaving three expensive shirts behind in the hotel, a Walkman, and said sexy toothbrush. But when I got back home I did, for some inexplicable reason, find the hotel's TV remote control in my bag. And you know what, it doesn't even bloody work because I still can't pick up Italian TV on it.

But all in all a fine trip, despite the locals reaction to many Reds. I don't know, they **still** haven't got over Michael Caine getting one over them all those years ago...

Welcome to Hell?
More like Heaven!

Fenerbahce 0 - Manchester United 2
European Cup Champions League, 3rd group match
October 16th 1996, Fenerbahce Stadium.
Schmeichel, Neville.G, Irwin, May, Pallister, Cantona, Butt,
Beckham, Cruyff, Johnsen, Solskjear. Sub used: Poborsky
Scorers: Beckham, Cantona
Attendance: 26,200

Alan Sewell
*Alan, the tender age of 34, is a Helioklischograph operator (WHAT!) and was
born in Hinckley, Leicestershire. He emigrated to South Africa when aged 11
and spent the next 21 years in Durban, South Africa (a city with golden
beaches on the Indian Ocean). He has supported United for many years and
when his parents emigrated back to Carlisle in 1985 he took six holidays to England in nine years, watching all the United matches whilst on holiday. In South
Africa he took up the sport of surfing with considerable success, representing
his county and participating in the South African Championships. He also
played football in the top amateur league for numerous years and represented
"England" (English born footballers in SA) in several 'mini World Cup tourna-
ments' until emigrating back to England in 1995. He is a Season Ticket holder in
the North Stand.*

Having watched previous memorable and, unfortunately, unmemorable United
European away games on TV in South Africa, the thought of going on my first
European away trip left me in a state of absolute excitement - so much that I
couldn't sleep the night before (how old am I!).

Being my first year back in England after a rather lengthy stay in South Africa (21
years to be exact) I somehow managed to 'burgle' a season ticket for Old Trafford.
I then made enquiries about travelling to away league games and the name
Martin Day and his Blackpool branch was mentioned (what a result!). I joined and
met loads of new Utd faces, unaware that I was soon to become a total beer
monster. Having missed Turin due to work commitments (what!) I was advised by
fellow Reds that a trip to Turkey was definitely not the place for a Euro away
initiation.

So here I was Tuesday, 4.00am, standing in the rain waiting at Bamber Bridge
railway station for the mini-bus to arrive. 30 minutes later and it was off to Knutsford
for the last pick-up before the four hour journey to Heathrow. Of the 14 settled in
the bus, thirteen seemed to be in high spirits, some talking about their previous trips
to Istanbul, and some even drinking! Needless to say one person (I wonder who!)
was sitting quietly, with all sorts of visions going through his head about what was

in store.

We arrived at Heathrow in good stead and after checking in, made our way to the bar for the pre-flight drink. It was here that we met the rest of the party, making a total of 56 hardy souls who had been encouraged by the reports of a trouble free trip by the twelve Reds who had travelled independently to the second journey back to Galatasaray, and had decided to forgo the relative safety of the official trip and sample the delights of three days in Istanbul. Mancunians, South Africans - we had the lot!

It was a major session before take-off, somehow even managing to seriously delete the free Whisky stall in the duty-free area (well spotted Phil!) and after the final call we eventually boarded the plane ready for the four hour flight, minus a 57th Red who has arrived incredibly late at check-in and missed the whole trip.

It is on the plane where I suddenly take a turn for the worse. Having only been used to 12 hour flights from South Africa and being a notoriously bad flyer I have an extremely big decision to make. Is it the sleeping pills or alcohol? Needless to say it was the latter.

After a nightmare take-off (I would say that!) and Ted sitting next to me trying all he can to calm me down, it's time to order drinks again, only this time they're free! With the stewardesses taking their time, it was here that Ted decided to operate Plan B, and using his previous experiences I'm sure, continually sending our stewardess up to the cabin, thus leaving the drinks trolley next to us unattended! A big mistake as Ted grabbed as many cans and bottles of wine as he could possibly hide. Little did he know how he was later to regret his actions.

We were soon to land and the worry started setting in again. Having seen the two previous trips to Istanbul on TV in South Africa my thoughts were focused on the Turks awaiting us in the terminal with the placards 'Welcome to Hell' being waved around.

Perhaps they hadn't expected any United fans travelling independently this time as it was thankfully not to be. The thought of the £10, cash in hand - with no receipt - visa payment I'd just contributed to some Turkish officials back pocket went straight out of the window as a Turkish tour rep awaited us with luxury coach to take us to our splendid hotel.

Onto the coach and my first view of Istanbul. It was one of a mixed reaction, reminding me of both Cape Town, one of the most beautiful cities in the world, and Soweto, one of the most poverty stricken townships. We arrive at the five-star Hotel Eresin via some very dodgy looking one-way backroads, only to enter it (a hovel) and discover it's the wrong one (thankfully!) - and the coach has left! A phone call to the driver and beer later and we're back on the coach to the right Eresin!

It's incredible - 3 bars, 3 restaurants, sauna, jacuzzi, swimming pool, cuddly toy, etc, and, most importantly, a young law students convention!

We book in and I'm rooming with Ari (is this part of the initiation!), we sort keys out and my new room-mates first words to me are: "Take my bags upstairs, I'm going for a drink" (nice one Ari!). We all succumb to our rooms for a quick shower and change and meet back in the bar for happy hour. For a five-star hotel the prices were very reasonable at £1.80 a pint. A few drinks later and arrangements were being made for the rest of the night. According to Phil (our tour guide) Ortakoy is our destination. A fleet of taxi's arrive and twenty minutes later we arrive at our first port of call. Good decision, it doesn't sell alcohol!

Not a great start to my Turkish bar crawl, and we then decide to try a bar which 'sells' peanuts at twice the price of the beer! We decide unanimously to move on, and so onto the strangest 'bar' I've ever experienced. I forget the name, so decide to call it the "Carpet Shop" - it was in fact somebodies house that sold beer! We went upstairs to the 'bedroom' where for some unknown reason they didn't believe in wallpaper. What the hell, carpets are a good substitute and to cap it off a door on the roof! A good laugh and a few beers later and it's definitely time to move on. Next stop is the appropriately named 'Sherlock Holmes'. A very lively English pub where we meet up with all the other Reds, all who've frequented some very strange bars/areas and decided to stick with what you know.

The beer was reasonably priced and the music was just bearable - at last we had found what we were looking for! It was now time for some serious drinking. After a few beers, Ted decided that double Brandy and coke was a good chaser and was to be the new round for the rest of the evening (terrible mistake Ted!). After a couple of them I decide it's definitely not my drink and wander off to join Martin for a stint of vodka and orange.

As the evening re-gresses I notice Ted is nowhere in sight. Carl and I have a quick look around to no avail and assume he's caught a taxi back to the hotel, little realising what was to become of him. For some unknown reason he decides it's time to take on the sights of Istanbul! The wine on the plane and the ridiculous double brandy's and lager have finally taken their toll.

His version of events fourteen hours later are that he wandered (staggered) out of the bar to presumably go back to the hotel, forgot he was on his own, didn't have a key which had the name and address of the hotel on it, forgot its name and didn't even know which side of the river he was on! Much anxious pacing the streets of the city later and a miraculously unharmed Ted is sorted out by the Consulate!

A few vodka's later and after being awake for nearly two days it's definitely time for a sleep. Arriving back at 4am all I could think of was my bed, but no way, Pete decided it was time to try out my mini-bar and have a chat, but after two cans and a bar of Toblerone later I carry him to his room!

Wednesday morning and up for breakfast with ten minutes to spare - and how I needed it. A top quality selection was on offer and after four helpings enough was enough. It was 11am, match day and decisions for the day are again left to Phil (a bad result!). Taxis are ordered, not that it was needed as they were all still outside from the rich fared previous nights drop off! And off we went on what I can only describe as a 'sheer nightmare' to the much acclaimed Lacoste Factory Shop.

If you're looking for the ultimate challenge in life, forget Nemesis or the Big One! Look no further than a taxi ride in Istanbul! They never - ever - knew where they were going, a journey never took less than 45 minutes, even if you were going a short distance you still managed to see most of the city (who needs a tour guide!)! Every driver smoked the equivalent of a Silk Cut factory on each journey. All, and I mean all, drivers had means of communication (and I'm not talking radio's) that was a type of Morse Code via the hooter!

The journey reminded me something reminiscent of the Hill, Schumacher dual in Adelaide in '96. Each driver tried to make as much bodily contact with other drivers as possible, it seemed the closer you came to crashing the better you were. One driver pulled off the Mission Impossible even Tom Cruise would have been proud of. He actually pulled up next to his mate in the next lane, lent out the window and grabbed a fag, all this and travelling at 50mph!

We eventually arrive over the river at the most elegant and expensive shopping mall in Europe, selling only the top name brands at extortionate prices! There is no Lacoste factory selling gear at cost and it results in the quickest window shopping expedition known to mankind. Next stop - where else but the nearest bar, which was conveniently across the road, part bar, part hairdressers!

The beer was cheap, warm and thanks to Gary's intelligent observation well past it's sell by date (by decades rather than years!). With Burgo (man of the trip) taking centre-stage, some legendary Euro away stories were told and the on-going debate on whether Andrew Cole is good enough discussed at length. I will leave the result of the latter to your own discretion!

Two hours later and it was time for that 'Kamikaze' taxi ride to the next destination - the Sultan Bar near to the famous and spectacular Tolpaki Palace where we met up with more Reds, including the official party who were now enjoying an hour's free time where they could do what they wanted...

Beers were ordered and everyone was in good spirits when suddenly Gary suggested food (Food! Is it normal to eat on match day?). We were immediately accosted by fourteen waiters, strange as there was only six of us at the table! It wasn't bad, just a pity they forgot to switch the electric on when they prepared them (nothing better than frozen pizza on a sweltering 80° day!), anyway it did the job of soaking up a few pints.

And so to my next weird and wonderful experience, a visit to the loo (yes, the loo) and a 'female' attendant sitting outside the gents. I thought nothing of it until my return where she stood in front of me mumbling something in which I presume was Turkish. I came to realise it was money she was after, so I reached into my pocket and handed her a note. She virtually snatched it out of my hand and gave me a look of pure disgust and sat back down. Little did I realise that I had handed her the equivalent of 8 pence! Embarrassed as I was I refrained from mentioning it to the others - so I apologise to Barney who nipped down straight away only to get involved in a tug-of-war as she tried to grapple more notes off of him!

By now most at the bar were ready for their expedition to the nearby 'Grand Bazaar' for that all elusive Turkish bargain - be it leather, handbags or carpets! What was it to be? Bargain hunting or on to the next pub which was conveniently situated ten yards away (I'm afraid no contest whatsoever).

We sat outside catching the last of the sun and again, somehow, I was the first to explore the toilet, and yet another horrifying experience awaited me (what is it with these Turkish toilets!). The fact that the toilet was somehow 8 foot above the floor was only half the problem, there was an absolute wicked stench of sewerage mingling all over the bar which was so unbearable I had to literally run out holding my nose.

Time was moving on and after one last drink it was a 'short' taxi ride back to the hotel , leaving a brave bunch of Reds who were going to travel to the ground via the ferry across the river and a tour of the bars by the stadium - they ended up having a surprisingly drunken and peaceful time!

It was happy hour at the bar again, and what a happy hour it was with several duty free bottles of Vodka doing the rounds. Onto the coach and the worry of what to expect was soon overshadowed by a tap on my shoulder which turned out to be Phil handing me his bottle of almost neat vodka! A few renditions of "There may be trouble ahead" were sung but thanks to my three cans and the vodka I was unperturbed.

We finally arrived at the ground - via a traffic jam of course - with plenty of time to spare only to find that our arrival had signalled the arrival of hundreds of Turks gesturing and drawing lines across their necks - wonderful! The Manchester Police boarded the coach and told us that the situation was a bit hostile and we were to be escorted straight into the ground. And if we were hit not to retaliate as we would end up in jail! We were searched at the turnstile, removed of all coins, lighters and any other form of objects deemed 'dangerous'.

Walking to our so called 'segregated' corner I turned right and up the stairs only to find to my horror I was amongst the Turks who had been abusing us outside! Whatever happened to the so called UEFA regulations? I was immediately ushered inside the slightly protected Utd area, by the main stand (sic), holding almost 300 Reds, which included our group and the loyal club trip members.

Schmeichel and Van Der Gouw soon arrived onto the pitch for their pre-match warm up only for the entire stadium lights to go out! Within seconds the tannoy announcer went hysterical and the crowd lit anything possible (with our lighters?) within their grasp. Intimidating to say the least, but nothing I believe to previous visits to the Ali Sami Yen.

The teams came out to wild cheers from the Reds and the game had finally arrived. We started off brightly and by half-time there was a lot of optimism. A little trouble started behind us but thankfully the local police were quick to react and calm things down. The tannoy announcer - with wild grunts and groans for the opening 30 minutes - was soon warned by the UEFA officials and his screaming was stopped.

The second half saw United in full control and inevitably we went 1-0 up thanks to the ever improving Beckham. This immediately incited the Turks and missiles began raining down on us as they threw whatever they could get their hands on - from lighters, to bottles to kebabs and pieces of paper! I was fortunate enough only to be struck by a half eaten Doughnut! (Very generous these fans as they even managed to throw back all our confiscated coins and lighters!).

What made this all the more ridiculous was that there was a self contained and separate section to our right where we could have been placed, but perhaps Fenerbahce enjoy the hostile ride they give other clubs. This though was enough to see Lee from Hull finally return from amongst their fans as he'd spent the first part of the match teaching the locals the words to various United songs and sharing his drinks!

King Eric soon made it 2-0 and the atmosphere and sheer joy amongst us was amazing. We weren't used to scoring in Europe let alone bloody winning and we were 20 minutes away from a vital win in Europe. The last few minutes seemed like an eternity but well worth the wait as Eric led the players over to applaud our support. We were kept in the ground for half-an-hour and escorted back to our coach only to be greeted by a similar scene to the 'Soweto riots of '74'. There were more police than fans, forming a barricade with the help of a few fully armed tanks! With that protection we all had no trouble getting safely onto the motorway. We arranged for the coach to drop us back at the Sherlock Holmes, where apart from a few Turks who had accepted their defeat the place was buzzing. Although being warned by the manager not to sing it didn't stop a few going absolutely barmy on the dance floor.

A few of us (Ted included - I wonder why?) decided to have a meal and were soon joined by a member of the British Consul in Istanbul. To our horror we were told a Turkish supporter, apparently a Galatasaray fan (why was he there?) had been kicked to death in the ground during the match in the end opposite to ours.

Back at the bar an excellent night followed and a gruesome photo session soon took place when several Reds decided to remove their clothes for the cameras (not a pretty sight - reminiscent of the annual World Sumu Championships).

It was soon 3am and as much as the manager loved us (record yearly takings in 4 hours) we had to leave.

Thanks to Ari's sense of bar smell we soon descended on another bar' something akin to an American drive-in take-away, anyway it sold beer which was the most important thing! After quite a few beers and the clock ticking towards aawn loads of locals dressed like they had just come from a wedding swarmed in, and much jovial mutual banter followed as we took the piss out of their one and only song (that had been sung during the whole game - 'Fuck You Manchester').

The manager and his seventeen hundred staff took exception to this and it took much buying of his stock to ease the situation. I finally raised the white flag (like the past seven City managers) and prepare for my last (hopefully) taxi ride back to the hotel. The end of a truly memorable day.

Fortunately I awake in good time for breakfast and am joined by five others (not bad out of 56!), Bags are packed and the impossible task of waking up Ari is a failure (to this day he still thinks I never made an attempt to wake him up). We have an hour before the coach so Shaun and I decide to take a walk looking for Turkish Delight for his wife to be! We were in for a shock as we walked about a mile before we found some in a shoe shop of all places. Strange.

We arrive at the airport with two hours to spare and, surprisingly, we head for the bar and duty free for those last minute bargains. Time really dragged but eventually the call came over for boarding, at last, or so I thought until I realised I'd lost my boarding pass! Sheer panic immediately set in as I searched everywhere to no avail and was soon scampering around the bar and duty free floor! I approached security and explained four times about my mishap only to be shunted onto to tell someone else.

This carried on for what seemed like ages as I was escorted to all sorts of airport personnel, only to be told I couldn't fly without it. The sweat was by now flowing profusely as one of them took my passport away, all at the time everyone was saying 'Good luck' and began boarding! As everyone left I stood at security 'guarded' by four officials like something out of Midnight Express in an absolute comatose!

The thought of having to spend another night by myself in Istanbul with £40 was frightening to say the least. After filling in endless number of forms and an official sprinting up and down like Linford Christie sending faxes back and forth I was eventually given the all clear, an agonising twenty minutes later.

I boarded to the cheers of 56 Reds and it was with a very great relief that I took my seat for take-off. We arrived at Heathrow at 4.30pm and began the trek home via a pub stop outside Birmingham.

A brilliant trip, great hotel, good company and above all an excellent win. An experience that will be remembered forever.

Hell? I don't think so.

"It means nothing to me..."

SK Rapid Vienna 0 - Manchester United 2
European Cup Champions League, 6th group match
December 4th 1997, Ernst Happel Stadium.
Schmeichel, Neville.G, Irwin, May, Keane, Pallister,
Cantona, Butt, Solskjaer, Beckham, Giggs.
Subs used: McClair, Poborsky and Casper.
Scorers: Giggs, Cantona.
Attendance: 45,000

Haz

Haz shot to fame with his trainspotting reports in RED ISSUE, although more re-cently has been involved in more serious exploits in Slovakian hotels and Geor-die Magistrates Courts! All these experiences, of course, have been part of the addiction, the NEED, in fact, to follow his first love across the world. According to his mates, Haz completely transforms when departing Ringway/Gatwick for foreign fields. This chapter gives a brief insight into just one of "Haz's Tours".

Sunday morning at 5am is not the ideal time to embark on a European away trip. In fact, when I woke at 6am, something, somewhere at the back of my very confused, hung-over mind said: "No - don't do it!". Fortunately, if only for the fact that I had possession of fourteen flight and match tickets, I ignored this warning and made the forty mile familiar trip to Ringway to meet the other thirteen, who by this time were extremely anxious, members of the trip.

We flew via Paris and the initial leg of the journey was, by our standards, fairly quiet, relaxing in fact. Just enough time for the body to become accustomed to more copious amounts of alcohol entering the system. By the time we hit the bar in Charles De Gaulles everybody was in high spirits, so much so that the onward flight to Vienna was held for us. This, as we began to realise running through passport control with full glasses of Stellas Artois without being stopped, was where the fun was about to begin.

Aside from your normal business travellers, there was an unusually large contin-gent of Japanese couples on board the flight. After at least half an hour of outrageous attempts at interpreting their answer to my: "So where are you lot off to?", it was revealed (we think) that they were on a trip to Vienna and were returning home on Concorde. Either that, or they were big Oasis fans. "We Supersonic, supersonic" was about all I could understand. Unfortunately, and granted I should have known better, they responded with: "So - you trav Vien O' Ho?". "No, I'm not really on holiday - we're going for the match on Wednesday night - Manchester United". Again, the obligatory breakdown of communication until suddenly this bloke was trying to force feed me with his best Parker Pen. "You play Man United?". "What?", I replied. "Look at me for goodness sake, do I look like I do?". Well, obviously, yes. I did actually refuse his kind offering, although as a token gesture, being the ambassador I am, signed his boarding card, much to his wife's delight. I then introduced them to the rest of the squad, Nicky Butt, Paul Scholes, David Beckham, even Chris Casper and the two most unlikely doubles of Andy Cole, who had bleached blond hair and Peter 'Robbo' Schmeichel, who, admittedly, looked the only possible goalkeeper amongst our 'squad'!

Photographs, gifts, autographs, kisses - it was great - in fact it was ridiculous. However on our arrival in Vienna we were actually beginning to believe we were the team. Sad, isn't it?!

For once we entered the country without any delays at customs and made our way to the hotel Kaiserpark, our home for the next week. Following a brief change, we headed for the lights (mainly Red, surprisingly enough) of Wien. One thing that certainly did have an impact on us was the weather; it was freezing. Therefore, the sooner we find a bar, the better. We visited a few - in fact we were thrown out of a few - considering Coley was dancing on the tables singing "Hello, Hello, we are the Busby boys!" it wasn't surprising. The Austrians attempting to eat their evening meal were unimpressed and, perhaps, were thinking that this was a sign of things to come. They weren't wrong.

After what seemed like the length of time since City last won anything, we eventually stumbled across a small, local bar hidden amongst a maze of back streets. "The Lambada" - owned by Ali. Ali, his broad smile stretching from ear to ear, along with his moustache was, seemingly, very pleased to see us. Schilling signs were evident in his eyes as we descended on his bar, bar staff and C.D. player!! It was debatable whether he appreciated the Stone Roses bellowing throughout his bar as much as we did, nevertheless the first fourteen beers and vodkas were served without delay. And then the next fourteen, and the next...

By the time Ali's bar was rocking to "Hello, hello, we are the first one's here!", Keano and Becks had made a move for Alis' newest member of staff - in fact it was the lovely Paula's first night at work. You couldn't fail to feel sorry for her. She was gorgeous, although as we were soon to realise, extremely gullible. Once Keano and Becks had convinced her that we were playing in the Ernst Happel Stadium against Rapid on Wednesday night, she was putty in their hands. Keano being Keano, happily married (almost) decided to make way for Becks. Becks being Becks, happily married (almost) went for it!

Nothing much happened that night, the cry of "Hello, hello, we are the first ones here" echoed around Vienna's 'First District' as we cruised the bars. the night life was pants, so myself and "Schmeichs" headed for the underground with the intention of caning the hotel bar. At one stop it became apparent that we had attracted the attention of three lovely young men, who were parading along the platform as though they were on a catwalk in Milan. We dived out of the carriage. Allegedly, Red Mist descended over my eyes as I had a 'quiet word'. There then followed a, let's say, scuffle in the concourse which soon spilled outside the station. Suddenly, this 'young man', using his secret weapon (no, not that one) slung his handbag round his head and attacked me with his finest chanel bag. Next thing, yours truly is in a pathetic heap on the floor, literally not knowing what had hit me. It could have actually done serious damage if it wasn't so funny. However, I was still sporting a far from small bruise on my return to work the following week.

Monday was the day when the fun really started. Months earlier, during an extremely drunken half-time in K Stand, Chet had suggested that we sample the delights of Slovakia and, in particular, Bratislava, if only for the extraordinary cheap lager which was available. There was also a mention of cheap drugs and sex. Although obviously our thoughts were simply of obtaining another stamp on the passport. On arriving at the Sudbahnoff five minutes after the train to Bratislava had left, we found that the next train was only four hours later - obviously a popular destination. After much deliberation and questions such as "Well, do we really want to go to this shithole?", it was decided that we would find a bar for the interim and have a 'quiet one'. After three and a half hours of "Eric The King" and five and a half thousand Schillings later, we left with the staff demanding the outstanding eight Schillings bar tab. Ungrateful and certainly no sense of humour. We were hoping things would improve over the border.

The journey, with the raid on the station buffet an essential appetizer (led, inevitably by the now infamous Phil 'He's got a cake' Bailey) was a scream. The jib was easy until we arrived at what seemed like an Austria/Slovak version of Twin Peaks. Despite initial fears of the dozen, or so, mean looking passport control officers we still managed to avoid purchasing tickets or, indeed, producing our passports for inspection. Throughout the confusion Benno also managed to pilfer a couple of bottles of champagne from the buffet trolley, as well as some poor bloke's wife whilst he went to the toilet! Dave's subtle approach of "Can I feel your tits?", as he launched his tongue down her throat went down a treat. The face on the poor bloke was a picture, when he re-entered their compartment. A lucky escape, if you ask me Dave.

On arrival in Bratislava, the world that is the former Soviet Bloc certainly lived up to our expectations - we stood out like Kings. The shell suit combinations and bad leather jackets being sported by the Slovakians, and taxi drivers in particular were, dare I say, on a lower level than seen on your average Saturday morning in Liverpool city centre. Within minutes of arriving it became obvious that the level of accommodation on offer did not compare with that in Vienna. After much deliberation we all piled into three taxis at the station. "Holiday Inn" was the call as it looked highly probable that this was, in fact, the best building in the city.

Our arrival at the hotel was not as smooth as anticipated. The taxi drivers, jumping to conclusions that we must, bearing in mind our destination, be loaded, attempted to multiply the fare five times over. An angry dispute followed with us refusing to pay, fists were raised and the row ended when eight, yes eight, policia arrived to sort it out. After much negotiation and with the police's patience at breaking point, we were politely informed (not) that unless we paid four hundred Crowns immediately we would be spending the night in one of Bratislava's, no doubt, luxury police cells. We paid.

Meanwhile, away from the commotion in the foyer, Benno and myself were tucking into a feast in the wedding suite. The guests had not yet arrived. The sight of Dave emerging from the room, a glass of champagne in each hand and a full trout in his mouth was a classic.

Checking in was a farce. Considering the chaos we had caused one would have thought that by this time we would have been shot, at least. However, Messrs. Keane, Cole, Schmeichel, T.Rigger of 1, Cockney Road, Peckham and, of course, D.Beckham of 1, Old Trafford Road, Manchester, obviously did enough to convince the lovely young ladies at reception that they were genuine professional footballers. They didn't even have the heart to ask for passports or any sort of payment or deposit. Bless 'em. This ridiculously naive hotel was just asking, no begging, to be abused. After all, we were the famous Man United - we could do what we wanted! Room 1002's bar bill began with ten tequilas, ten lagers and two bottles of champagne, none of this was paid for.

As we began to relax we were, sheepishly, informed by Phil that the 'young darling' he thought he had pulled at the station - the one who grabbed him and led him to a large bush - was, in fact, a "Money grabbing Slovak-Scouse bitch!". His pockets, including wallet and passport had been totally emptied. Perhaps as well for Phil that the hotel was providing free ale!!

We had been informed that Charlie's Bar was the only Bratislavan bar worthy of our presence and had arranged to meet Colin and the aptly named Adam "Quick" here at 8pm. Considering this was their best offer, the 500ml Budvar bottles at 65p and, even better, Becks at 27p were gratefully received. Despite spending most of the night here our visit to Charlie's ended somewhat abruptly when a dispute between - who else? - Benno and a barmaid led us to be ordered out by the biggest bouncers, with blades, any of us had ever laid eyes on. Despite Rhys' valiant attempts in "fighting for United" he ended up spark out, in a heap on the floor. Myself, Dave, Benno and Nige piled into a cab and asked for a club.

We were actually quite surprised to find a club in Bratislava at 2am, although on entering we found it to be only one-quarter full. After D.J. Keano had written off the resident Slovak Dance Master's 12-inch version of Jamiroquai's "Space Cowboy", we headed upstairs to "Bar Erotica". Our eyes lit up when we realised that we were the only four in the place aside from a dozen, or so, Bratislavan whores. We ordered our drinks, around £4 each, a world away from the peanuts we were paying earlier that evening. At £65 an hour for straight sex and £75 for a sauna the anticipation and excitement of shagging a Slovakian soon wore off. Also, it has to be said that, with hindsight, they were all fucking horrible. I personally quite fancied the sauna idea but after enquiring, quite innocently, whether we could have a quarter of an hour each we were told, once again in no uncertain terms, to leave. Now this bouncer was the biggest ever - he had obviously graduated from Charlie's bar. Four very bloody, bruised faces, and ribs, crawled out into the -30° night. A very long walk followed and we arrived back at the Holiday Inn to top up the room bill. We even ordered dial-a-pizza - which arrived in a Lada at 7.30am the following day!

One final point on the subject of the hotel jib. Having booked in under false names, do not, no matter how many beers you have sunk, make the mistake of 'phoning home from your hotel room'. On the Tuesday evening, with the squad long since having disappeared back to Austria, "Mrs Keane" in deepest Cheshire received a call from the Slovak authorities enquiring about the whereabouts of a certain T.Rigger (my European room-mate) of Peckham. That took some explaining when I got home.

Probably the most enjoyable few hours of our Slovak experience was when we left the hotel and headed for the border. We picked up cabs outside so as not to be traceable and ended up spending the afternoon in the lovely village of Devinska Nova Ves. It was grey. The sky was grey, the buildings were grey. It was almost like being at Southampton away a couple of years ago. Amongst the grey, we found a bar. Despite Kenny's pleas to return to Austria, as "they're coming!, they're coming!" (he was referring to the Bratislavan policia), we could not resist the twenty pence vodkas which were being forced down our necks by one very bemused barman.

Miraculously, everyone made it back to Austria. Even Benno eventually paid the five pence train fare and we arrived back in Vienna around 7pm. By this time the main bulk of Reds had descended on the city. We started again, back in Ali's bar, the Lambada, where Paula informed us how much she had missed us. Touching. She was also particularly concerned at the amount of alcohol Keano was consuming, only hours before a big game. She did have a point - I was leathered!

We left to explore the rest of Vienna's nightlife and spent most of the evening signing autographs for more gullible Austrians. To finish the day on a high, somebody suggested a strip show. It was the most pathetic 'entertainment' I had set eyes on since Neil Webb's performance against Forest on Easter Bank Holiday Monday. The only curtains we got to see were the cloth ones that closed all too quickly just as their nether regions came into view. The highlight of the show was Benno's strip on stage, which was, without doubt, the most erotic and tantalising. In fact, he probably had the best body of the lot! After which, incidentally, we were asked - no, told - to leave.

Match day. Vienna was awash with the usual Red, white and black (oh, and of course Eric), talk of jibs, many stories of Prague which was the favourite stop off point en route. However, despite the massive consumption of alcohol everybody was on edge knowing that United had to win against Rapid. We came across a bar with a restaurant in the basement, which by 4pm was absolutely rocking. People were on the chairs, tables, bar, even a couple trying to hang from light fittings...you've seen it all before, but when you're there, you're part of it, God it makes you feel good. The Steins were being hammered on the tables..."If the Reds should play..." and so on.

Tram 21 was the route to the stadium. The scenes at the city centre interchange were unforgettable. The office workers, Bratwurst sellers and newspaper men were flabbergasted by the crowds of Reds singing for all they were worth as they all tried to squeeze into the tram.

Outside the ground we met the Cockney contingent who by this time did not know whether they were outside the Ernst Happel or Upton Park. The overriding memory, certainly for Dave and myself, was the temperature. Agreeing that if we wore jackets we were bound to leave them somewhere, we opted for shirt and sweater, an outrageously poor decision. Neither of us have ever, ever been so cold watching United. In fact, we are still debating whether to approach the club for compensation. Considering events in Bratislava, however, we're happy to call it quits for the time being!

On entering the stadium we found that United occupied the whole of one end of what was a fantastic ground. Around five thousand, possibly more, had made the trip, at that point, our biggest away following of the season. We proceeded to our seats, next to the Rapid boys, who seemed surprised at our "Stand Up For The Champions". Truth was it was the only way to keep warm. Nigel was somewhat delayed as his tongue was unfortunately (for her) caught around Zoe Ball's tonsils, only withdrawing to enquire whether Dwaine had recognised his "new bird".

Dwaine was unimpressed and only had eyes fore the substantially large Bratwurst thing in his mouth. Zoe seemed to like that, too.

The match itself was what we had come for, and did we get our moneys worth! Schmeichel pulled off one of the best saves I've ever seen which gave everyone the confidence and belief that we may, just may, be nipping over to Oporto the following March. It was Giggsy who broke the tension and basically his goal was the signal for everybody to go mental. Of course, when King Eric notched in the second half, that was it. We were going to enjoy ourselves. The relief on the players faces was there for all to see. Fantastic scenes followed, the flags, the firecrackers.."Que Sera Sera...we're going to Portugal" was the warmest feeling I had experienced all week. Honest.

Despite this, the best result since Montpellier in 1991, we left the ground singing: "Sha la la la Summerbee...". The V.I.P. lounge, which was actually a tent, were unimpressed by our entrance and not for the first time this week, we were asked to leave. We didn't really think we could get away with the players blag this time although, not surprisingly, 'Becks' had a good go!

Back at the Lambada the party was in full swing when I made my entrance. However I was greeted by a mass cry of "limp!" as I walked through the door. Of course, I had been stretchered off with a badly gashed shin a few hours earlier and I was touched to receive such concern and close attention from the lovely Paula. She was horrified when she had seen me taken off on TV and was not expecting to see me tonight! Poor old Ali certainly earned his crust that night, the beers, tequilas and vodkas were flowing freely, so much so that I woke up the following morning with a french stick lodged up my arse. Mr Taylor was apologising profusely for his actions and in the meantime Dave was, frozen solid, stuck on the end of the hotel's flagpole, four floors up, after exchanging their's for our United flag.

Thursday was planned to be the quiet one. After all, we'd spent three days in this lovely city and only seen the inside of bars and brothels. The joint sightseeing/ present buying expedition was arranged. Unfortunately, the George & Dragon was en route...

Despite the worst hangover I can remember for years, we spent the whole day deteriorating with other Reds, of course with the odd song thrown in for good measure. With Paula still in tow, a few lads who had been previously briefed approached us seeking autographs and 'photos' we were still, in Paula's eyes, "the team".

Come last orders, we piled into the next bar and subjected the poor staff to a squad rendition of: I am the resurrection". This proved especially confusing for Tony, who, on entering the bar stopped in amazement and gave his mates the classic line of "Fucking hell - they're playing the Stone Roses in here!". For one moment you could see their glee and pure amazement that a cafe owner in the centre of Vienna owned, and played, an album of Manchester's finest! Actually lads, there's something we should tell you...

For an hour or so we were made most welcome, then the bar was to close. We left with a couple of pineapples (I'm not sure why) and came across some Rapid fans outside. They had bottles and glasses and we sense immediately that they disapproved of our presence. As we disarmed them of their weapons, my cry of "Do them with a pineapple" just left everybody in stitches on the floor. In fact, this probably broke the ice and we realised that there was not going to be a scene. The fact was though, had we attacked them with our 'weapons' they would have been seriously injured. It would have been a laugh though. The group of lads told us that they would take us to a club and began to lead us down a maze of back streets. We thought this was a ploy and regretted ditching the fruit, although as it turned out the club really did exist.

It was in a basement and very claustrophobic although our entrance and immediate request for decent tunes gained the attention of the Austrian crowd and in particular, Austrian females. We could not have dreamt for a better attention seeking incident when the stage we were crowded onto, singing "City, you're so shitty" to the tune of Oasis' 'Wonderwall' collapsed. Legs, arms, heads, broke through wooden planks, tables and young girls. Their concern for our wellbeing was touching. Once they were quietly informed that we were the team (as if they didn't know!) they just could not do enough for us. I did not pay for a drink all night and after an hour of autograph signing at the bar it became a little boring. It was amusing, however, watching Liam supervising the orderly queue, urging the crowds of Austrian Reds to stop pushing. One twenty stone Rapid fan almost ruined things as he took delight in trying to convince everyone that we were blagging it, until he got a slap! I cannot remember an awful lot more about the evening apart from yet more cheesy sausage Frankfurter burger objects around 5am.

We, somehow, managed to wake up in time to carry out the obligatory insurance blag at the local police station before ordering our taxis to the airport. Dave had been released after his arrest following a drunken drive in Paula's car. They were travelling the wrong way in a one way street - he was steering and she was in control of the pedals.

After Scholesy had weighed in with the beers, G&T's and vodkas in the airport bar, the return flight was a black-out. We consumed bottle after bottle of Air France's red wine, we drank even more during our couple of hours in Paris and still managed to graciously accept gifts from more Japanese passengers after posing for pictures. Ambassadors of the club, that's what we were. We even sat next to the two most horny women you are ever likely to see in your life and did not even abuse them. The week's activities were beginning to take their toll.

It would have been pleasant to have had a quiet week following Vienna and perhaps a chance to plan for Oporto. No such luck. After a few hours sleep we were off to Crewe Station to catch a train to London. United were at West Ham on Sunday. The buzz was about to start again...

The Wrong Hangover: 10,000 Reds In Porto

FC Porto 0 - Manchester United 0
(aggregate 0-4)
European Cup, Quarter-Final 2nd Leg
March 19th 1997, Estadio Das Antas.
Schmeichel, Neville.G, Irwin, May, Johnsen, Pallister,
Cantona, Butt, Solskjaer, Beckham, Keane.
Subs used: Scholes, Poborsky and P.Neville.
Attendance: 40,000

Adam Brown

Adam Brown is a life long United fan who works and lives in Manchester. He is a member of the Football Supporters Association National Committee and the Government's Football Task Force and he is a Research Fellow at the Manchester Institute for Popular Culture currently editing a book on football called "Fanatics!"...he is also notoriously last minute in getting his work in!

Sometimes you wonder how stupid the powers that be can get. Or whether it's more sinister than that. You know the occasions - when you cannot believe your eyes and ears, what you're witnessing and how badly things are going wrong. And how it's almost all "their" fault. Our visit to Porto for United's second leg European Champions League quarter final was one such time - with over 30 fans hospitalised, several shot, many batoned, many more tear gassed, and a near-Hillsborough crush at the stadium gates - and must be the most serious incident involving English fans for many years. But it is nothing really new, just more extreme.

Most Reds had their trips sorted well in advance, booking those days in the sun in the sheet-metal grey heart of December, having seen the boys dispatch Rapid Vienna with some class. The first European Cup quarter final (the quaint old name for this grand competition, for those younger readers) for nearly thirty years; the first Euro quarter final of any kind since Blackmore and Bruce wowed us in Montpellier back in 91. This was always going to be a big one as attempts to get flights to Portugal in January would have shown. Remember those baffled looks as the travel agent tries to work out why she can't find any free seats to Portugal in March?

By the time we went, the tie was something of a formality, or as close to a formality as you get with United. Porto - unbeaten in their Champions League group games - were given a hiding at Old Trafford on a night many Reds reckon was one of the finest ever. Four goals to the good, flights and accommodation sorted, this was just going to be the biggest party we'd enjoyed on foreign shores since we requisitioned Rotterdam to lift the Cup Winners Cup six years earlier. Funny thing is no-one in authority appeared to have learnt a single thing in that intervening time. But more of that later.

There were five of us going and I was in the lucky position of having a Portuguese friend, Porto fan and all-round good mate - Joao - to sort things their end. He'd been over two weeks previously for Porto's downsizing and had taken it all on the chin very well even writing a piece for the United Magazine inviting us all over for a bit of a do. He'd got us a flat to stay in up the coast from the city itself and with flight tickets in our hands we were all set.

Of course no build up to a European away would be complete without the usual traumas over match tickets. United were given 4800 by Porto for the tie, the bulk of which were kept for travellers on United's official trips. Everyone knew this wasn't enough as everyone knew people who were still ticketless. Joao was on the starting blocks in Porto for the tickets they had, waiting for them to sell to non-season ticket holders and extra money was transferred over to cover another mate of mine's group of ten who were also left short. Back here United were being their usual obstructive selves about the tickets they did have. Having been given a bloody nose over not selling to either independent agencies at the time of Barcelona, they did let 500 out to Miss Ellies but there were pitifully few for those of us wanting a bit of a holiday, a different route or a bit of peace and quiet from the chaperoning of the official trips. A ballot of sorts was held for the independent travellers and many of us were left wanting.

Unfortunately, to say that you want to go to a European nation under your own steam is only a short hop short of being a brick-wielding hoolie. If you're a football fan, of course. Go on business, as a tourist or for any other reason and people take you at your word. Say that you want to go to a football match, however, and you suddenly become some potential monster, a "likely troublemaker" to be watched, to be handled with utmost suspicion, to be dissuaded from going. Or so it seems in the eyes of the club, FA, government and UEFA anyway.

Both Walshy at IMUSA and yours truly at the FSA put considerable pressure on all of the above warning of the numbers going to Porto, calling for proper and fair distribution of tickets to fans however they wished to travel and arguing that fans were still not being listened to - over tickets, over preparations and over managing the crowd. After all this time and after all that has happened - Hillsborough, Rotterdam, Galatasaray, Barcelona, Juventus - they still don't listen. Hence the FA's response to a letter I wrote to Adrian Titcombe, their security advisor. I told him that very large numbers of fans were going to travel, that at that time many didn't have tickets and that preparations were inadequate. He said, "a television set in England should be the recommended option." How crass. How stupid. How like an incompetent ostrich.

Now I don't know about you, but if you've just paid for a flight, taken time off work and have good experience of getting into games, you're not going to change plans and lose your money just like that. It illustrated how grossly out of touch the FA are in these matters. We know how to get ourselves there, how to get accommodation and have a fair idea that there will be tickets available. Why can't the authorities accept that and accept it as it is, rather than presuming that we are all going to turn into a rampaging mob as soon as we're out of sight of a steward. If they are concerned about segregation (and at times they should be) then they need to make sure that as many tickets as possible are available - however you want to travel.

As it happened, of course, most of us got sorted one way or another for tickets in the end - not that anyone ever checked mine! - and United did manage to extricate extra tickets from Porto at the last minute. They were, however, at least double what was being paid in Portugal: another characteristic of being a travelling English fan is that you get fleeced at every opportunity by the opposition.

What really sticks in the gullet about these ticket hassles, though, is that we're constantly being told what infinite choice we have in everything else we do from buying a car to the flavour of Polo mints. We're told that the customer is king, that football is a business and that us going to games is merely part of an "integrated leisure experience". We're also told that we now live in an open Europe with freedom to work and travel as we please. What total hypocrisy, then, to impose the kind of restrictions on us that should have civil libertarians fuming. One minute we're in the free West, the next it's bloody communist China.

So there we were at Manchester airport flying out for a week in the sun. We'd lost Sean, one of our number, who had to cancel at the last minute due to business difficulties but it was definitely high spirits as we landed in the Porto heat on the Friday before the game. We were missing the game against Sheffield Wednesday, but we were in Porto and got to take another look at the opposition before United met them. They'd hit a bad patch, Porto, having been cruising it all season in the Portuguese league. They were threatening a United 92 -style collapse as they met Sporting Lisbon at home.

We went along and it was refreshing to go to a top of the league clash and be able to walk up and get tickets on the night - a far cry from the secret intelligence work, ticket office doublespeak and military manoeuvre needed for some of our games here. Sporting won the game and increased the pressure on Porto.

More important than the football - we weren't going to lose five goals, were we? - was it meant we had a chance to look at the stadium. I'd been before one summer and they'd done some work in putting seats in, or at least bolting plastic buckets onto two foot high concrete steps. Not the sort of wholesale rebuilding we've had here and it was nowhere near complete, although Porto are one of the European clubs to have sunk their pitch into the ground to increase capacity, giving the pitch an unusual closeness to the concrete bowl stands. The steps were a bit disconcerting to say the least, created by simply placing long blocks of concrete - loose, mind - onto the terrace. Facilities were minimal and you knew it would never have passed the most basic safety assessment here. The stand was effectively a flight of two feet high steps from the back to the front without so much as a cursory crush barrier in sight. I tried to imagine what it was going to look and feel like with 10,000 Reds crammed in - but could never have foreseen how bad it would be.

The crowd wasn't bad - about 30,000 - but it was no Galatasaray cauldron. The Sporting fans were great, as far as we were concerned anyway, singing "Manchester, Manchester, Manchester" and "Ooh Aah Cantona" to our delight and the consternation of our Portuguese hosts. They don't like each other much, the Oporto people and the Lisbonites, a rivalry rooted in Portuguese history and vented in football: indeed, the allegations of corruption at FC Porto were dismissed by everyone we spoke to as the jealousy of FC Porto's domination of the Portuguese football world. The capital's media dishing it out to a successful northern football club, now where have I heard that before?

We met Joao's family who showed an unwavering hospitality which will never be forgotten, inviting us into their family birthday party, feeding and watering us beyond the call of duty and generally acting in a way which was to be repeated over the next few days. By everyone except the police. We then hit the Porto's Saturday nightlife and Super Bok ("Superstar!") had already established itself as a firm favourite. Christ Almighty, it gets you pissed. The drinks vendors at the local station were pretty handy, too, as we staggered back to our seaside resort at 6am.

Me and Joao had arranged a football match between United and Porto fans to be held on the Tuesday. I'd lined up a couple of lads and United We Stand's Andy stepped into the breach with the rest of the team. As we recovered from the Saturday night, Joao and his mates were training for the game. Training! It was too much to even contemplate - so we hit the beach.

On the Monday we headed off inland up the river, which was quite breathtakingly picturesque, and had a slap up meal which cost about thirty five pence including a healthy jug or two full of the local brew straight from the barrel. By the time we were back in town it was nightfall and, as we wandered down to the Riberos area, the strains of "Red Army" were wafting across the city's night. The Reds had arrived.

If the locals looked a bit stunned that night at the drinking, the singing and the look of almost desperate hedonistic determination, what, I thought, were they going to make of the next two days? A bit like your impression of Old Trafford at a reserve game compared to the ground in full, European-night voice. Except more so. A reassuring sight was one woman living above one of the bars in Placa de Reberos getting her clothes pegs out to help Reds hang their banners from her balcony! She was about eighty and gave us all a toothless smile.

The Tuesday was all about the match. Our match that is, rather than "the formality", as Joao kept referring to United's game. We met Andy, Blackie and the boys at the station and headed off to the pitch on the outskirts of the city. It had unintentionally turned into a bit of a media circus, with both Manchester TV stations there along with their Portuguese equivalents. Although this wasn't what we had had in mind at all, and at times seemed a bit intrusive ("can you just run out the dressing room again, lads, we didn't catch it quite right"), it seemed churlish to complain when they were, after all, reporting a good news story about fans getting along. Not many of those around.

We lost, which in the circumstances was kind of good - throw them the crumbs as we take the big prize, a place in the European Cup semi-final. It didn't feel like that at the time, though, even though we were equipped with three ringers in the form of the rock-like Ibbo, the midfield dynamo elder Mitten and the free-scoring Simmo. However, for the rest of us fitness, ability, heat and the ever-present Super Bok played their inevitable parts in our downfall. My humiliatingly sliced shot, broadcast across the Granada region some months later (cheers!), was only eclipsed by Blackie's dismissal ("friendly" just isn't in his vocabulary) and Andy Mitten's impersonation of Andy Cole on a bad day with his potential game-saving header going wide.

So we trudged off for a recuperative meal supplied by our hosts, more Super Bok and a display of some of United's finest vocal talents. Then into town and Reds had arrived in force, the reluctance of the local constabulary to let us carry on the party beyond 1am being the only dampener on the party. And so it was Wednesday.

Reports on Portuguese television said that 25 flights were arriving that day bringing yet more hoards of Reds into Porto and even our sleepy seaside resort was feeling the overspill. Nothing could have prepared us for the sight as we wandered from the station down through the main square and toward Riberos. You could hear United fans singing almost anywhere in town. Reds were sprawled across the grass, draped over the statues and filling any open air seat going., bottles in hand. The Placa de Riberos was crammed, bar owners frantically drafting in extra help and extra crates of Super Bok. The entire area just brimmed with United fans of every description: from the air it must have looked like someone had splattered a dollop of Tomato Ketchup onto Porto's map; from the ground you wondered how long it would be before it all slipped into the river.

Of course there were those who'd had a bit too much - one lad dozed on his Leigh Reds banner-come-beachmat; another slumped across a table - but it was an overwhelmingly good atmosphere. Given that our cities planned for two years to host fans at Euro 96 and that it appeared that Porto had done roughly nothing to accommodate so many visitors, the vast majority of Reds were brilliantly behaved. Drunk, sure, but just having a party. The locals made half-hearted attempts at telling us that it was going to be 5-0 but joined in the laughter and banter and scarf and hat swapping. At the match I think there were more United fans with Porto colours on than the usual red.

The lack of planning was first evident when trying to get to the ground. There weren't enough buses, no-one knew which to get, taxis were at a premium (I got ours after chasing it up a hill - not to be recommended) and no-one had provided any serious maps or guides. Tourist city, Porto ain't. However, most were in good time for the game and the whole area near the ground was completely mobbed. As darkness descended, however, the police began to get twitchy.

There were a host of problems which combined to create complete havoc at the Stadio Das Antas, however, let's dispel two myths first. One: many United fans may have been drinking, some heavily but this is not an excuse to start hitting people let alone firing bullets at them. No-one says a word when its Directors and their mates quaffing champers in the VIP lounge, which leads you to the conclusion that its the people who do it rather than the drink itself that they don't like. Snobbery, mate. Also, if we'd all been dressed in Irish tricolours or wearing kilts they'd all have been talking in quaint terms about how we knew how to enjoy ourselves. Two: almost all United fans had tickets and there were only about 200 forgeries - less than 2% of those who travelled, rather than the 40% claimed by Portugal's more imaginative journalists.

The frailties of the ground became apparent very quickly. Access to our end of the ground was, from the main road, via a narrow, enclosed alleyway formed by the walls of the ground itself and the backs of nearby buildings. There were no signs whatsoever directing United fans to their section; lighting was exceedingly poor; there was no adequate means of communicating to us; there was no means of monitoring how many fans were outside the stadium; and three entrances for 10,000 or more fans was woefully inadequate. We were split up almost immediately in the chaos which was rapidly gestating and tried to make our way to the entrance to which the police were directing us.

The Portuguese police outside the stadium were directing Reds to the entrances behind one goal regardless of where their tickets were intended for. This decision seems to have taken no account of how many fans could be accommodated in that area of the ground. Significantly, around 2,000 fans who travelled with independent travel agencies, who had valid tickets for other sections of the stadium, were directed by police to Gate 5, behind the goal at the Manchester United end. Many of these Reds were subsequently turned away from the ground because - surprise, surprise! - the computer ticket-reading systems at the turnstiles correctly identified the tickets for other parts of the ground.

The Portuguese police then appear to have taken the extraordinary decision that rejected tickets must be forgeries - although it was they who had directed fans to that entrance - and closed these entrances. We were in a build up of Reds all in good time for the match, with valid tickets and just wanting to get in. But as the gates remained closed, a severe crush developed in the narrow alleyway around Gate 5. At some point in the hour before the match the decision was taken to let fans into the game through the main Gate 5, without going through the turnstiles, and without checking any tickets. After all the hassle getting match tickets, no-one wanted to see them. I felt a bit cheated and almost felt like showing mine to the police anyway, even handing them the stub. Just to feel better, like. They let people in by opening and closing a metal "curtain-style" gate at intervals and letting us into the small tunnel which led directly to the staircase on the terraces behind the goal.

Naturally the opening and closing of this gate caused further crushing as fans moved forwards and then found their way blocked as the gate was closed again. People who could either see what was going on or were feeling the brunt of it began crying out about Hillsborough and it was then that I started to get really worried. You know that feeling in your stomach when reality dawns on you that you are in an uncontrollable situation, you have no way out of it and all around you people - especially those in blue uniforms - are making matters much worse. Neither Portuguese police, nor stadium stewards communicated to fans what was happening, nor were they able to, given the lack of an adequate PA system or megaphones. Worse, there did not appear to be anybody who spoke English except confused and worried Reds.

We eventually got to the front of the crush - which was good, because you knew you were going to get in shortly (I think the teams were already on the pitch at this point); but bad, because you were getting more crushed. Worse still was what was waiting on the inside.

Inside Gate 5, riot police formed two lines on each side of the tunnel. When fans were pushed by those behind them, or when they struggled to get through the closing metal gate, police lashed out, batoning fans causing head and body injuries. People were falling down around us as we hurtled through the welcoming committee. Many fans had blood-splattered shirts. I turned and saw one Red fall to the ground to be pounced upon by four officers.

Meanwhile, those fans, including one of our number, who were still trapped outside - many trying to enter the stadium because they feared for their lives because of the uncontrolled crushing - were beaten by riot police stationed on the outside of the gate. Fans who had managed to get in, and who had run the gauntlet of police in the tunnel, were naturally anxious to get as far from the scene as quickly as possible. However, that section of the ground was already seriously overcrowded with as many as three fans to each "seating" space, and the staircase down the middle of the section was full of supporters.

There were no crush barriers or other means of preventing fans from falling from the top of the staircase to the bottom other than by falling on other fans. There were no stewards from either club, no police and no announcements made to advise fans of the situation, of how they might get to available space and to make them aware that any strong movement from the back would cause an avalanche of fans down the staircase. Inside the ground, there appeared to be no numbering to regulate how many fans should sit in any one area and the ability of the physical space to cope was in serious question. The calm and spaciousness of the game against Sporting suddenly seemed a very long time ago.

I had a hell of a time trying to tell the police to stop what they were doing and to at least use a bit of common sense - if you want to stop people running into an overcrowded stairway you don't make them run there by clubbing them with batons. Stupid, stupid, stupid. If it wasn't so serious it would have made a great sketch by Monty Python in their blacker moments of humour. I found one officer who spoke English and, with my jaw dropping to the ground, he told me that not only was the officer in charge outside the ground and therefore unable to see what was happening, but that none of them had radios so they couldn't communicate with each other. Policing a football match. With ten thousand visiting fans. No radios. Staggering.

The situation at the top of the staircase was so serious that fans were being hoisted by their hands up the walls of the tunnel opening in a frightening re-enactment of scenes from the Hillsborough disaster. Although many fans suffered injuries from the police action, and a number of fans were injured by pressure pushing people on top of each other as they fell down the staircase, it was only through their good sense and behaviour that further physical harm was averted.

Eventually most Reds outside managed to get into the ground, although some, clearly shaken by what they had seen and been involved in, decided it was safer to leave the ground and watch the match on television. Adrian Titcombe got his wish after all then. Glad someone was happy.

It is clear to me that a major disaster and fatalities were very narrowly averted. And I don't write that lightly. It was that bad. It is also clear that the Portuguese police did nothing but worsen the situation by their inability to cope with the numbers of fans, their attempt to push all Reds through one small entrance regardless of where their tickets were for, and their inexplicable desire to lash out with batons and shields indiscriminately and completely without justification.

The situation on the terracing remained dangerous during the game. Had there been a Manchester United goal, and fans had celebrated, injuries may have been much worse. Further, the thin wire gate separating the left side of the end (looking onto the pitch) from the middle section was not opened and therefore the congestion could not be eased by spreading fans to less crowded areas, despite the fact that it must have been clearly visible from the position of the police and stewards on the pitch.

We were crammed in to the side of the entrance and so had a great view of the stragglers coming in, heads bleeding, eyes in startled disbelief. "I'm fucking sick of this. Everywhere we go we're treated like shit." I was inclined to agree with the bloke holding his head as another wave of batons came down on the Reds. What had happened to the party? It had got busted.

I did an interview with GMR's Andy Buckley during the second half and felt distinctly like Kate Adie must feel in those war zones. Riot police were amassing outside and then started to move to the door. My last words to Andy were that I hoped they weren't going to shut the gate.

So naturally, having only let fans in once a crush outside reached crisis proportions, the police decided to close the gates and not let anyone out again. This did fray tempers on the inside - fans were trying to leave up to fifteen minutes from the end so they could get out safely found themselves being pushed against the other side of a closed door which they had only recently come through.

The police response to fans banging on the door to get out (all police had gone outside by now) was to open up and fire three volleys of tear gas into a totally confined space. Smart idea. Where could anyone go except to shove others down the staircase? To follow these up with guns firing plastic coated ball bearings seems to me to be more about a vicious maliciousness than incompetence. They were shooting us. For pity's sake they were shooting us!

There were two attempts at making announcements to us - the first sounded like a gagged moose, the second, although louder, was like someone talking under water. There was enough to make it recognisable as a well-known European language, though, and we understood that they were telling us to go to the gate at the right hand end of the section. Trouble is, which was the right end? As we faced the pitch? As they were looking at us? And if it was our gate they were on about, didn't they know there was a small army of baton-happy police stopping us get out? Confusion reigned. With uncertainty, anger and fear on the inside it really wasn't the best place to be - especially as there were some seriously criminally negligent police officers waiting outside - and the whole thing didn't feel much like a celebration.

The knowledge of what had happened before the game - the overwhelmingly good natured party in the city centre, the swapping of scarves and the banter, as well as events such as the fans' match on the Tuesday evening made it all seem so sad. The Porto fans were genuinely impressed and happy that so many of us had come to their city, but the applause which rang out from the FC Porto stands for the tremendous United support, just as the first tear gas exploded, was the ultimate in poignancy.

You don't fire bullets at football fans. Save them for a war. You don't fire tear gas at people who have nowhere to go to - any fool knows that it's a dispersal tool. When police finally opened the gate they then continued to baton charge and fire bullets and tear gas at us leaving the ground. More supporters were injured as many saw on television pictures. It was like pouring half of Siberia's mines onto the wounds.

We staggered out of the nightmare and, having managed to meet up with at least some of our party, headed off to try and salvage the night. Joao re-emerged the next day as we hadn't been able to meet up again that night. He was distressed and apologetic about the chaos. We told him it wasn't him who should be apologising. We went for a beer together.

30 fans were taken to hospital that night to be treated for head wounds, to have bullets removed from their bodies and heads, and to be treated for the effects of crushing. I got back to Manchester to be phoned by two supporters - one of whom had had the three bullets remaining in him x-rayed confirming that they were not plastic but metal - and the other, with seventeen head stitches, was beginning the long, convoluted legal process of trying to get compensation. Many others didn't seek medical attention, rightfully fearful of giving their names to Portuguese authorities. The media frenzy waiting for us when we got back is a different story.

This was the wrong kind of hangover. What an abdication of responsibility on all sides of authority! From the top to the bottom, despite all we're told about the brave new football world, supporters are not listened to, are not involved in preparations for European travel, and are treated in much the same way as we were here before Hillsborough. What is most frightening of all is that, as with match organisation in England, it will probably take a death, or deaths, before anything changes. That is a price which we shouldn't have to pay for a bit of recognition and a bit of respect. Fortunately for us, it didn't happen. Not this time.

By way of a postscript, the media here, although sympathetic for once, did keep throwing up the red herrings of alcohol and tickets (take a bow, Alan Green, Rob Hughes, David Lacey, you ignorant gits). The FA denied that they had anything to do with what happened and absolved themselves of responsibility in their own, expert manner ("your comments have been noted", said Graham Kelly, pushing the boat out). The Portuguese authorities issued a Stalin-like tissue of lies.

UEFA, bless 'em, for the first time ever, absolved English fans of any responsibility and punished the Portuguese club - OK the fine was a nominal fifty grand, but there was no doubt where the blame lay.

Since English clubs returned to Europe we have had Liverpool supporters crushed into terracing in Auxerre; United fans beaten, imprisoned and deported from Turkey; Norwich supporters arbitrarily arrested in Milan; diabolical ticket distribution to us at Barcelona and elsewhere; Leeds fans deported without justification (apart from the usual) from Eindhoven; Chelsea fans detained at Bruges; the appalling treatment of Leicester City fans in Madrid and the batoning and tear gassing of us in Turin last year.

At the time of writing the press and authorities are wringing their hands at the prospect of 10,000 England fans descending on Rome for their country's World Cup qualifier against Italy. Talk of "rings of steel", "cordons" and "firm policing" suggest that the message still hasn't filtered through.

More bad hangovers on their way, it seems.

DEVILS DROP IN DORTMUND

Borussia Dortmund 1 - Manchester United 0 (aggregate 2-0)
European Cup, Semi-Final 1st Leg
April 9th 1997, WestfalenStadion.
Van Der Gouw, Neville.G, Irwin, Keane, Johnsen, Pallister,
Cantona, Butt, Solskjaer, Beckham, Giggs.
Subs used: Cole and Scholes.
Attendance: 48,500

Andy Mitten

Andy Mitten is 23 years old and has edited the fanzine 'United We Stand' since its formation back in 1989. Great nephew of the United legend Charlie, Andy's hobbies include discussing new structures at football grounds, collecting ticket stubs which he views in private with his girlfriend and watching planes take-off. He has a head full of useless facts ranging from the capital of Tanzania to the longest A-road in the UK. He's been lucky enough to watch Manchester United play in over twenty countries.

The trip to Dortmund had come around too quickly for the dozen youthful United fans kicking around Manchester Airport on Tuesday 8th April. It wasn't that they were complaining about reaching the Semi final of the European Cup, it's just that the, "honestly boss, I've got to have another wisdom tooth out and will require three days off work," type excuses were starting to wear a bit thin with the trip to Porto just three weeks previous.

Of course we could have conformed to the wishes of opinionated know-nothings in the media telling us to stay at home and watch the game on television. What, and miss out on the most important game in many of ours life time? It wasn't even an option.

Dortmund was going to be very different to Porto. For one, United didn't have a 4-0 cushion as the first leg was away from home. Nor would there be a 10,000 strong travelling red army as just 3,400 tickets had been allocated to United fans. Beating Borussia in their own home would be a tall order but if this particular group of reds were nervous, then it didn't show on the one hour scheduled flight to Germany's richest city, Dusseldorf.

Alex Ferguson had taken his team out the previous day and didn't intend to take them back to Manchester until Thursday. A new strategy in light of the disappointing league results following our European away games this season. Whereas the players would be relaxing with a spot of gentle training, the only training most United fans would be doing was picking up their steiners of beer. We'd chosen Dusseldorf because previous visits to Dortmund had not really impressed and also because Claudia Shiffer is from the city and we fancied knocking off any of her mates that happened to be knocking around the bars on a Tuesday night. If only. Dusseldorf was a pleasant city and but for a smattering of reds on United's executive trip, a football fan free zone. That was fine by us because we had a free run of the many bars in the old town down by the Rhine.

Early on Wednesday morning we caught a train from Dusseldorf for the one hour journey to the nearby city of Dortmund. The collection of reds loitering around Dortmund station had only one rumour to confirm, that there was an acute shortage of accommodation in the city. Two police officers, clocking just who was turning up in Dortmund amidst rumours of rival German hooligans turning up to stir it up, recommended that we went back on ourselves to the neighbouring city of Bochum to find accommodation, which is exactly what we did.

Back in Dortmund it soon became apparent that the city has about as much to offer the casual visitor as Coventry. Like its Midlands counterpart, the city was flattened by bombs during the second world war. But it was football, not architecture, that had brought us to Dortmund and we didn't waste any time making our way through the busy shopping area towards the market square where a festival had been organised for both sets of fans by the local authorities.

In the centre of a square, a stage, dressed in balloons of United's red and black and Dortmund's yellow had been erected. Pea soup, a local speciality, was distributed gratis, a commendable gesture from our German hosts - shame it looked and tasted like vomit. What next? Lancashire hot pot dished out to visiting fans in Manchester's Albert Square. The big attraction was the beer. Dortmunders like their beer, they drink more per head than in any other European city and were happy to sell local brew in plentiful amounts from stalls on the square's periphery. It didn't take long for the wiser heads to suss out that you could get the same beer in nearby off licenses for a third of the price and the sight of a procession of reds carrying crates of Becks from local shops was soon the norm.

The sun was shining, the atmosphere spirited. Kids, from Manchester and Dortmund, played 5-a-side until their dads dragged them away. Nearby, a shop stocked only with Borussia merchandise, witnessed queues all day, too many fanoraks like me buying Borussia pin badges the shop assistant reckoned.

On the stage Pat Crerand thanked our hosts for their hospitality, local dignitaries thanked United fans for travelling, drunken fans slurred drunken terrace tunes, one United fan boasted about chasing ten City fans with a baseball bat. The organisers looked bemused if not amused. In the drab buildings overlooking the square, Police, armed with surveillance cameras, binoculars and batons kept a watchful eye. Controlled, contrived, congenial and a far cry from the fracas three weeks earlier in Oporto.

With three hours to kick-off, an announcement was given for fans to start making their way, under Police surveillance of course, towards the Westfalenstadion a mile away.

The Westfalenstadion was built for the 1974 World Cup finals and forms part of a huge sporting complex. Fans walk up to the ground almost in a procession along a single road like Wembley way. The atmosphere was like a carnival as fans marched along forming a sea of day-glo yellow interspersed with the odd drunken red. Next to the stadium is Borussia's old ground, the 'red earth' stadium which was scene of United's two previous clashes with the German giants. In one, the reds drew 0-0 after a 3-2 victory at Old Trafford in 1956. In the other, United beat Borussia 6-1 with a hat-trick from Bobby Charlton and further goals from Best, Law and Herd.

An equivalent result tonight would be unthinkable but I'd settle for the hard earned goalless draw which those Busby Babes achieved.

It was an impressive sight inside the ground, especially the packed terrace holding 18,000 at one end of the ground, a swirling mass of bodies, yellow flags and scarves. The other three stands towered high above the pitch, the fact that the stadium has no running track, unusual in Germany, has made the Westfalenstadion a favourite with German players and fans. What makes it so popular is that the Germans consider the atmosphere it to be 'typisch englisch'. If only they knew how bad the atmosphere had become in the biggest English stadiums they would probably think of another description.

Despite years of under achievement Borussia have always enjoyed a vast support. The recent Rhur renaissance at Dortmund has boosted that support further and can be attributed to coach Ottmar Hitzfeld who joined the club in 1991. Hitzfeld succeeded in attracting recognised German internationals back to Deutschland when he poached stars from Italy's Serie A. Matthias Sammer came from Inter, Karlheinz Riedle from Lazio and Jurgen Kohler, Andreas Moller and Stefan Reuter all arrived on a one way ticket from Turin's finest, Juventus. These players still provide the backbone of the squad but are by no means the only stars. Portuguese international Paulo Sousa, Brazilian defender Julio Cesar and Swiss international Stephane Chapuisat all combine to give Dortmund an extremely powerful squad.

The UEFA Cup final was reached in 1993, the domestic Bundesliga championship won in 1995 and 1996. Demand for match tickets hit new heights, two new tiers of seating were built above existing stands to boost the capacity to 54,000, sales of Borussia's distinctive day-glo yellow shirts outstripped even those of the institutional Bayern Munich. Both on and off the pitch, it's a story from which Manchester United can draw many parallels.

For all their success, Borussia could do nothing about the four first team regulars missing in the line-up against United. Not that it eased our nerves for despite the absence of Sammer, Riedle, Kohler and Chapuisat, I've never been so nervous at a football match in my life. The home side, no doubt encouraged by Schmeichel's non appearance, pressured but created few genuine chances. Dortmund's pre-match hyperbole that the United back four would be run ragged was just that. With the score pegged at 0-0 at the break, hopes rose amongst the reds that United could sneak a goal and maybe a victory.

At half-time the P.A system boomed out James Brown's classic "Get on up" and "I feel good". United fans certainly got on up and sang along with a passion. The German fans responded with rapturous applause, they'd never witnessed anything like it.

I'd have settled for a 1-0 defeat before the game, a case of damage limitation before frightening the lives out of Dortmund back to Old Trafford I thought, but once United starting creating chances I became hungry for more. Butt had the best chance of the lot, only the post prevented a further explosion of noise from the United fans. Then Dortmund scored. Nothing special, a speculative shot that went in off a deflection. The luck of the Irish? The luck of the Germans more like. A 1-0 defeat.

As the travelling fans spilled out of the ground, they were only United by their glum expressions. The pessimists would mumble, "gutted", the realists, "If only Butt had put that chance away", and the optimists, "We'll do 'em at O.T".

It's amazing how a good nights sleep can change your moods, your outlook, and by the following morning the consensus was that a 2-0 victory at Old Trafford was an achievable result amongst reds on an Amsterdam bound Inter City. If only.

Pockets of Juventus fans were still loitering around Amsterdam's lad-enticing attractions after their game against Ajax the night before. Despite beating Ajax 2-1 in the new Amsterdam Arena they looked sullen. Maybe their success has made them complacent and blasé.

An English newspaper at Amsterdam's Schipol airport criticised United's stars on their performance, a bit over the top, but I was too exhausted to discuss it. It was time to go home. We were tired, weary, but above all, optimistic. Down but definitely not out.

Two weeks later Dortmund came to Old Trafford to defend their slender one goal lead. A seventh minute goal from Ricken knocked the stuffing out of United and despite wave after wave of United attacks, the German champions held out. At this level, United needed to put away the chances they created. A simple philosophy but one which cost us a place in the European Cup final.

If somebody had told me at the start of the season that come April, United would be five points clear at the top of the league with a game in hand and be in the semi-final of the European Cup, I'd happily have settled for their prediction. As it transpired, being knocked out at the penultimate stage was hard to take, especially with all the talk about a return to Munich being destiny. The thing that made our defeat by Dortmund harder to take was the fact that a month later they defeated Juventus 3-1 in the Bavarian capital. Juventus, as far as I could see, were by far and away the best team in Europe. Skill coming out of their ears, strength almost by deception and the style of Armani models. Then a Dortmund team who we deserved to beat go and trounce them.

It could have been us, it should have been us. Never mind, there's always next year.

IF THE REDS SHOULD PLAY IN ROME OR MANDALAY - WE'LL BE THERE!

SUBSCRIBERS LIST

1. TONY HUGHES
2. MARK
3. NIGEL APPLETON
4. MIKE DOBBIN
5. HOWARD COOMBER
6. JOHN
7. PHIL HOLT
8. CARL HAYES
9. ARTHUR ALBISTON
10. STEVE
11. STEPHEN
12. MICK
13. MARTIN DAY
14. PETE
15. TOWER POWER
16. JOHN SAYER
17. CHALLY
18. ARI
19. DR.EDWARD MARTINS
20. STEFANOS TSICHRINTZIS
21. NIGEL SWINBANK
22. PHIL WILLIAMS
23. PETE BOYLE
24. MR ANON
25. WAYNE IBALL
26. PAUL WOOSNAM
27. ROB PATTINSON
28. TERESA McDONALD
29. BARNEY CHILTON
30. ALAN SEWELL
31. HAZ
32. ADAM BROWN
33. ANDY MITTEN
34. TONY BECK
35. ROGER PURDUE
36. TIM BURTON
37. SEAN GILMARTIN
38. SAMANTHA SMITH
39. LEE GABBIE
40. ROGER BRIERLEY
41. CALLUM FERGUSON
42. CHRIS READE
43. PAUL 'BELLY' BELSTON
44. BARNEY O'LEARY
45. TREVOR COOKE
46. EMYR EVANS
47. MICHAEL LIAM GEOGHEGAN
48. STEPHEN J.HUGHES
49. PADDY McANEA
50. ROGER SAFFERY
51. GRAHAM MENZIES
52. PETER QUICK
53. ROB UNDERWOOD
54. JAMES BRIDGES
55. ANDY FLACK
56. COLIN C. O'KANE
57. ROBERT BRIMICOMBE
58. JOHN BIRD
59. TAFF WILTSHIRE
60. KERRY DAVIES
61. TERRY & KAREN PATTEN
62. MICHAEL BIRD
63. STEVE LEGGOTT
64. RICK HOLLAND
65. MICHAEL R.HEATON
66. KATHLEEN JOHNSON
67. MARTIN KERSHAW
68. PHILIP JONES
69. MICHAEL TAYLOR
70. ROB FERRARI
71. JOHN NORRIS
72. PAUL R SMITH
73. EDDIE THOMAS
74. JANET TALBOT
75. LEO AUTIO
76. PAUL NICHOLAS
77. JIM CONNOLLY
78. KATHRYN HUGHES
79. CHRIS PORTER
80. ALISON WATT
81. BARRIE PURDUE
82. EDDY SNAPE
83. HOWARD MARTIN
84. HARRY LINFORD
85. PETER SHAW
86. D.CARTWRIGHT
87. LEE PRICE (WELSH)
88. DARREN SMITH
89. RAY EVANS
90. KEVIN IBALL
91. SIMON COOK
92. JASON CARTER
93. SEAN MURCHAN
94. UNITED BY FOOTBALL
95. JULIE JONES
96. STEVE & BEV, LEE, NICKY, MATTHEW, LORRAINE HUBERT
97. ROY (MACKER) MACDONALD
98. WAYNE OCCLESTON
99. STEVE MORAN
100. FRANK NEWBY
101. DAVID F BELFIELD
102. PAUL ANTHONY COOPER
103. MARTIN JOHN COATES
104. ANDY WRIGHT
105. MATT DOWNEY
106. STUART CAWTHRAY
107. D.J. WRIGHT
108. STEVIE CARROLL
109. PAUL O'HARE
110. PAUL ROUGHLEY
111. GARY PARTINGTON
112. PRIYA MAHAWATTE
113. ANDREW CROZIER
114. JOHN WILLISCROFT
115. G. STILL
116. PAULA. J. SMITH
117. BRIAN BUTTERWORTH
118. PADDY McANEA
119. PHIL MALKIN
120. SHANE MATTHEWS
121. STEVEN HEALEY
122. GARY BRAMWELL
123. KIRSTIN MOON
124. MARTIN MOON
125. ROY SWINBANK
126. MARK 'EGG' SIMPSON
127. WILLIAM B.KILMURRAY
128. WILLIAM B.KILMURRAY
129. OYSTEIN EIIE
130. STEVE GAFFNEY
131. KATHRINE BLACKBURN
132. WILLIAM PARTIS
133. DEAN BIRTWISTLE
134. PAUL COOPER
135. GARY HAYES
136. MICHAEL DEAN
137. TONY MYERS
138. LIAM CALDWELL
139. 'BUD'
140. MARK LANCASTER
141. SHAUN.M.FORREST
142. BEN GODFREY
143. DERMOT BASSETT
144. STEPHEN POOLE
145. STEWART BAKER
146. PAUL CHAPMAN
147. KIM MILFORD
148. SHAUN ROGERS
149. VIC HATHERLY
150. ROGER FERRIS
151. ROY STEPHENS
152. FAY SWINDLEHURST
153. BRIDGET SWINDLEHURST
154. KEVIN (NOSH) BURSTON
155. AMY & HANNAH TAYLOR
156. BRYN THOMAS
157. M. BETTNEY
158. J AXTON
159. CHRIS HORNE
160. GORDON TAYLOR
161. MARK & LISA LYON
162. MARK BRENNAN
163. PAUL HANCOCK
164. PHIPPO (BRUM)
165. GEORGE DYSON

ALSO AVAILABLE FROM $\mathcal{J}uma$ -
The home of Britain's most interesting football books

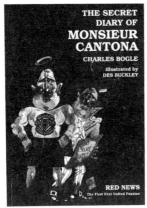

THE SECRET DIARY OF MONSIEUR CANTONA by Charles Bogle
128pp A5 paperback ISBN 1 872204 20 1 £5.95 (+£1 p&p/ Europe £2/ Rest £4)
The king may be gone, but his secret diary lives on. Since 1993, when the first instalment was - allegedly - discovered by a down-and-out searching for dog-ends, these mysterious documents have been turning up in a Manchester rubbish skip, whence they have been painstakingly rescued, restored and reproduced by *Red News*, the first Utd. fanzine. Could they be the genuine secret diary of a certain French footballer?* If so**, this contains the most startling and frank revelations ever to emerge from behind the scenes at Old Trafford, and a fascinating insight into the mind of a genius - baffled by the idiosyncrasies of the English, frustrated by the inadequacies of the mere mortals around him. (*Almost certainly not. **Which we doubt)

WE ARE WOLVES Wolverhampton Wanderers - The Fans Story edited by Charles Ross
200pp sub-A4 paperback ISBN 1 872204 35 X £9.95 (+£1.50 p&p/Europe £3/ Rest £6)
In the fans' own words, the special appeal of a club that has spent nearly forty years trying to recapture the glory days of the 50s, when the team of Stan Cullis and Billy Wright turned Wolverhampton Wanderers into Europe's finest. This is the story of rollercoaster ride since that golden post-war era. Nostalgia: from charting the fortunes of the team and a young follower in the 60s to rites of passage tales from the 70s and 80s. Hero worship: of two great strikers, John Richards and Steve Bull. Despair: as Wolves' decline in the 80s took them to the Fourth Division and to the brink of extinction. Delight: as Wolves climbed out of the abyss with two successive promotions. Frustration: of the wilderness years of Division One and the heartache of two play-off defeats. Over twenty authors from the *A Load Of Bull* fanzine provide a rivetting insight into what Wolves mean to them.

PINNACLE OF THE PERRY BARR PETS The Men And Matches Behind Aston Villa's 1897 Double
by Simon Page
102pp sub-A4 paperback ISBN 1 872204 30 9 £6.95(+ £1 p&p/ Europe £2/ Rest £4)
1897: Aston Villa complete the League Chapionship and FA Cup Double. 1997: The true and complete story of the men and matches that made history is finally recorded in a single volume. Pinnacle Of The Perry Barr Pets details every match played by Villa's finest ever line-up during the club's most successful season ever. An exhilarating journey through the last days of the Wellington Road ground, via Crystal Palace and arguably the greatest Cup Final of all time, to the opening of Villa Park, then the best stadium in the World. Includes biographies of all the players and major backroom staff and offers a unique insight into the running of a 19th Century footballing giant, aswell as the lives of footballers before the days of multi-million pound signings, extortionate wages and television.

GLADYS PROTHEROE... FOOTBALL GENIUS! by Simon Cheetham with foreword by Graham Taylor
220pp A5 paperback ISBN 1 872204 10 4 £5.95 (+£1.25 p&p/Europe £2.50/Rest £5)
From the sun-baked terraces of the Maracana to the frozen teahut at Vicarage Road, supporters throughout the world love and respect Gladys Protheroe. Who discovered John Barnes (and Bruce Springsteen)? Who persuaded Alf Ramsey that Geoff Hurst was a better prospect than Jimmy Greaves? Who punched Ron Atkinson on live TV? And the astonishing truth behind Stuart Pearce's suicidal back pass against San Marino. Over half a century of football history and - sometimes shocking - revelations from inside the game. "*Quite Brilliant ★★★★★*" - **FourFourTwo** magazine. "*A footballing masterpiece... kept me sniggering and dribbling to and from work for the next week*" - **Beesotted** magazine.

FOOTBALL AND THE COMMONS PEOPLE edited by David Bull & Alastair Campbell
320pp A5 paperback ISBN 1 872204 05 8 £9.95 (+£1.50p&p/ Europe £3/ Rest £6)
30MPs and former MPs describe their experiences of, and opinions on, 'the people's game'. Serious issues such as Denis Howell on the politics of the '66 World Cup and David Evans justifying his policies as chairman of Luton Town and Maggie's lapdog! And fans-eye confessions: who indulged in the rather unparliamentary activity of "Taunting Rangers supporters" out of the car window (and not when he was a teenager either!). Was one MP really among the Tartan Horde ripping up Wembley in 1977? And which MP has an Irish Cup-Winner's medal - an Ulster Unionist playing for Derry City! Includes Roy Hattersley, Kenneth Clarke, Michael Howard, Michael Foot, Gordon Brown, Ann Taylor, Stan Orme on Manchester United and more. Fascinating reading throughout.

FROM SPORTSPAGES AND ALL GOOD BOOKSHOPS OR DIRECT FROM THE PUBLISHER ADDING p&p AS SHOWN. Credit card (Visa/Mastercard only) orders taken by fax.

Juma Printing & Publishing, 44 Wellington Street, Sheffield S1 4HD.
Tel. 0114 272 0915. Fax 0114 278 6550. Email ml@jumaprint.demon.co.uk

Juma mail order

We can supply almost any British book in print, football or any other subject, also videos and multimedia. Request our latest football list or visit the 'virtual bookstore' at www.jumaprint.demon.co.uk. Alternatively fax or email your enquiries whereupon we will let you know cost and availability by return.

Juma printing

We are small press, self-publishing and fanzine specialists, established since 1983. We also offer a full commercial printing service for all business require-ments. Unbeatable value, fast, friendly service and nationwide delivery. Call Martin Lacey or send a sample of your current material for a quote.

Juma Printing & Publishing
Trafalgar Works, 44 Wellington Street, Sheffield S1 4HD
Tel. 0114 272 0915; Fax 0114 278 6550; Email ml@jumaprint.demon.co.uk